Planning, the market and private housebuilding

The Natural and Built Environment series

Editors: Professor Michael J. Bruton, University of Wales, Cardiff
Professor John Glasson, Oxford Brookes University

1. *Introduction to environmental impact assessment*
John Glasson, Riki Therivel, Andrew Chadwick

2. *Methods of environmental impact assessment*
Peter Morris & Riki Therivel (editors)

3. *Public transport*, 3rd edition
Peter White

4. *Planning, the market and private housebuilding*
Glen Bramley, Will Bartlett, Christine Lambert

5. *Housing policy in Britain and Europe*
Gavin McCrone & Mark Stephens

6. *Partnership agencies in British urban policy*
Nick Bailey (with Alison Barker and Kelvin MacDonald)

7. *British planning policy in transition*
Mark Tewdwr-Jones (editor)

8. *Urban planning and real estate development*
John Ratcliffe & Michael Stubbs

9. *Controlling development*
Philip Booth

Planning, the market and private housebuilding

Glen Bramley
Heriot–Watt University
Will Bartlett
University of Bristol
Christine Lambert
University of the West of England

First published in 1995 by UCL Press

UCL Press Limited
University College London
Gower Street
London WC1E 6BT

and
1900 Frost Road, Suite 101
Bristol
Pennsylvania 19007-1598

British Library Cataloguing-in-Publication Data
A catalogue record for this book is available from the British Library.

Library of Congress Cataloging-in-Publication Data are available

ISBNs: 1-85728-162-4 HB
1-85728-163-2 PB

Typeset in Times Roman and Optima.
Printed and bound in Great Britain by Page Bros (Norwich) Ltd.

Contents

Acknowledgements

The research on which much of this book is based was funded by the the Joseph Rowntree Foundation, whose support is gratefully acknowledged. This was initially through the Housing Finance Research Progamme, directed by Professor Duncan Maclennan, and subsequently through support for a specific project on "The local supply response of private sector housebuilding to the market in the British land use planning context".

Research in the Bristol area, reflected particularly in Chapters 4 and 5, was greatly assisted by the co-operation of the Avon County Planning Department, five district councils and over a dozen housebuilding companies.

Many organizations contributed to the assembly of data required for the modelling exercise reported mainly in Chapters 6–7. These included 13 County Planning Departments, the Department of the Environment, National House Building Council, South East Regional Research Laboratory, Population and Housing Research Group at Anglia Polytechnic, the Nationwide Building Society, and the NOMIS database at Durham University. Particular thanks are due to Gill Court who undertook the bulk of the painstaking task of assembling the dataset.

The detailed data on individual houses sold in Bristol underlying the density adjustment model presented in Chapter 8 were collected by Colette Pozzo. Thanks are due for her special efforts in generating this dataset.

We are indebted to the Universities of Bristol and the West of England for their support in enabling us to bring this project to fruition, in terms of general encouragement, time, library and computing resources. We have also benefited from the comments and encouragement of colleagues too numerous to mention. However, we would single out for special mention colleagues at other institutions who have been particularly helpful in the development of the work, particularly Duncan Maclennan, Christine Whitehead, Alan Holmans, Jed Griffiths, Sarah Maak and Stephen Manett.

Glen Bramley   Will Bartlett   Christine Lambert

CHAPTER 1
Introduction and background

1.1 Planning and the housing market

> A key element in understanding what has gone wrong lies in the British obsession with providing incentives for owner-occupation. This artificially stimulates the demand for residential land, yet the planning controls on land use are some of the tightest in Europe. Land and house prices are inherently unstable . . . , and booms in them have previously been a source of difficulty for the British economy. (Muellbauer 1990a: 16)

> The supply of land for housing has been restricted by planning controls. The prices of land and of houses have risen in consequence. As a result land has been used with increasing intensity with infill, "town cramming" and smaller houses on less land – "rabbit hutches on postage stamps"; a destruction of the urban environment of the many to preserve a rural environment for a few. (Evans 1991: 853)

These quotations from key commentators capture much of the concern that has arisen in recent years, in Britain and elsewhere, about housing in its relationship with the economy and with planning and public policy. Housing is intrinsically important to us all, but it seems to play a special role in the economy. When there are massive booms and slumps in housing, as in the period 1987–92, the ramifications are very widespread. Housing supply through new housebuilding is vulnerable to economic fluctuations and tends to exacerbate them. It is also strongly constrained and influenced by the land-use planning system, particularly in Britain, which makes this distinctive form of public intervention particularly crucial in understanding the housing market. The effects of failures in the housing market, whether or not exacerbated by the planning system, may be felt not just in the "housing" problems of quality, affordability, and homelessness but in the wider fields of national and local taxation, the distribution of wealth, unemployment, and the performance of regional and national economies.

This book is about the interaction between planning, private-sector housebuilding, and the housing market. It is an attempt to bring academic research to bear on problems of policy and practice. As such it presents at the same time an exercise in both market analysis and in policy analysis. As a market, housing is quite distinctive and it warrants specialized study, albeit set within a broader framework in which urban economics plays an important part. Planning is also a rather special arena of public policy, in which the State exercises very extensive powers of regulation. Thus, the policy analysis comprises both an examination of planning as a particular policy process and evaluation of the wider policy impacts of what is happening in the housing market.

Before going on to describe the research background to this book and the way we approach the subject, it is useful to focus briefly on some special features of housing and on the policy issues that have arisen between planning and housing and which have motivated our work.

Special features of housing

Textbooks generally start by identifying the features of housing that make it rather special and different from other commodities (Garnett et al. 1991, Gibb & Munro 1991). The following features would typically be identified as distinguishing housing:

- a house is a very durable good or asset;
- outright purchase of a home is very expensive relative to average household income;
- housing is generally fixed in its location, and attributes of that location (e.g. amenities, access to particular facilities) are consumed jointly with the housing itself;
- housing is a heterogeneous and multi-dimensional commodity;
- bad housing can generate certain adverse external effects (social costs), and vice versa;
- many would support the proposition that a certain minimum standard of housing is needed by and should be available for all households, regardless of ability to pay.

Clearly, the first two of these propositions are related. Different methods of solving the problem of how people are to pay for their very expensive but durable housing give rise to the different forms of housing tenure that dominate discussion of housing. These mechanisms include: mortgage-financed owner-occupation; private landlordism; public landlordism, funded by taxation or public borrowing; provision by employers; co-operatives. Historically in Britain, private landlordism was predominant, while now owner-occupation with mortgage finance through such intermediaries as building societies has become pre-eminent. Market solutions to this problem exist but require a certain legal and regulatory framework to function effectively. Housing finance remains sensitive to economic and monetary conditions, particularly rates of inflation and interest.

The third proposition ties housing closely in to the urban land market and urban economics. The land that a house stands on is locationally fixed. Like any fixed factor, land attracts a "rent" which reflects the returns to be earned or value of a particular use of that land (e.g. housing) at that point. It is important to add in this context the point that housing is normally the largest single urban land use, typically occupying half or more of built-up areas, and hence the housing market may often be the most important influence on the urban land market. This puts housing production in a situation different from other commodities, in that the price of one of its key inputs (land) is determined to a considerable degree by the demand for housing itself. Urban land values vary greatly, because of differences in accessibility to city centres and other key locations, and differences in environmental and social amenities. The field of urban economics, discussed further in Chapters 2 and 3, is primarily concerned with analysis of these relationships.

The heterogeneity of housing (d) stems in considerable measure from locational specificity. Every house is different, even every 1930s semi or 1950s former council house, because, even if the design is identical, the location, and hence the view, the access, the neighbours, are different. Houses are adapted over time in use, acquiring extra features and equipment, so that heterogeneity tends to grow, especially under owner-occupation where the occupier has more individual control. Reinforcing this point, housing should be viewed as a multidimensional good, in the sense that it provides different kinds of benefits to its users: shelter, warmth, security, hygiene; space for eating, sleeping, working, socializing, storage of goods; status symbol; attachment to a local community. This makes it more difficult to define and measure the quantity of housing which people are consuming, or its effective price, issues which are discussed further in Chapter 2 and later in the book, particularly in Chapter 8 which addresses increasingly important issues of quality.

The last two features identified (externalities and minimum standard needs) provide perhaps the most important basis for public intervention in the housing market and the provision of subsidized housing. These arguments are discussed further in Chapters 9 and 10 (see also Hills 1991: 11–21; Gibb & Munro 1991: 35–41, Le Grand et al. 1992: 91–105). Justifications for land use planning intervention, which partly overlap, are discussed in Chapter 3. The problems of durability and high cost interact with the need for access to adequate housing in what is increasingly seen as a problem of affordability. Planning may exacerbate such problems, yet also offers new ways of promoting affordable housing opportunities, as discussed in Chapters 4 and 7. Access to housing in a market-dominated system depends on wealth as well as income, both of which are increasingly unequally distributed in Britain. The spread of owner-occupation represents an important component of personal wealth for many households, but the uneven development of house prices and access to the sector may reinforce inequalities in wealth distribution.

Housing analysts have long recognized that some of the problems of the housing market may be exacerbated by the unresponsiveness of housing supply, particularly in the short term. This characteristic of supply is inherent in housing's durability and high cost, but may be worsened by the spatial immobility of housing in the face of shifting patterns of demand. The problem may be further compounded by planning controls on land for housing. Yet the bulk of research effort on housing has tended to concentrate on the demand side, on issues of finance, needs and distribution. This book and the research underlying it attempt to right the balance somewhat, by looking afresh at housing supply in theory and practice. This necessitates looking in depth at two areas, the housing construction industry itself and the planning system which determines the supply of land for new housebuilding.

Policy issues

This book addresses issues for public policy that arise out of the interaction between the housing and planning systems and which have attracted attention over the past decade. It is worth identifying these policy issues at an early stage, as they provide much of the context and motivation for our work.

House prices are of widespread popular concern, unsurprisingly given that two-thirds of British households are owner-occupiers. They are also a matter of concern for public policy, for several reasons some of which were alluded to in the quotations with which we began this introductory chapter. Macroeconomic policy-makers are concerned about the disturbing effect which large fluctuations in house prices can have on the economy as a whole, for example through their effects on savings, consumption and inflation. Large and changing regional house-price differentials can interfere with the processes of households mobility and labour market adjustment. High house prices generate problems of access and affordability for lower income groups, problems that increase pressures on local authorities and social housing providers, while increasing the cost these agencies face in procuring housing for those in need. Research that can shed light on the generation of house-price fluctuations and differentials, such as the work we report in Chapters 6 and 7, can inform policies to lessen these problems and alleviate their effects.

The *adequacy of land supply* for housebuilding is a second major area of policy concern. Since the 1970s this has been a major bone of contention between the private housebuilding industry, the planning authorities and environmental pressure groups. Government has intervened in planning at both the strategic and the implementation level to try to ensure an adequate supply, in ways which are described in Chapter 4. Adequacy can be defined in different ways which may lead to different views about the effectiveness of the system. Official attention focuses upon adequacy of immediate land availability to meet planning targets, but there is a wider issue of the adequacy of the targets themselves, which may be more important for the overall market outcomes. The process of land release may itself be part of the problem, giving rise to what we identify in Chapter 7 as an "implementation gap" in planning at the local level. Solutions to this problem may involve either or both of a greater degree of market sensitivity and awareness in planning and a more proactive role for public agencies in land supply.

A central preoccupation in our research has been to try to model and measure the *responsiveness of housing supply* to market demands, taking explicit account of planning policies and land availability, and linking local responses to national conditions. Although this work (reported in Chs 6 and 7) is of analytical interest, it also provides a basis for answering certain key policy questions. First, how much of a change in housing demand nationally will result in changing output, and how much in changing house prices? Secondly, how much difference would changes in the amount of land released for housing through the planning system make to house prices and output? Thirdly, does it matter what kind of land and in what areas? Only by quantifying these relationships can we begin to get away from contradictory assertions and identify the realistic policy trade-offs available.

In the field of housing policy, increasing attention is given to the issue of *housing affordability* and its relationship with the need for social housing provision and subsidy (Bramley 1994, Whitehead 1991). As already mentioned, house prices are a key element in the affordability equation, along with the distribution of income and wealth. Thus, an ability to understand and predict house price changes and differentials must increasingly underpin attempts to measure and forecast housing needs. Local authorities are required to engage in such attempts, in their capacity as both "enabling" housing authorities and as planning authorities with an enhanced role in facilitating the provision of affordable social housing as well as general market housing (DoE 1992).

This new role for planning is effected both through the preparation of new-style local plans and through the mechanism of *planning agreements* with developers. Planning agreements have become an increasingly important if controversial mechanism by which local authorities seek to secure resources for infrastructure or community facilities and to alleviate the impacts of development. We examine the planning agreement mechanism in Chapter 4 and consider housebuilders' attitudes to it in Chapter 5. Chapters 7 and 9 attempt to quantify the scope for and market impact of planning agreements for social housing and infrastructure costs respectively.

Planning agreements can be viewed as a form of taxation on development, albeit of a flexible and negotiated kind. The impact of *taxes and subsidies* on the housing market is an important policy topic in its own right, and one which led us into our research on housing supply to start with. Subsidies or tax reliefs specific to housing can affect house prices as well as the output and consumption of housing, and these price effects may distort and even defeat the ostensible purpose of the subsidies. Housing attracts a range of subsidies in Britain, and the tax treatment of owner-occupation has long been very favourable. In Chapter 9 we examine the quantitative impact of mortgage tax relief on the housing market, this being the particular focus of critical concern. We also discuss the impact of changes in local property taxes which were an important feature of the period 1989–93.

The *housing construction industry* was, in the 1950–70 period, the focus of considerable government concern, when the aim was to maximize the quantitative output of housing and when as much as half of that output would be purchased by the public sector. In the changed conditions of the 1980s, a more laissez-faire stance has been adopted. Nevertheless, there are grounds for policy concern about the industry. For example, it is argued by Ball (1983, 1988) that the response of the industry to extreme market instability has been to adopt a mode of organization reliant on subcontracting which gives flexibility and low overheads at the expense of technical backwardness, low skills and poor quality. Despite this flexibility, some believe that the overall supply is still insufficiently responsive. Ball and others also argue that the high level of development profit (i.e. gains in land value) on new housing have been substituted for profits earned from efficient and high-quality construction; implicitly, the planning system, by restricting land supply, increases the likelihood of this happening. The industry may put too many resources into trying to work the planning system, and it may be more tempted in some circumstances to defer development in the expectation of higher gains later. Chapter 3 discusses these general possibilities, and Chapter 5 looks in a more qualitative and descriptive way at the industry.

The *density* of housing development is an important issue, both in the theory of housing supply and urban structure (Chs 2 and 3) and in the practical world of planning. In an unconstrained market system, density adjusts to reflect market conditions, subject to time-lags involved in changing the built stock. Planning interferes with this process, partly indirectly by changing the overall availability of land for housing, and partly directly through the imposition of policy norms or limits on density. The direction of these effects can vary; sometimes planning is criticized for "town cramming", while elsewhere (particularly in America) it may be accused of "exclusionary zoning". Such intervention appears adversely to affect welfare by reducing the choice of housing consumers, but there may be balancing benefits elsewhere and good design may make higher densities acceptable. Chapter 8 examines the density issue, highlighting the more limited adjustment of density to market prices in Britain and the role of planning in this.

Density may be regarded as one of a range of aspects or dimensions of *quality* in new housing. Chapter 8 also considers other topical examples of quality attributes that might be subject to planning or regulatory policies: design guidance, size mix, energy conservation, accessibility for people with disabilities. In all these cases the general issue is how far very prescriptive regulation is justified, or rather whether it is better to offer information and advice on good practice and to rely more on individual choice in a market.

1.2 The research background

Past research

At the beginning of this chapter we indicated that we saw this book as an attempt to bridge the gap between academic research and practical policy. Thus, part of its function is to draw on recent and past research by others and interpret the findings in the context of particular issues about the operation of the system or about policy. This we do in particular chapters, especially the earlier ones. It would not be appropriate to review all of the relevant literature at this point. However, it is worth making some general observations about the research literature on the relationships between planning, the housing market and housing supply.

We see these issues as being quite strongly related to the academic field of urban economics. Urban economics appears to be a thriving "industry" in North America but verging on the moribund in Britain in the 1990s. In other words, there is an American-dominated literature, which is very useful for (a) studying methodological development and (b) making comparisons and contrasts. However, the planning and land-supply situation, policies and institutions are very different in Britain, which mean that we cannot read American results directly across into the British system. Monk et al. (1991) usefully review some of this literature, for example work on zoning, which is interesting but not directly applicable.

Economic modelling of the housing market in Britain in recent years has mainly focused on the national level, attempting to explain house price changes, for example, in terms of mainly demand-side factors. Such models do not link in any way to the effects of planning and land supply on the supply of housing, even in those cases where regional variations are examined. Models to explain individual house price variations (so-called hedonic models) have been used for various purposes, including the analysis of housing subsidies and the valuation of environmental effects, but again these have not linked into planning. The main economic contribution to debates about planning and the housing market have come from the University of Reading, through the work of Evans (1988b, 1991) and Cheshire & Sheppard (1989). The former has argued mainly in an informal theoretical mode, backed up by descriptive data; the latter developed a modelling approach but only for a single city.

Researchers in the urban geography tradition have taken a considerable interest in planning and housebuilding, for example Rydin (1985), Short et al. (1986), Couch (1988) and Barlow (1990). This work is reviewed in Chapters 3 and 5 and also in Monk et al. (1991) and Monk (1991). In the 1980s such researchers tended to adopt less of a quantitative modelling approach and more of a qualitative approach, emphasizing institutions and processes and utilizing mainly case-study material. Their preoccupations were often with questions of political economy, with power and influence over policy and outcomes, and how this might vary between different localities, rather than with the general behaviour of the housing market.

Research on land availability for housing continued from the mid-1970s onwards, but was mainly of a very practical and descriptive kind, measuring development pipeline times and delays, tracking the origins of sites, and so forth. Chapter 4 reviews this work. Some relevant work on aspects of planning, but without specific focus on housing, continued through the 1980s, for example Healey et al. (1985) on implementation and Elson (1985) on green belts. At the end of the 1980s there was renewed interest in research on planning and the housing market, perhaps as a result of the boom but also because of policy developments relating to planning agreements and affordable housing. Various projects were sponsored by the DoE (1992b) and t#he Joseph Rowntree Foundation, including our own work described below. Nevertheless, the 1980s saw rather less research overall on the issues of concern in this book, and certainly nothing as ambitious and comprehensive as Hall et al. (1973) in their study of *The containment of urban England*.

Overall, the research background we found at the end of the 1980s seemed very patchy, with some notable gaps. In general, there was less analysis of housing supply than of issues of demand, need and distribution. Applications of the standard urban economic model, common in the American literature, were surprisingly rare for British cities. In particular, there were virtually no economic models of the supply of housing, or the determination of house prices, which took explicit account of planning policies and land-supply constraints. Neither had systematic statistical modelling techniques been applied much to the behaviour of the planning system itself. Furthermore, apart from the work of Ball (1983, 1988), there seemed to be relatively little research drawing on social science perspectives (e.g. industrial economics, organization theory and sociology) into the housebuilding construction industry itself.

The SAUS research

Between 1988 and 1993 the authors were engaged in various linked pieces of research at the School for Advanced Urban Studies (SAUS), University of Bristol, mainly supported by the Joseph Rowntree Foundation, on aspects of the relationships between planning, the housing market and private housebuilding. This research may be seen as an attempt to fill some of the gaps just identified.

In fact, we came to be involved in this work, if not accidentally, at least by a rather indirect route. In 1987 the Joseph Rowntree Memorial Trust (as it then was) established a major programme of research on housing finance, under the direction of Professor Duncan Maclennan. The major part of this programme comprised six city-region studies, and the present authors took responsibility for one of these, Bristol. The aim of the research programme was to examine the "incidence and impact" of the housing finance system in Britain, recognizing that the effects of housing subsidies and other policies could operate rather differently in different local and regional contexts. Although "incidence" refers mainly to distributional effects, who gets what out of the system, the term "impact" was taken to refer to the response of the housing supply systems, public and private, to the different financial subsidy arrangements. The overall outputs of this programme are reflected in Maclennan et al. (1991) and Joseph Rowntree Foundation (1991).

It was envisaged that the studies would devote considerable attention to the supply side of the housing system. Although it would be fair to say that, across the initiative as a whole the work on supply was less complete, systematic and integrated than the work on incidence, in the Bristol study we did attempt to look at some aspects of this quite closely. In particular, we carried out a review of the literature on housing supply, published in a more technical version as Bartlett (1989) and reflected in a more accessible form in Chapter 2 of this book. We compiled site-level and aggregate data on land available and housebuilding activity, and on housebuilding companies. We documented and discussed the planning policies of the constituent authorities. A qualitative interview survey was carried out with a sample of housebuilding firms active in the area; findings from this exercise are reported in Chapter 5 and more fully in Lambert (1990). And a rather crude statistical analysis was carried out of the pattern of new private housing completions over time. Other aspects of the study, which is reported as a whole in Bramley et al. (1990), included a household survey on what people pay for their housing and how, a study of the reviving private rented sector, and detailed work on public sector rents and subsidies.

In undertaking this work, we became aware of the limitations of what could be done in one case-study area, but also aware of some new opportunities opening up in terms of data availability. A further project was proposed, which gained support from the Rowntree Foundation, entitled rather clumsily "The local supply response of private sector housebuilding to the market in the British land use planning context". One part of this project involved developing the local Bristol case study further, and applying the standard urban economic model of housing supply through density adjustment (see Ch. 2) to data for this particular British city. The results of this exercise are reported in Chapter 8. The second and larger part of the project involved compiling a database at the inter-urban (district) level and using this to establish quantitative economic models to predict housing supply and house prices taking account of local planning policies and land availability. This work is reported fully in Chapters 6 and 7, while Chapters 8 and 9 both refer to evidence derived from these data and models. Chapter 9 picks up the theme of the impact of financial policies (taxes and subsidies) on the housing market, which was our starting point.

Although this book in part represents a report on the findings of the research project just described, as so often the work accomplished in the finite timescale and resources of this one project is not complete or final. Other avenues suggest themselves for exploration; models fitted in one context may need to be modified in a different context. In this instance the Rowntree Foundation have approved a further project to extend the geographical and temporal coverage of the model, in particular to take account of more recessionary conditions in the market and to study market adjustment processes more closely. This further study will also look more closely at the impact of the changing planning system.

Rowntree are also supporting a research initiative on the housing construction industry, to help plug another of the gaps identified earlier. One of the present authors is carrying out a study within this programme of the role of small firms and subcontracting relationships in the new housebuilding sector. Although some of the preliminary and pilot work on this study has informed this book, the fuller results will not be available until some time in the future.

1.3 Different approaches

Economists and planners

It will be apparent from the above discussion of research that there are different approaches possible to the study of planning, housebuilding and the housing market. The choice of approach may be affected by the background discipline and skills of the researcher, the particular research question at issue, and the resources available for the research. We see this book as linking the disciplines of economics and planning (and hopefully not falling down the gap between them!). This is partly because we see these two disciplines as the ones that are both most concerned about and have most to contribute to the issues we are addressing. Partly of course it also reflects our own background as authors.

One of us is an economist who has mainly worked on "urban" issues, including housing, employment and local government finance. The second is also an economist, but with a background more in the economics of industrial organization, small firms and co-operatives, and in international comparative work. The third of us is a geographer, also qualified as a town planner, who has undertaken a wide variety of urban and planning research and who currently teaches professional town planners.

Economics as a discipline is distinguished, among the social sciences, by its strong interest in formal, deductive theory and quantification. Canons of good practice in these endeavours are highly developed, and economists tend to use their techniques to explore particular issues narrowly but in great depth. Economists tend to favour assumptions which are consonant with received theory and amenable to mathematical analysis, whether or not these are necessarily most appropriate in particular circumstances. For example, they tend to assume that agents act rationally and individually to maximize their material interests, and that markets are efficient and reach equilibrium, unless they have strong reasons to believe otherwise.

Town planning presents a very contrasting picture. It is mainly an applied, pragmatic subject which draws eclectically on a range of background disciplines, including geography, economics, demography, sociology, law, architecture and engineering. Its strength is breadth rather than depth and its orientation is empirical rather than theoretical. Quantitative modelling to support planning developed rapidly in the 1960s and 1970s, but more recently there has been less enthusiasm for grand modelling solutions, although modelling techniques in specific fields (e.g. transport, retailing) have continued to develop. The preoccupations of town planning have changed over time, reflecting the differing phases of urbanization and urban policy in Britain. Thus, in the 1980s, the focus was less on large-scale urban growth and more on economic decline and restructuring, urban regeneration, and conservation. The nature, rationale and function of town planning is discussed further in Chapter 3. In general, planners are engaged in dealing with problems of "market failure". Thus, it would not be surprising to find that planners habitually make rather different assumptions about the properties of markets than do economists.

Economic models

In parts of this book we examine the operation of the housing market, particularly its supply side, by using economic models. Economic models fall into two broad categories, theoretical models and econometric models. Theoretical models seek to provide a simplified account of the relationships between certain key economic variables (for example, house prices, incomes, housing stock), based on logical deductions from a set of assumptions about behaviour, institutions and rules. For example, how many houses will a firm which owns a piece of land with planning permission build, if we assume that the firm tries to maximize its profits and knows about past and present house prices and costs? The emphasis is upon formal logic and its expression in the form of algebraic equations (or graphically, which can be a more accessible form), supplemented by discussion of the reasonableness of assumptions. Such models are examined explicitly in Chapter 2, which looks at the theory of housing supply, and they underlie some of the material on the impact of planning in Chapters 3 and 6. Chapter 9 refers to the standard economic analysis of the impact of a tax or subsidy.

Econometric models are the empirical application of such economic models to data from the real world. In essence, such models seek to quantify the relationships between economic variables (house prices, completions, land supply, etc.) on the basis of systematic statistical data on the values of these variables across many cases. Econometrics is a branch of applied statistics developed for the analysis of economic relationships. The main techniques used are multiple regression analysis and variants on it. Regression analysis is the standard technique used to measure the effect of one or more "independent" or "explanatory" variables on a particular variable of interest, known as the "dependent" variable (see Targett 1984 for a simple explanation; Kennedy 1985, Maddala 1987 or Stewart 1976 are intermediate texts).The variables we are particularly interested in explaining or predicting in this book are house prices and the amount of new housebuilding (completions). However, we also explore the use of the technique in Chapter 7 to explain "outputs" of the planning system, particularly planning permissions, while Chapter 8 applies it to housing density.

Regression is based upon statistical correlations between variables, and it is fair to comment that correlation does not itself imply causation. However, in econometric work generally the approach involves starting from a plausible *a priori* theoretical model of behaviour, which does imply that a change in variable x causes a change in variable y, given a set of assumptions. If these assumptions are reasonable, then the relationships established from the statistical fitting of the model to data can be reasonably interpreted as causal effects. The purpose of the statistical analysis is to establish (a) whether the relationships do actually exist, and have not arisen simply by chance, and (b) how strong those relationships are (e.g. the magnitude of the elasticity of supply). Statistical tests can also indicate whether some different forms of model fit the data better than others.

Econometric models can be fitted to various different kinds of data. First, they may be fitted to data for a given system (e.g. the national economy or housing market) for different points in time (e.g. quarters or years), known as time-series analysis. Secondly, they may be fitted to data for different units (e.g. cities, small areas) at a point in time, known as cross-sectional analysis. Thirdly, they may be fitted to data for individual economic agents such as households or firms, known as micro-data. Sometimes these approaches are combined, with data for areas or units for different points in time combined, known as panel data. Each of these approaches raises some special issues and problems. For example, time-series raise particular issues about dynamic adjustment processes and time-related processes within the data. Cross-sectional data raise analogous issues about the underlying spatial trends within the data. Micro-data often involve special problems with variables which can take only restricted values, categorical data and yes/no dichotomies.

The models described in Chapters 6–9 of this book, based on our own research, are mainly cross-sectional. The units of observation are mainly local housing-market areas defined approximately by district authority boundaries. The assumptions and limitations of this approach are rehearsed in Chapter 6. Some of the studies referred to in Chapter 2 fall into this category also, particularly models fitted to data drawn from different cities. The urban economic models following the tradition of Muth (1969) and discussed in Chapters 2 and 3 are also cross-sectional, but set within the confines of a single city. Our own test of this model within Bristol uses micro-data on individual houses.

By contrast, most of the economic models of the British housing market are national time-series models (Whitehead 1974, Mayes 1979, Tsoukis & Westaway 1991, Meen 1992). These models are good for studying the dynamic relationships governing short-term fluctuations in house prices and housebuilding, but their supply-side components are usually simple and partial. In particular, they are not able to take account of the crucial land-supply function and its relationship with planning. A simple time-series model for new housebuilding in the Bristol area was explored in Bramley et al. (1990: ch. 4) but this also suffered from inadequate variation in the land supply component.

1.4 Guide to the book

The broad structure of this book follows a relatively straightforward logic. First, it proceeds from theory (in Chs 2 and 3) to practice (in Chs 4 and 5). At both stages, a focus on housing supply and construction (Chs 2 and 5) is balanced by a focus on planning and its effects (Chs 3 and 4). Secondly, we move from discussion in these early chapters based mainly on past research and literature, to the results of our own recent work utilizing a modelling approach. This approach is explained in Chapter 6, which develops the core element, our model of the supply of housing. Chapters 7–9 develop this model further and apply it to the analysis of some of the policy issues identified earlier: planning issues about the overall supply of land and housing needs; issues about housing density and quality; and issues about taxes and subsidies affecting housing. In the final chapter, we take stock and look to the future, in terms of some key themes.

The book does therefore develop in a logical way and most readers would probably find it most helpful to tackle it in this order. However, some readers with a particular knowledge of the subject may wish to dip in to particular parts. For example, someone interested in the issue of planning and land availability for housing might wish to look at Chapters 3, 4 and 7. Someone interested in housing density could advantageously concentrate on Chapters 2, 3 and 8. Someone interested in how the housebuilding industry is changing would find Chapters 5, 8 and 10 of most interest. Someone interested in the impact of the housing finance system on the housing market would find Chapters 6 and 9 the key ones.

Inevitably, in a book that attempts to explain, interpret and report on research, there is fair amount of material about the techniques used, some of which is a bit technical. We intend that this book should be readable by interested lay people, practising professionals and students, and not just by other researchers. Therefore, we have tried to avoid situations where technical material interrupts the flow of the main text. At several points, certain technical material (for example, equations or worked examples) are presented in a box, clearly separated from the main text. In general we have tried to minimize the use of algebra and to use simple graphics where these are helpful. The main modelling technique used, regression analysis, was briefly introduced in the earlier discussion of economic models. We do include tables showing some of the key results from applying these models, because these provide a great deal of valuable information about the relationships discussed in the text.

Readership

This book is intended to fulfil three overlapping functions. First, it is a supplementary textbook for students of planning, housing, construction, surveying, economics, geography, social policy and other allied disciplines, at under- and postgraduate level. In our own teaching we have found a noticeable gap in existing textbooks, with few covering the relationships between planning, housebuilding and the housing market. We would see the book as complementing existing texts on planning, housing policy, housing economics and finance, giving a more in-depth treatment and bringing the student up to date with contemporary research and policy debate.

Secondly, it is intended to provide a review and distillation of recent research, interpreted and elaborated in the light of current issues of policy. We stated at the outset that we see the book as providing market analysis linked to policy analysis. As such, we hope it will be of value to a wide range of readers, including other researchers and teachers, central and local government officials, practising professionals in planning, housing, surveying and allied fields, people working in the housebuilding industry itself and related financial and consultancy services, economic/business forecasters and analysts, and lay people interested in planning.

Thirdly, the book brings together the results of our own research, some previously published in rather disparate form and some previously unpublished. This will be of particular interest to others in the research community, both academics and those in government and other agencies with research interests and responsibilities. It will also be relevant to researchers in other countries, for whom the British experience with a highly developed planning system is of considerable interest. Although not primarily a comparative study, the book has been written with an awareness of national differences and adds to the stock of published material available for comparative assessment.

The book does not assume a high level of prior specialist knowledge. Readers are assumed to have some general knowledge of or interest in planning and housing, but in general we try to explain specialist terms or concepts as they are introduced. A basic knowledge of statistics and an appreciative understanding of some basic concepts in economics would be helpful; otherwise some arguments may need to be taken on trust.

CHAPTER 2
The economic theory of housing supply

2.1 Introduction

In this chapter we examine the contribution of economic theory to understanding the supply of housing. We review the relevant literature and explain how economic theory approaches this question, expanding in some detail on approaches which are particularly important. The relevant parts of economics are primarily the microeconomic theory of production in a competitive market where producers are motivated by profit. We also examine the branch of theory known as urban economics which deals with the location of economic activities in a spatial framework, where behaviour is affected by the cost of transport and communication.

Economic theory is distinctive within the social sciences by its reliance on a formal, deductive style of reasoning, where behaviour and outcomes can be predicted using formal models that start from explicit assumptions. Work within this tradition can be intimidating in its emphasis or formal algebraic models, although graphical presentation can often aid understanding. In general we keep the algebra to a minimum in our presentation, confining the detailed derivation of the theoretical results to a box to avoid interrupting the flow of the text. A fuller treatment can be found in Bartlett (1989).

Housing is a complex commodity distinguished by its heterogeneity, high cost and durability. Housing supply can be conceptualized in different ways and we discuss this first. Correspondingly the analysis of the determinants of supply may focus on different aspects, ranging from the construction of new housing, the redevelopment of existing housing, and upgrading, repair and maintenance, and changes in intensity of use of the existing stock. All these aspects are discussed at least briefly in this chapter, although the main emphasis in this book is upon new building rather than maintenance and rehabilitation.

One reason for being interested in housing supply is because of concern about the impact of housing subsidies and financial arrangements on the housing market. Another reason is that changes in the national economy can have a big impact on the demand for and price of housing. The impact of such changes depends mainly upon the responsiveness of supply to changes in price, known technically as the *elasticity of supply*. If supply responds strongly to demand and prices (elastic supply), then the impact of subsidies or macroeconomic changes is mainly on the output of housing (new building, upgrading, etc.); if supply responds weakly (inelastic supply), then the impact is mainly on prices. The elasticity of supply is defined as the proportional (percentage) change in supply divided by the proportional change in price which induces the supply change. This elasticity is the primary focus of this chapter, which reviews an extensive literature on the subject. The impact of land-use planning on supply and the market is picked up mainly in Chapter 3 and later on in the book.

2.2 The nature of housing supply

That the supply of a produced commodity can normally be expected to increase when relative prices rise (or decrease when they fall) is a fundamental characteristic of a market economy. In a market economy, individual consumer preferences are taken account of through the market mechanism via changes in relative prices. Demand patterns shift through changes in taxation, real income, life-styles and culture. Relative prices operate as signals to producers, at the same time as providing them with material incentives, to increase or reduce their level of output from existing productive facilities, or to undertake investment to expand those facilities. A supply increase, following an initial increase in relative prices, will tend to moderate the rise in prices. If the "elasticity" of supply with respect to the price is high, then the prices will fall back towards their original level by the time the process of supply increase is ended. If the elasticity of supply is low, then the supply increase and associated negative feedback will be small, and relative prices will stay high. It is therefore of considerable interest to know the magnitude of the supply elasticity in the housing market, as this will provide information about the expected distribution of the effects of a demand increase between ultimate changes in output and changes in price.

Conventional microeconomic theory has a well worked out theory to describe these effects. In the Marshallian tradition, a distinction is made between the short period where land and capital are fixed and any increase in supply has to come about through the utilization of the existing capital stock more intensively, and the long period in which both land and capital can be expanded through a process of investment expenditure, by existing or new firms. A distinction is also drawn between the supply function of the individual firm, and the market supply function. In the short run, the market supply function is just the horizontal summation so the individual firm supply functions, but in the long run the market supply function depends upon the number of firms in the industry and hence upon the ease of entry and exit.

Complexities of housing

This theoretical structure would be valid in the case of most produced commodities, whose output was homogeneous and could be easily altered, where expansion of facilities was less dependent upon the architecture of existing structures, and where the exact location of produced output was less important. However, in thc housing market, economic analysis is beset by the related problems of heterogeneity, durability and locational specificity. It is these factors that have made the analysis of housing markets particularly tricky and that give rise to fundamental problems in the conceptualization of the market. Several questions are posed by these problems:

- How should the commodity "housing" be defined and its quantity measured?
- What are the principal features of the market?
- Are there separate submarkets for housing in different cities or districts?
- Is the market for new housing distinct from that for existing housing?
- Is the market competitive?
- Should houses be treated as consumer goods or capital goods? Should housing be treated as a stock or a flow?
- What is the role of the associated market for residential land?
- What place should be given to an analysis of the structure of the construction industry?

Such issues lie in the background of the debate on housing supply.

The most promising approach, providing a unifying framework within which the issues can be coherently addressed, is provided by the "competitive theory of housing markets" developed *inter alia* by Muth (1969) and Mills (1972). The central unifying concept they introduced is that of a homogeneous good called "housing services". This is distinguished from the stock of housing assets (the dwelling as an investment good) which produces the flow of housing services per unit of time (the consumption good). Thus, the dwelling(s) owned by a landlord can be treated as the asset belonging to the housing "firm", and the output produced by this asset is the flow of housing services consumed in a period (a year, say) by the tenant.

Since the market for housing services is assumed to be competitive and no individual landlord can influence the price, each unit of housing service will achieve the same price. Strictly, this applies to housing in a given location or at a given distance from the city centre. Since dwellings differ in quality and hence provide different quantities of housing services per unit of time, the actual rent paid per dwelling will not be a good measure of the price of housing services. In addition, price and quantities traded in the market are not separately observable. What we see are packages of housing services and an overall price for the package (i.e. a house). This accounts for much of the difficulty involved in the empirical analysis of the housing market, and in the estimation of supply elasticities.

This theory of the housing market is most easily set out when the market is actually a rental market. However, most housing markets in developed countries have a significant sector of owner-occupied housing; in Britain this sector is predominant. To deal with this difficulty, the theory makes the heroic assumption that owner-occupiers can be treated as landlords who rent housing to themselves. This glosses over any behavioural differences that might exist between owner-occupiers and absentee landlords. Landlords are more likely to act like profit-maximizing firms. However, the fact that most dwellings are owner-occupied makes the assumption that the market is a competitive one rather realistic, since no owner can have much influence over the market price.

A dwelling can therefore be loosely equated to the firm of microeconomic theory, producing units of housing services as a flow of output per period of time. Viewed in this way, housing has both a consumer good and an investment good aspect, and one can conceive of distinct markets for the investment good (the asset market in dwellings structures) and for housing services as the associated consumer good (the rental market in "standard rooms per month" or some such measure of quantity). There are thus two markets to analyze and, although the connections between them are close, the connection need not always be direct or exact. The markets should be especially close under circumstances of pure competition where the asset price should equal the discounted value of expected future rents.

Market imperfections can have wider consequences for the operation of the housing market. For the demand side, these have been explored in extensive literature on tenure choice (Henderson & Ioannides 1983, 1986). However, the implications for the supply side have received less attention, with the exception of Cronin (1983) who argues that

> even if the supply of housing is competitive on a highly aggregative level (e.g. all types of housing across an urban area), the degree of market power on the part of housing suppliers may reach significant proportions if the relevant market is some subset of the total. (365)

In addition, the capacity of individual sellers to resist a downward reduction in market price by varying the date of sale in periods of market slack suggests that there may be some peculiarities in supply behaviour. These may be associated with the way in which expectations are formed over time. For example, in the early part of a demand boom, there may be a large increase in the number of homes offered for sale, as delayed sales come onto the market. As the boom gathers pace, the market tightens and the supply elasticity may fall.

In the rest of this chapter we review the theoretical and empirical work that is relevant to understanding the forces determining the elasticity of supply of housing services. In §2.3 the short-run decision concerning variations in the supply of services from the existing stock of housing is examined. In §2.4 we consider the case of long-run adjustment with free entry and exit, i.e. the variation in supply resulting from new construction and conversion of property for alternative uses. Conclusions are set out in §2.5.

2.3 Housing services supply in the short run

The short-run supply of housing services can be altered through a change in the intensity of use of existing structures. For example, an increase in the supply of housing services in the short run would be achieved through an increase in the use of "operating inputs" such as energy, cleaning services and/or a more dense occupancy of existing dwellings. The marginal cost of an extra unit of housing services is the extra cost of these inputs; and this rises steeply as intensity of use increases (Fig. 2.1). With a given house, the profit maximizing landlord will increase the utilization rate to the point where the rent income equals the marginal cost per extra unit.

As rents rise, in the short run the dwellings will be used more intensively, and the output of housing services will be increased by increasing the density of habitation (e.g. through multi-occupation). The quantity of housing services per inhabitant could also be increased by increasing the quantity or services used per inhabitant, for example by using more fuel for heating, or electricity for lighting. This type of adjustment is what Ingram & Oron (1977) have called the "current period operating decision".

The analysis also highlights the existence of a "shut-down price", a rent level which is so low for the landlord that continued operation of the stock becomes unprofitable. Price fails to cover even the minimum short-run variable cost. This situation can lead to the existence of vacant properties, and is an important aspect of short-run adjustment to price changes, which has been highlighted by Rydell (1982). The sensitivity of the vacancy rate to changes in price is likely to vary in different market conditions, falling off as a zero vacancy rate is approached,

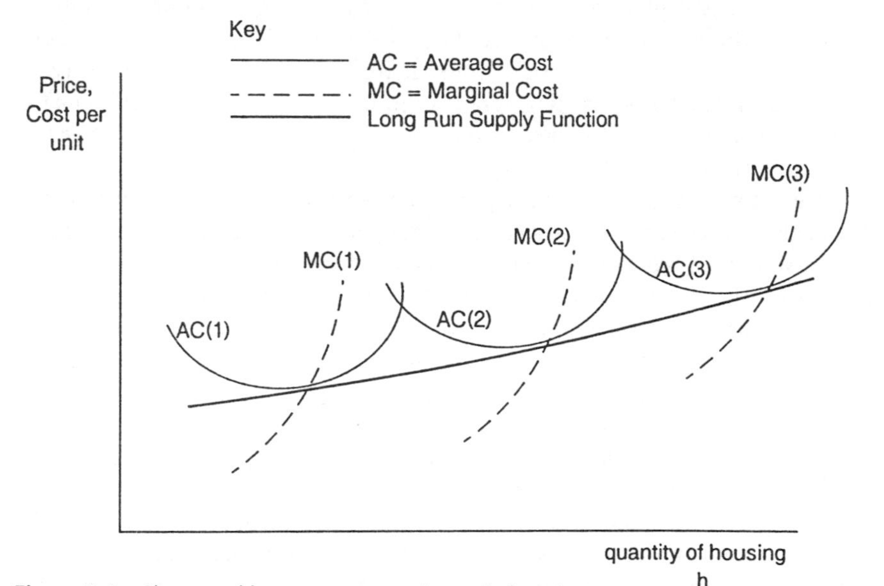

Figure 2.1 Short- and long-run cost and supply functions.

and being greater during periods of market slack when there are many vacant properties available. Rydell has estimated the very short run elasticity of supply, defined as the ratio of relative change in the occupancy rate to relative change in price using data from a cross-section of 59 metropolitan areas in the USA, together with price indices calculated by Follain & Malpezzi (1980). This very short-run elasticity is found to vary between 0.24 at a 96% occupancy rate, and 0.83 at a 90% occupancy rate. Using a figure of 93% as the long-run equilibrium occupancy rate, the "average" elasticity is found to be 0.5. So, even in the short run, occupancy changes prevent the supply elasticity from dropping to zero.

In the slightly longer run, even in the absence of new houses entering the market, the supply of housing services from the existing houses can be increased by changing the condition of the building structure. This involves some investment in maintenance of one type or another (repair, improvement, renovation or conversion). Each of these types of investment changes the capital stock embodied in the existing houses, and also changes the average cost of providing housing services. The extent to which average costs vary with changes in the building structure on a given plot depends on a technical relationship known as "the elasticity of substitution" between capital and land. For example, the substitution elasticity would be high if it were relatively simple to add extra storeys to a building, whereas it would be low in the typical case for a normal two-storey house with a pitched roof, where this would be very costly. It might be relatively easy to convert the loft to an attic room, but for more than that the process might become more difficult and costly. Such differences reflect both technical constraints (e.g. thickness of load-bearing walls) but also legal regulations and constraints, such as planning restrictions on density (see Ch. 8). If the relationship between land and capital were relatively fixed, there would be a low elasticity of substitution. In general, given the presence of the fixed factor - land - it would be reasonable to expect that a each further increase in the quality or quantity of housing services from an existing house could be achieved only at a continually increasing average cost. The lower is the elasticity of substitution, the tighter the relationship.

More detailed analysis would require separate attention to the various types of adjustment mechanisms involved under the general rubric of "maintenance". The possibility of the existence of several distinct technologies to describe the adjustment of a housing unit to its optimal size is a reflection of the durable nature of housing, which was referred to earlier on, as well as the "lumpiness" of some of the investment expenditures involved (if only because of building regulations). Indeed, the distinction between short- and long-run adjustment itself is not entirely obvious. Some repair work can be achieved relatively quickly, whereas other types of renovation may take a relatively long period to design and implement, especially where planning permission is required. Moreover, the term "long run" is often given the theoretical interpretation of a situation in which all factors of production are variable. Clearly, in the present case this cannot be taken to apply to land, and so there would be a case to treat all repair and maintenance and renovation activity as "short-run" activity. In the economics literature, maintenance elasticity is often referred to as a "short-run" elasticity. However, since fixity of land inputs is a rather fundamental feature of housing services production, and to preserve the distinction between supply response associated with given structures and from changes to the structure, we will use the term "long run" to refer to all those supply responses that involve some form of alteration to the structure.

Different approaches have been adopted to deal with this feature of supply adjustment. For example, Ingram & Oron (1977) distinguish between "quality capital" (interior finish, fixtures & fittings, etc.), which depreciates relatively quickly, and "structure capital" (the building foundation and shell), which depreciates relatively slowly. Within this framework, the various maintenance technologies could be associated with the various types of changes to the capital stock. For example, quality capital would be amenable to repair and improvement, whereas structure capital would be altered by renovation and conversion, each process being a distinct technology. Ingram & Oron follow a dichotomy of this type, distinguishing the "current period maintenance decision" which causes changes to quality capital, from the "structure type decision" which involves changes to the structure capital. Arnott et al. (1983) similarly distinguish between a maintenance and a rehabilitation technology, although the major distinction for them is the discontinuous nature of rehabilitation.

The particular classification used will vary with the needs of any particular analysis, but the essential point is that capital stock adjustment can take place over a succession of "long runs" with associated movements along the long-run average cost curve. In the absence of new houses entering the market, the long-run supply function would be upward sloping, given the presence of the fixed factor (land), but more elastic than in the short run. Figure 2.1 illustrates the relationship between the long-run cost/supply function and short-run cost functions relating to different levels of housing stock (possibly at different points in time).

In the absence of new entry (through new construction or change of use of structures from commercial or industrial activities), the market supply is the sum of the individual supplies of housing services from the existing stock of dwellings. The elasticity of this market supply is likely to be fairly low, especially in urban areas where it is difficult to increase the size of the individual dwelling units on fixed plots of land. Of particular interest also is the possibility of external economies and diseconomies affecting the cost structure of individual dwellings: the output of housing services (and their associated average and marginal costs) from each dwelling in a neighbourhood depends not only upon the stock embodied in the dwelling and the level of operating inputs employed but also upon the output levels associated with all the other dwellings in the neighbourhood. In this case, the supply elasticity can be expected to vary from area to area and to depend upon the locational and neighbourhood characteristics of the area.

Empirical studies of repair and maintenance elasticities

Several empirical studies have been made in the USA of the supply elasticity of housing services from the existing stock, notably those by Mendelsohn (1977), Ingram & Oron (1977) and Ozanne & Struyk (1978). Mendelsohn constructs a model for home owners' home improvements, which shows that home improvement activity is positively related to house price, expected length of tenure, and income, whereas the choice between own labour and outside labour depends upon own wage rate and own productivity in house improvement activities. This model is important because, in contrast to the standard profit maximizing model of the firm, it is based upon the assumption of utility maximization drawn from consumption theory, which is more satisfactory for the case of the owner-occupier. In addition, it is one of very few that recognize the importance of domestic labour (DIY) in the production of housing services, and in day-to-day maintenance without which a structure would deteriorate relatively rapidly. Mendelsohn tests his model on data from a national sample of residential alterations collected quarterly by the US Census. The sample covered about 5000 households over two winter quarters between 1971 and 1972. The variables used to explain improvement expenditure statistically were income, housing value, race, owner's age, age of house and duration of occupancy. The dominant result is that higher income increases the frequency and size of expenditures, and increases the probability of hiring outside labour. Higher housing value significantly influences the decision to undertake house improvements, but does not significantly affect the amount of expenditure once the decision to make some improvement has been made. These results are consistent with the notion of a positive elasticity of housing supply from the existing stock of owner-occupied dwellings, but one which is highly variable between locations and personal circumstances.

Ingram & Oron develop a simulation model of an urban housing market. The supply side of the market consists of two levels of neighbourhood quality (good and bad) and two types of structure (high-rise and small multi-occupied units). Input prices vary by neighbourhood and the "production function" for quality varies by structure type (a production function describes the quantitative relationship between an output and one or more inputs). The empirical element of this study involves estimation of parameters of the production function. Time-series data are used from a sample of 29 apartment buildings in the Boston area over the period 1942–69. Alternative measures of the price of operating inputs are derived from a fuel and utility index and a consumer price index. The output is defined as the annual average rent per room divided by a local rent index. The input variable is defined as real operating expenditures, which are calculated by deflating actual operating expenditures by the price index of operating inputs. The estimated value of the "elasticity of substitution" varies between 0.32 and 0.65 depending on the exact specification of the equation adopted (the exact meaning of this term is discussed further in §2.4 below). Once the parameters of the production function have been estimated, it is possible to combine that information with price data to develop a picture of the way in which production costs vary with output levels. Although not altogether successful, the study highlights the importance of the supply response attributable to changes in operating intensities, and suggests that it might be of some considerable significance. It also highlights the difficulty of empirical work in this area.

Some further progress has been made by Ozanne & Struyck (1978), who are able to use panel data on 2500 dwellings in the Boston Metropolitan area for 1960 and 1970 derived from the CINCH (Components of Inventory Change) data from the 1970 Census of Housing. The sample includes 1500 owner-occupied dwellings and 1000 rented dwellings. Quantity changes are measured by statistical models, and price variations are computed as the residual variation in gross rents. These data facilitate a direct estimate of the supply elasticity of housing services from the existing stock of housing. The estimated supply function is a cross-section estimate which relates the quantity of structural services provided by a dwelling in 1970 to the 1960 quantity, the 1970 rental price, a measure of factor input prices (e.g. wages), and a proxy for producer expectations. Factor input prices vary across neighbourhoods, and so perform a useful role in the regression model. In particular, the existence of local labour markets implies the existence of some spatial variation in wage rates among repair and maintenance contractors, and there is even some spatial variation in non-labour inputs such as cleaning aids and paint, household appliances, floor polishes and lawn-mowers, due largely to variable trade discounts. Spatial variation in mortgage costs was associated with "red-lining" of poor neighbourhoods with relatively large populations of Black households. On the basis of their statistical analysis they conclude that the lower limit to the supply elasticity from existing structures is around 0.3, which implies that a 10% increase in house prices would give rise to a 3% increase in the quantity/quality of housing services provided from the existing stock. Nevertheless, since the existing stock is large compared to any possible short-run increase in new construction which might follow a demand shift, a large part of any increase in housing service supply is likely to derive from this source, despite the low numeric value of the elasticity. The study is useful in that it develops a methodology for making use of cross-section data to provide estimates of the supply elasticity which would be relatively easily replicated in other contexts.

Maintenance over time

An important feature of the repair and maintenance decision, neglected in the discussion so far, is the intertemporal nature of decisions to add to or remove from the capital stock, precisely because the stock is durable. The flow of benefits from an improvement is expected to endure over a significant future period of time, and this means that the dynamic nature of the investment decision involved will need to be taken account of in a fully acceptable theory of supply. Several attempts have been made to introduce the element of time into the analysis of housing supply, building upon intertemporal investment theory, having included studies by Moorhouse (1972), Dildine & Massey (1974), Sweeney (1974), Margolis (1981), Arnott et al. (1983) and Vorst (1987). Models such as these generally proceed by investigating the behaviour of a landlord who owns a single dwelling on a given plot and adopts a maintenance policy so as to maximize present discounted rents over some time horizon. Some studies assume a fixed economic life of the building, (Moorhouse, Arnott et al.), but in other cases the simpler assumption of an infinite time horizon is used. Maintenance is carried out within the constraints of a maintenance technology where diminishing returns apply as improvements are increased. Using the technique of optimal control theory, it is relatively easy to derive the time pattern of optimal maintenance expenditures, and to show that this leads to a stable equilibrium solution (Margolis 1981). Arnott et al. (1983) further show that, if construction costs are sufficiently low relative to maintenance costs, maintenance may be neglected, the building may be allowed to depreciate and may be demolished in finite time, when a new building would be constructed in its place. If demolition costs are high, the building may just be abandoned, although this phenomenon is more common in US cities than in Britain.

The great advantage of dynamic models is that they make it explicit that maintenance takes time, and that the supply response is spread out over a succession of time periods. Therefore, the supply response itself has a time dimension, and this means that, in housing, supply will take time to adapt to changes in demand. This has rarely been made explicit in empirical studies, with the exception of Rydell (1982), who provides estimates of the timescale of the supply response. Rydell finds a composite price elasticity of 11.5, for data on Brown County, Wisconsin and St Joseph's County, Indiana; of this composite elasticity, the repair elasticity alone was 0.2 (comparable to the findings of Ozanne & Struyck), the inventory elasticity attributable to factor input substitution was 6.7 and the elasticity attributable to new construction was 4.6. The time dimension of the supply response is illustrated in Table 2.1.

Table 2.1 Variation in composite supply and elasticity over time in the USA.

Years since demand increased	Supply elasticity
0	0.24
1	0.49
3	1.22
5	2.35
7	3.86
9	5.5
10	11.5

Source: Rydell (1982), 25.

The time dimension of supply response also features in our analysis of new-build supply and its relationship with planning in Chapters 6 and 7.

2.4 Long-run models of supply with new construction

In addition to maintenance activity the housing stock can also be adjusted through the entry of new dwellings into the market, both in existing residential locations, through infill and conversion of use, and through construction on new green-field sites. Dwellings may exit from the stock by demolition or change of use. In this way the existing housing stock can be expanded and the demand for new services can be met by the addition of new dwellings. The size and location of this new stock should adjust as far as possible to meet the current pattern of rents and demand. New housing will be constructed whenever the price of housing (related to rents) rises above the minimum level of construction costs, since positive profits can be made. The ensuing expansion of supply shifts the long-run supply curve outwards (see Fig. 2.1). This in turn reduces the market rent until excess profits are eliminated, and new construction comes to a halt. In practice, of course, new construction takes time because of planning delays and the length of construction times, and so the process would be far from smooth. The construction industry is notoriously cyclic, and so periods of above- or below-normal profit can often persist for some time. Typically, the perfectly competitive model treats these effects as subsidiary influences, arguing that the long-run trends are the important aspects of the supply-side model, about which any cyclic fluctuations take place.

This process can lead to a change in the elasticity of supply for housing services. As each individual dwelling adds new supply to the market, the long-run supply function (associated with the existing stock of dwellings) is shifted outwards. If perfect duplication of units were possible, the long-run supply would be perfectly elastic. Of course, this formulation as it stands makes no concession to the issue of locational specificity. If it is meaningful to define a limited submarket in a particular location, then the supply of housing has to be considered separately for each location. In the extreme case of a completely isolated housing submarket, for which there were no substitutes in other locations, a land supply constraint would ultimately come into operation and duplication of units would cease to be possible. This type of quantity rationing on the supply side (because of the immobility of land) could be important in some cases, particularly where there are planning restrictions on the development of new sites, or where for technical reasons the available land is unsuitable for residential development. In the very long run, one would expect that the development of other aspects of the urban economy would diminish the force of any such constraints, through the development of new forms of transport to make new supplies of land accessible, or through the development of new construction, maintenance and rehabilitation technologies. These issues are taken up and discussed further in Chapters 3 and 6.

Very long-run changes affecting all markets are covered by what economists call "general equilibrium models". However, such models and effects are beyond the scope of most analyses of the supply of housing services, which generally focus on the housing sector alone and take the state of other markets as given; this is called partial equilibrium analysis. However, one general equilibrium feedback mechanism that is particularly important is the impact of any change in supply conditions on the markets for the particular factors that go into the production of housing, i.e. the markets for construction labour, finance, materials and land. Since the housing market is sizeable in relation to the rest of the economy, it would be reasonable to expect that an increase in demand for these factor inputs, which could arise from an increase in maintenance and construction activity, would be associated with an increase in their price. In this case, the average costs facing landlords and construction firms would rise, shifting up the average cost curves, and giving rise to an upward sloping curve, even under conditions of free entry. This situation (often referred to as one of "external diseconomies of scale") is quite likely to be observed in the case of housing, making this an "increasing cost industry".

The microeconomics of the supply of housing services

Within the neoclassical paradigm of perfect competition, the first fully worked out theoretical model of the long-run supply of housing services was that of Muth (1969), whose seminal work on cities and housing has inspired much empirical research on housing supply. Muth presents two models of housing supply, the first of which abstracts from durability and heterogeneity, and focuses on the influence of locational specificity in the housing market. From the analysis of optimal consumer choice it is shown that the demand price for housing services varies with distance from the city centre, since the farther the consumer resides from the city centre the greater are transport costs (assuming all work and other opportunities are located at the city centre), and so the unit price of housing services must fall with distance to balance increased transport costs. This gives rise to a mark-up on the unit price of housing services as one approaches the city centre from the city edge, and the price of housing services rises along a "residential rent gradient" (Henderson 1977). These gradients are illustrated in Figures 2.2, 3.1 and 3.2.

At each location, at a distance u from the city centre, housing producers face a given demand price $p(u)$ for housing services, which declines along the residential rent gradient.

Associated with the residential rental gradient is a land rent gradient which reflects the maximum land rental price $r(u)$. This is associated with the highest bid per unit of land that landlord producers of housing services are likely to make to landowners. If the supply of land were perfectly elastic at a rental price r^*,

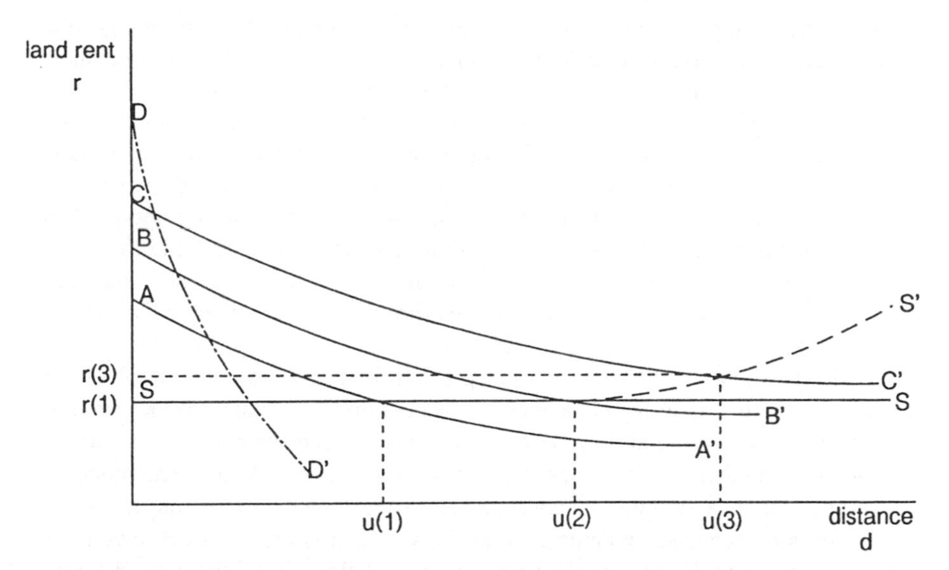

Figure 2.2 Land rent and distance, with different levels of demand.

then the size of the residential zone of the city would be given by that area for which the bid price for land for residential use exceeded the supply price of land. This would be the bid price (or opportunity cost) of that land in its best alternative use. Near the city centre, this use would probably be commercial, with its steeply sloping bid-rent curve DD'. At the city fringes it would probably be agricultural use that would represent the best alternative.

In Figure 2.2, the line SS' shows the supply price of land at various distances from the city centre. The rents r are indicated along the vertical axis. Land supply is shown as being elastic up to distance $u(2)$, but possibly inelastic thereafter, represented by the rising dashed curve SS'. In other words, as the limit of the land area is reached, land rents must increase to attract more land into residential use. The demand for land is shown by the land rent gradients AA' and BB', reflecting successively higher levels of demand for housing. At any given level of housing demand, the land rent gradient, derived from the residential rent gradient, falls with distance from the city centre, i.e. as one moves from left to right along the horizontal axis in the diagram. Given the land rent gradient AA', the residential zone extends to distance $u(1)$ from the city centre. Should the demand for housing services, and hence the derived demand for land, increase, the land rent gradient would shift to the right. If a perfectly elastic supply of land were assumed, new entry into the housing services industry as a result of new construction activity responding to an increase in demand from AA' to BB' would extend the city limits to $u(2)$, with no consequent final increase in land rents or house prices. In this example, the long-run supply elasticity for housing services would be infinite.

In a more realistic case, the supply price of land into residential use might well be increasing, because land is in overall fixed supply, there are alternative uses of land against which the housing industry has to bid, and additional transport and other urban infrastructure may have to be financed. This case would be illustrated by a further shift of the land rent gradient to the right, with rents increasing from $r(1)$ to $r(3)$. This is the case of an increasing cost industry described earlier. This, together with planning controls on the supply of land, would give rise to a less than infinitely elastic supply of housing services. This would apply, even if the housing market were competitive, and there were free entry and exit, perfect information, divisibility, and so on. Some reasons for inadequate land supply, including planning and its implications, are discussed further in Chapter 3.

In the formal model set out by Muth, an explicit expression is derived for the elasticity of supply of housing services per unit of land area. This involves the shares of the two main inputs land and construction (also sometimes referred to as "capital" or "non-land") in the value of housing, and the elasticity of substitution between these inputs in the production of housing services. The model is developed on the assumption of constant returns to scale in production. Dwelling unit size is determined by demand conditions, and it is assumed that dwellings of different types (flats, detached houses, etc.) belong essentially to different industries, with their own distinct residential rental gradient, each dwelling type affording the maximum achievable rent at a particular distance from the city centre, and hence being dominant at a particular location.

Muth shows that the elasticity of supply of housing services (Es) can be expressed as

$$Es = x.\sigma$$

or in value terms as

$$Es = 1 + x.\sigma,$$

where x is the ratio of construction cost to land value per dwelling and σ is the elasticity of substitution between construction and land inputs. Box 2.1 shows the formal derivation of these formulae from the theoretical model.

Muth (1969) estimates the elasticity of substitution to be around 1. This means that the shares of construction and land costs are unaffected by changes in relative factor prices. With a ratio of factor shares (i.e. the ratio of construction costs to land values) of around 20 in the USA, this implies that the elasticity of supply of housing services per unit of land area was very high (around 20). In a later article, Muth (1971) revises his estimate of the elasticity of substitution downwards to 0.5 on the basis of newly available US cross-section data on new house sales, so that the supply elasticity would be about 10. However, the interesting point here is that with an elasticity of substitution less than unity, factor shares will vary with factor prices. And, since land prices vary with distance from the city centre, so too would the supply elasticity. He calculates that the supply elasticity for a city with a six-mile radius would remain high at the city edge, at around 18.5, and fall steadily towards the city centre, where it would be only

Box 2.1 Formal model of long-run housing supply

The housing producer chooses inputs of land, L, and capital N to produce housing, given the price of housing services p and the price of capital inputs w to maximize profits π.

$$\pi_u = p_u.Q[L_u,N_u] - r_u.L_u - w.N_u$$

An optimal location in terms of distance from the city centre, u, must also be chosen. Since price varies with location, so do the optimal factor input levels, so these variables will be indexed by u, The rental price of land (r_u), is determined as the maximum any producer is willing to pay at a given location. Since bid rents fall with distance from the city centre, $r'_u < 0$. Output of housing services, Q, is produced with a constant returns to scale production technology, and so can be written in terms of output per unit land area, i.e. in terms of density as:

$$q_u = q[n_u];\ q' > 0;\ q'' < 0$$

where $q = Q/L$ (the quantity of housing services produced per unit of land area) and $n = N/L$ (the capital:land ratio, or the density of housing). Thus, the profit function can be expressed in terms of profit per unit land area as:

$$\pi/L = p_u.q[n_u] - r_u - w.\,n_u \qquad (1)$$

If producers maximize this profit function, the optimal density, n^*, can be determined from the first-order condition:

$$p_u.q'[n^*_u] - w = 0 \qquad (2)$$

The comparative statics with respect to distance are then derived by implicit differentiation of (2) as:

$$dn^*/du = -p'.q'/p.q'' < 0$$

The sign is negative since both p' and q'' are negative. This result shows that the optimal density decreases with distance from the city centre.

Competition between producers drives r to a maximum achievable value, r^*, at a given location. This underpins the following free-entry, zero-profit condition where we drop the location indicator u for notational convenience:

$$p.q(n^*) - r^* + w.n^* = 0 \qquad (3)$$

Locational equilibrium requires that no change in location can increase profits. We assume that the price of capital does not vary across locations in the city so that $dw = 0$. By totally differentiating (3) we obtain:

$$dp.q + p.dq.dn - dr - w.dn = O \qquad (4)$$

From the first order condition (2) we can simplify this to

$$dp.q = dr, \text{ or:}$$

$$d[\ln(p)] = x_L.d[\ln(r)] \qquad (5)$$

where x_L is the share of land in total output, i.e.

$$x_L = r.L/p.Q$$

This expression (5) shows the close relationship between the residential rental gradient $d[\ln(p)]$ and the land rent gradient $d[\ln(r)]$.

Now we can return to expression (1) to finally derive the elasticity of substitution of the value of housing output per unit land area. First we totally differentiate to obtain:

$$d(pq) = dr + w.dn$$

This can be re-arranged as:

$$p.q.[d(p.q)/p.q] = r.\,[dr/r] + n.w.[dn/n]$$

or:

$$d[\ln(pq)] = d[\ln(r).x_L] + d[\ln(n)].x_N \qquad (6)$$

From the definition of the elasticity of substitution between capital and land, we have that:

$$d[\ln(n)] = \sigma.d[\ln(r)]$$

So, (6) can be written as

$$d[\ln(pq)] = d[\ln(r)].[x_L + \sigma.x_N]$$

Using the relationship between the land rent gradient and the residential rent gradient established in (5) gives the supply elasticity in value terms as:

$$e_s = d\ln(pq)/d\ln(p) = [1 + \sigma.\,x_N/x_L] \qquad (7)$$

or in real terms as:

$$e_s' = d\ln(q)/d\ln(p) = \sigma.\,x_N/x_L \qquad (8)$$

1.5. So, rising demand for housing in a city will tend to boost prices and rents near the centre, and give rise to much housing construction on the periphery.

A complete formulation for the supply elasticity would have to take into account both the elasticity of factor input substitution between construction and land (i.e. density), and also changes attributable to the increase in the residential land area, i.e. in new construction on formerly non-housing land. Rydell (1982) refers to this as the "composite" elasticity of supply of housing services, which on the basis of cross section US data he calculates to be 11.3, as an average figure for the USA as a whole. However, as we have seen, the actual figure is likely to vary with location and so would need to be calculated separately for different city regions in any disaggregated study. Rydell also estimates the components of the composite supply elasticity, and shows that of the total figure 60% was attributable to input substitution and only 40% to variations in the amount of residential land.

Indirect empirical studies

Many empirical studies of housing supply have been designed to establish the magnitude of the elasticity of substitution between land and other factor inputs into the production of housing services, in an attempt to make the Muth elasticity formula operational. Virtually all of these studies are American. McDonald (1981) has reviewed 13 such studies, concluding that they support an estimate of unit elasticity of substitution between land and construction. From the definition of σ we can write:

$$\ln(wN/L) = c + \sigma.\ln(r) + (1\text{-}\sigma).\ln(w)$$

where L and N are land and construction inputs supplied at prices r, and w as before. This equation, or variation of it, has been widely used to estimate σ empirically, using standard econometric (regression) methods as briefly described in Chapter 1. The range of estimates reported by McDonald lies between 0.36 and 1.13, with 9 out of 12 valid estimates being significantly less than 1. The studies by Koenker (1972), Rydell (1976), McDonald (1979) and Sirmans et al. (1979) use data from single metropolitan areas (Ann Arbor, Chicago, Brown County, Santa Clara County). They use the estimation equation (with w assumed constant):

$$\ln[pQ - rL)/L] = c + \sigma.\ln(r) + u$$

As McDonald points out, measurement errors for r induce bias, which has a downward impact on the estimated value of σ. Re-estimation of the Sirman et al. study on a different database, using a technique involving "instrumental variables" to eliminate the bias, gave McDonald an estimate of σ insignificantly different from unity. Clapp (1980) devised an independent measure of land value that was derived from a regression of total property value on the characteristics of the structure and site, and then deducted the value of the structural characteristics of the house from its total value.

Nevertheless, Neels (1981) is critical of these studies on account of the possibility of measurement error. He attempts a direct estimation of the production function for housing services (the production function relates the output of housing to the quantities of inputs). He uses a particular function (known as "translog") to represent the production technology in a very general form, with the advantage that more than two inputs can be modelled in a flexible way. In addition to land, Neels investigates the role of capital, energy and other current inputs in the production of housing services using data from a survey undertaken in Brown County, Wisconsin and St Joseph's County, Indiana. The results provide evidence of a rather low value of σ of 0.32 when energy and other current inputs were entered separately, which compared with a value of 0.67 when these current inputs were entered as a composite input. Overall, these results once again imply that a value in the range 0.5–1.0 provides a reasonable estimate of σ.

Most other studies have been based upon a form of production function that assumes a constant elasticity of substitution (CES). Sirmans et al. (1979) object that this is too restrictive, and they introduce a variable elasticity of substitution (VES) production function which allows σ to vary with factor proportions. The appropriate estimation equation is then linear rather than logarithmic. After making the appropriate calculations, their reported results for a sample of single-family housing from Santa Clara County, California, give an estimate of σ which varies from 0.66 to 0.92.

The studies by Muth (1971), Polinsky & Ellwood (1979) and Sirmans & Redman (1979) used data on cross-sections of metropolitan areas. Their estimating equations took the logarithmic form:

$$\ln(rL/wN) = c + (1-\sigma).\ln(r/w) + u$$

The possible biases associated with errors in the independent variables r (rents) and w (wages) tend to cancel each other out in this type of specification. However, since it is likely that the measurement error on r is greater than that on w, McDonald concludes that a downward bias still probably exists. Nevertheless, all these studies give rise to estimates of σ significantly less than unity. Muth's (1971) estimate was 0.5. Sirmans & Redman's estimate from a cross-section data on 10000 single-family houses in 31 metropolitan areas in 1969, provided an estimated value of σ of 0.45. These results are well in the range of Neel's study, mentioned above. They indicate that the downward bias which concerns McDonald is probably not sufficient to support his contention that the true value of the elasticity of substitution is as high as 1.0.

Finally, Rosen (1978) and Stover (1986) estimate translog cost functions (cost functions relate unit costs of outputs to the price of different inputs, the scale of output, and other factors). Rosen's study is based on a cross section of 10000 single-family houses from 31 metropolitan areas in 1969. Stover uses data from 61 SMSAs for 1976 to 1981. Rosen's estimate of σ is 0.43; Stover's is 0.35.

The conclusion from these attempts at estimating the elasticity of substitution must therefore be that the value of unity is an upper bound and that it is quite likely that there are considerable difficulties in substituting construction/capital inputs for land in the production of housing services. In Chapter 8 we report on our own application of this approach to British data, which very much reinforces this conclusion. This implies that variations in house prices, which pull up the price of land, will be associated with an increase in the share of land in production costs, which it would be difficult to avoid through changes in the factor mix. Evidence showing an increase in land's share in housing costs during periods of rising prices would also support the finding of a less than unit-elastic elasticity of substitution.

Smith (1976) extends the model to incorporate the case where the quantity of housing services is to be split into the product of quality and density. This approach may be thought to be appropriate where quality and density are not substitutable in the production of housing services. Smith derives an estimating equation from which the respective elasticities can be recovered, which involved regressing assessed land value on housing expenditures per area. Using 200 market transactions for single-family housing in Chicago between 1971 and 1972, he derived values of the supply elasticity of density of 5.26 and the supply elasticity of quality of 3.75, which are significantly different from each other at the 99% level. The estimated elasticity of substitution lies between 0.96 and 1.36 (this corrected result is reported in Grieson & Arnott 1983). However, as Grieson & Arnott point out, the usefulness of the approach is in doubt as in practice it is not usually required to estimate the two elasticities separately. Since normal profit-maximizing quality and density vary simultaneously with price, for most practical purposes the composite supply elasticity of quantity of housing services discussed above would be the relevant variable. Thus, although ingenious, the approach developed by Smith has not been carried forward by other researchers. We discuss quality and density issues further in Chapter 8.

Direct empirical studies

The major alternative to the inferential method of estimating the long-run supply elasticity is to estimate a supply function directly on either cross-section or time-series data on prices, costs and quantities traded. The major problems involved are of correctly identifying the supply function, given simultaneous determination of price and quantity by supply and demand forces. Also, it is sometimes difficult to interpret the results, and it is not always clear whether the estimated elasticity is indeed a genuine "long-run" elasticity or not. In addition, there is the difficulty of measuring quantities separately from prices (because each house is a different package). The problem could be addressed by the use of so-called "hedonic indices" of quantity in the manner of Ozanne & Struyck (1978); these involve the use of statistical models that predict individual house prices from data on house and locational attributes. However, the normal practice has been to make use of data on new housing construction (Whitehead 1974, Bradbury et al. 1977, Follain 1979, Mayes 1979, Topel & Rosen 1988; see also Ch. 6). This restricts the usefulness of the results, since what is effectively being measured is the elasticity of supply of additions to the stock, of new entry. This is only a part of the total supply response to a price change, which also includes any changes to the intensity of use of existing stock, through increased utilization, increased occupancy rates, and increased maintenance and conversion activity. Some of these elements are more important in the short run, and some in the long run. It should be remembered that elasticities relating to new-build are measures of annual *flow*, not of the housing stock, although changes in stock are clearly related to new-build flows.

In an early study, Whitehead (1974) investigated the supply response of new housing starts in the UK on national time-series quarterly data for the period 1955 to 1972. For the period 1955 to 1970 the best model tested gave an estimate of the elasticity of new construction to current house prices of around 2; but when estimated with the addition of two more years, up to 1972, the elasticity fell to only 0.5. The reasons for the observed parameter instability of the model were not adequately explained at the time, but the greater impact of planning constraints on land supply during the 1972 boom (see Ch. 4) might be a plausible explanation. In any case there were admitted shortcomings in the specification of the supply model. Although construction costs, interest costs and financial flows were included in the equation, little attention was paid to the possible effect of time-lags. As Whitehead acknowledged, "perhaps the most important factor on the supply side was the massive increase in the amount of house improvement work undertaken. This sometimes requires almost as much skilled labour as in new building, but is has a fairly certain rate of profit and does not require so much finance on the part of the builder" (p. 170).

A later study of new construction in the UK by Mayes (1979) used a more robust specification of the supply of starts, which takes account of lags and delays in the construction process. This enables the estimation of both short- and long-run elasticities. The estimated short-run supply elasticity was 0.27 and the long-run elasticity (calculated on the assumption of long-run equilibrium) was 0.55. This is a surprisingly low value for the long-run elasticity of new construction starts when contrasted with the findings from US studies, even accounting for the differences in land availability and planning regulations, and it points to the clear need for further research on the supply conditions in the UK market.

Several studies of this type of the US housing market have also been carried out. An early study by de Leeuw & Ekanem (1971) argued that data from cross sections of metropolitan areas would indeed yield the required long-run supply elasticity since "studying differences among cities amounts to studying how housing markets behave in the long run, in the sense of having had ample time to adjust to basic market forces. The reason is that differences among cities in size, costs, tax rates, real income, and so on, tend to persist for years or even decades". de Leeuw & Ekanem use an indirect method of estimation involving rental values, a single equation, and prior information on demand elasticity. The implied supply elasticities fall in the range 0.3 to 0.7, which is evidence of a highly inelastic supply of housing services. The low values suggest that the cross-section method, insofar as the specification is correct, may not really capture "long-run" values of the variables. In fact it is rather implausible that all agents are operating at long-run equilibrium values, and so the estimated equation is likely to be a hybrid measure of an unknown combination of short- and long-run effects. In addition, as Olsen (1987) has commented on the de Leeuw & Ekanem paper, "their specification of the long-run supply function is inconsistent with standard economic theory and hence the results cannot be interpreted" (p. 1017), since they included in the structural supply equation both the quantity of housing services and the input prices instead of just prices.

A further cross-section study on US data by Bradbury et al. (1977) takes advantage of the insight provided by the Muth model that the supply elasticity should be expected to vary across locations (e.g. in the basic model with distance from the city centre), as output prices vary with location. In practical situations, a variety of locational, neighbourhood-specific factors will affect the supply elasticity. Bradbury et al. model this by estimating an interaction effect between price changes and locationally specific vacancy rates in their study of data on percentage changes in the number of housing units in 89 Boston metropolitan area subregions. Although the estimated equation does not fit the data very well, the individual coefficients are all significant. Other variables included are the change in competing uses of land, the change in the vacancy rate and a dummy variable for the strength of planning controls. The estimated supply elasticities are once again low, but they vary across locations in the manner predicted by theory, from almost zero at the city centre to about 0.9 at the suburban fringe.

Dynamics and expectations

Progress has been made in integrating the supply of new housing construction into a coherent dynamic model of the housing market, particularly by Poterba (1984). In this "rational expectations" model, construction sector producers respond to a demand increase by accelerating the rate of new house construction. Rational expectations implies that actors in the market, particularly producers, form their expectations on the basis of a logical and realistic forecasting model (generally equated with the model favoured by the analyst!). Models of this kind are sometimes called "forward-looking". With static expectations, the initial response to the demand shift would be a pure price effect, and new construction would begin to increase supply to meet demand only after a time-lag. However, with rational expectations, the initial price-jump required to set the market onto the "perfect foresight" path towards a new equilibrium is lower, and the associated supply elasticity higher, than it would be if expectations effects were absent.

Poterba estimates an investment supply function with an equation in which investment in new construction depends on the expected real price of houses adjusted for length of time to sale, the real price of alternative construction projects, and the prevailing wage in the construction industry. He explicitly rejects the inclusion of variables such as income or demographic trends in the equation as, he argues, the asset price of housing is a statistic sufficient for these demand-side forces, and that the flow of new construction should therefore depend only on the real house price. The model was estimated on quarterly US data for the period 1974–82. In the best fitting equations, the estimated supply elasticity ranged from 0.5 to 2.3, depending upon the model specification. These findings can be compared with the results of earlier studies that included real house prices in residential investment functions. Kearl (1979) found a supply elasticity of about 1.6 for new investment, and Huang (1973) reported an elasticity of nearly 2 for housing starts. Poterba uses these results in developing a simulation of the effects of eliminating mortgage-interest tax relief in an economy with a 10% inflation rate and a 25% marginal tax rate. He finds that the policy change would lead to an immediate fall of 26% in real house prices and a long-run decline in the stock of housing capital of around 29%. The simulations suggest the importance of using explicitly dynamic models with forward-looking expectations when studying policies that affect capital accumulation and asset prices.

A further study of the supply of new housing starts has been made by Topel & Rosen (1988), who carry Poterba's analysis forward, emphasizing the importance of expectations of future house price changes in influencing construction decisions, and introducing internal adjustment costs to explain how supply takes time to adjust following a price increase. Rational expectations induce landlords to build ahead of anticipated demand in order to distribute costs over an extended interval of time. This means that expected inflation enters into the supply function. A regression model relating quarterly US data for new starts between 1963 and 1983 to a real hedonic price index for new standard-quality single-family homes, the real interest rate, expected inflation, a time-to-sale variable and lagged starts. Time-to-sale has a significantly negative effect on housing starts, as does expected inflation, and the best estimates of the long-run supply elasticity with respect to a permanent price increase is about 3. For the short-run (1 quarter) elasticity is around 1, with the short-run elasticity converging to the long-run elasticity within one year. This fairly rapid response rate is attributable to the non-specialized nature of the resources used in the construction industry. As Topel & Rosen comment, "perhaps the pronounced seasonal and cyclical fluctuations in construction promote a certain adaptability and built-in flexibility in the organization of the industry that allow resource movements to respond quickly to changing economic conditions" (p. 737). This echoes the qualitative British evidence emphasized by Ball (1983) and discussed further in Chapter 5.

Rational expectations have exerted a considerable influence on recent economic modelling of the housing market. Nevertheless, the qualitative evidence on housebuilder behaviour and expectations cited in Chapter 5 casts doubt on this as a realistic portrayal of typical firms in the industry.

2.5 Conclusion

The determination of the elasticity of supply of housing services is an important input into the estimation and measurement of cyclical behaviour of the housing market, the impact of housing subsidies and other topical policy issues in housing. We began this chapter by considering the meaning or definition of housing supply and considering the different ways in which this can adjust, in the short and the longer run. Thus, housing occupancy, maintenance and upgrading can represent important elements in the overall adjustment of supply, alongside new building itself, the main focus of this book.

In this chapter two main methods for deriving the supply elasticity have been discussed. First, an inferential method uses information on the production technology as described by the key elasticity of substitution parameter to derive, indirectly, an estimate of the supply elasticity. This method has the *disadvantage* of being sensitive to the theoretical assumptions of the characteristics of the market: the market structure, the ease of entry or exit, the size of returns to scale, the rate of technical progress in the construction industry, the extent of spillovers from labour and capital markets into the housing market, and the effects of planning controls on land release and conversion of use. Some estimate of the impact of all these factors needs to be made before estimated values of the substitution elasticity can be used to infer the supply elasticity. The *advantage* of the method, however, is that the substitution elasticity poses relatively few problems for econometric estimation, provided appropriate data are available.

Secondly, it is possible to attempt a *direct estimation* of the supply elasticity from a supply function estimated on cross-section or time-series data for house prices or rentals. The *disadvantages* of this approach are that the price of housing services is not readily observable, and so the difficult problem of constructing a price index for housing service needs to be solved separately. Models of this type often focus upon the supply of new housing starts or completions alone and so pick up only a portion of the supply response to a price change, a further part emanating from an increased supply from the existing stock. In the short run this takes place through changes in the occupancy rate and the intensity of use of existing structures, and in the long run through factor substitution brought about by a more intense development of existing sites following improvement and rehabilitation of the stock. Also, since price and quantity are simultaneously determined, problems of econometric estimation are more difficult, and the conditions for the identification of the supply function need to be carefully considered. A further and final difficulty is that care needs to be taken to build into the estimation, through the specification of the estimated equation, some means of distinguishing short- and long-run effects, otherwise the estimated supply elasticity will be a hybrid measure which it will be difficult to interpret. The *advantage* of the approach is its relative directness, so that the results are less sensitive to the assumptions made about the housing market under study. The model described in Chapter 6 exemplifies the application of this type of approach to British data.

Most of the studies reviewed in this chapter have been undertaken in the USA. The US context differs considerably from that in the UK, especially regarding the supply of land (Bramley 1989). Therefore, adjustments would need to be made to the underlying assumptions that feed into the indirect calculation of the supply elasticity, such as the ratio of factor shares for example. To illustrate, by way of a hypothetical example based on values that may be appropriate for the UK, for a value of the substitution elasticity of 0.4, and with land value representing 40% of the overall price of housing, the implied long-run supply elasticity of housing services per unit of land area would be 0.6. However, it should be emphasized that, once the induced increase in new housing construction is taken into account, this figure would necessarily be augmented, to an extent dependent upon the elasticity of supply of land into the housing sector, and hence upon the strength of demand for land in alternative uses.

The significance of the long-run elasticity is that it provides an upper bound upon the responsiveness of the housing market to changes in price. Since short-run elasticities differ by time and place, is it not surprising that empirical measures of short-run elasticities are extremely variable. More interesting, perhaps, are attempts made to estimate the time taken to adjust to full long-run equilibrium, such as is done in the studies by Rydell (1982), and Topel & Rosen (1988). The later in particular, and also the study by Poterba (1984), indicate the importance of dynamics and expectations to the analysis of the supply responsiveness of the housing market.

Finally, whenever the price of housing services varies across locations, if the substitution elasticity is less than unity, then factor shares will vary over space as well. Since these variables enter into the determination of the long-run supply elasticity for housing services, that elasticity will also vary in reflection of the spatial structure of house rental prices. It therefore seems justified to make separate estimates of the elasticity for each distinct geographical unit.

CHAPTER 3
Planning and housing supply in theory

3.1 Land-use planning

What is planning?

"Planning" can mean different things to different people or in different contexts. The former USSR organized its economy through a planning system, as an alternative to a market system. The British Treasury engages in an annual exercise for the planning of public expenditure. Large and complex capital investment projects require careful planning, as do military operations. All of these examples have in common that they involve "predicting the future in order to formulate normative policies to influence it" (Lichfield & Darin-Drabkin 1980: 5). They also all involve systems of considerable complexity in which different elements are interdependent. Planning can also imply an emphasis on space rather than time; thus, for example, the word "plan" can mean map or diagram of the layout of a building, or a city, in two-dimensional space.

In this book we are concerned with a specific meaning of the term "planning". We are interested in the system variously known as "town & country planning", "land-use planning" or "development planning". Planning in this sense represents a particular form of public policy intervention in the arena of private decisions with regard to the use of land, governed by particular legislation (in Britain, chiefly the Town and Country Planning Acts). This particular form of planning contains elements of all of the kinds of planning suggested in the previous paragraph, both forward-looking forecasts and deployments of resources, and drawing up plans in two-dimensional space. Land-use planning is restricted in the sense that it deals only with changes in the use of land, rather than all aspects of socioeconomic life. On the other hand, it does have to respond to and accommodate a wide variety of interests, and some complex interactions between different activities, insofar as land is required as "a platform" for all activities and the spatial arrangement of different activities may matter.

In this book we are concerned not with the totality of planning but only with the ways that it may impinge upon housing supply. The focus of the discussion is primarily upon the British institutional arrangements for planning. According to Cheshire & Leven (1982: 1) Britain has planning controls "among the most comprehensive of those operating in Western industrialized countries"; other authors (Lichfield & Darin-Drabkin 1980) paint a picture of Britain's planning system as a leading example for much of the rest of the world. Thus, although the British focus of this book might be seen as unduly restrictive, it has the advantage of providing an insight into the effects of a fairly strong and comprehensive planning system.

Planning activities

What is involved in land-use planning? Planning activities fall into three broad categories:

- *forward planning*, which mainly involves the preparation and updating of regional strategies, county structure plans, and local plans; such plans typically involve setting quantitative and qualitative targets for new housing provision, and local plans normally allocate (or zone) particular pieces of land for housing development;
- *development control*, which involves local planning authorities responding to applications for the right to undertake specific developments from landowners or developers; the response may involve granting or refusing permission, negotiating to modify the application, or participating in an appeals procedure.
- *implementation*, which involves direct industrial, commercial or housing development by or involving public authorities (e.g. town centres, new towns, comprehensive redevelopment, Community Land scheme).

The main institutions involved in planning in Britain are elected local authorities, for which it is one of many functions. When talking loosely of "the planners", we should remember that most planning decisions are made by elected local councillors, advised by professional officers, and not by a completely autonomous group of bureaucrats. Central government is also involved, in the form of the Department of the Environment ministers, officials and the planning inspectorate, especially where developers appeal against planning refusals, and through policy guidance. Mention should also be made of the bodies that provide the infrastructure necessary for development to proceed, as they play an important practical role in constraining and shaping development. These include departments of local authorities in the case of roads and schools, and the (increasingly privatized) public utilities responsible for water, sewerage and other services. An even wider range of bodies, for example representative organizations and pressure groups, form part of the "policy community", which seeks to influence planning and housing development, as described in Rydin (1986). The institutional framework for planning is discussed further in the next chapter.

The aims of planning

What does this elaborate apparatus of intervention seek to achieve? From the literature (Harrison 1977: ch.1; Curry 1978: 55–6; Pearce 1992), as well as observation of practice, one can discern some general aims that could be said to constitute the main operational objectives of land-use planning in Britain:

- *Spatial containment* of urban development, particularly the clear separation of town and country and the prevention of sprawl. This goal is clearly central to the best known feature of British planning, the green belts (see Hall et al. 1973, DoE Circular 14/84, Elson 1986, D. Hughes 1988).
- *Separation* of different and potentially conflicting land uses, for example housing and industry. The term "zoning" is often used abroad to describe this type of planning, although it may also encompass density below. Probably the most common reason for refusal of planning permission is that the development would be "non-conforming" with the predominant and/or planned use of the zone in question.
- Influencing the *density* of development, for example through plot ratio controls, as discussed in Harrison (1977: ch. 11), can be an aim of planning, as discussed further below.
- *Co-ordinating* the volume and location of different kinds of development (housing, industry, retail) to try to ensure balance and reasonable self-containment in local labour markets, shopping and services. This may involve an explicit, redistributive goal of improving access to job and other opportunities for certain groups or areas, but equally it may be a simple efficiency goal of minimizing transport costs.
- Co-ordinating development with the provision of expensive public *infrastructure*. The supply of investment in roads, sewers, schools, parks and other facilities is rationed, and concentrating development in particular areas maximizes the use of these limited resources. Increasingly, planning agreements are used to secure major financial contributions from developers towards these costs.
- Influencing *urban design* in order to achieve certain standards of appearance, layout, and facilities considered desirable.
- *Conservation*: the protection of certain features of both urban and rural environments that are valued for historical/cultural, aesthetic, scientific or other reasons.

This list may not be exhaustive but it conveys the main range of concerns of planning in Britain and, to varying degrees, other countries.

Stepping back from these operational objectives, is it possible to relate these to higher-order objectives? For example, does planning contribute to economic efficiency and performance, to equity and social justice, to the quality of life, or to environmental values such as sustainability?

One framework within which a coherent theoretical rationale for planning can be erected is that of welfare economics (e.g. Harrison 1977, Curry 1978, Walker

1981, Le Grand et al. 1992). Within this framework there is a heavy emphasis on the role of externalities, both direct environmental neighbourhood effects and financial effects relating to infrastructure and transport costs.

The flavour of the approach can be conveyed by a relevant example of externalities. People derive benefits (or welfare) from having a house with a garden. They also derive benefit from the existence of open countryside adjacent to the town where they live; they enjoy looking at it, using it for recreation, and possibly value the knowledge that it provides a habitat for diverse species of plant and animal. The first benefit is a normal private economic good; you choose and pay for the size of house and garden that you prefer within your economic means. The second benefit is an external benefit derived by one person (the resident) from the decision of another (the owner of the land) to maintain it in its rural state. However, in a normal market situation the second party (the rural landowner) has no financial incentive to take account of the benefit of the amenity to the first party (the resident). In practice, on the fringe of typical British towns the landowner would have a financial incentive to sell the land for housing development. The occupiers of this new housing would enjoy private benefits of new houses with gardens, which they would pay for, but the existing residents would lose their beneficial amenity. This is an example of an economic externality.

In general, economic external effects can mean that markets may fail to operate in their usual "efficient" manner in allocating resources, so that overall we are worse off. In this case, we lose the valued amenity of undeveloped rural land adjacent to our city residences. Externalities thus provide one possible justification for public policy intervention in the market, which may take various forms, including regulation, taxation, or direct public service provision.

Externalities are one reason why markets may fail to perform their usual role of allocating resources efficiently. Other causes of market failure also relevant to planning include the provision of local public goods (e.g. parks), inadequate information about future needs and developments, or the monopoly control over particular pieces of land. The welfare framework may also draw attention to issues in the distribution of benefits or costs of urban development between different socioeconomic groups (Le Grand et al. 1992). Some have tried to encompass environmental issues within the same framework, although others might argue that this may be stretching economics too far.

Planning and implementation

It is one thing to plan, but another to see those plans realized in the form of developments on the ground, within the timescale originally envisaged. In the study of public policy, increasing attention has been paid to "implementation gaps" or "deficits" dividing policies from action (Barrett & Fudge 1980, Hill & Bramley 1986: ch. 8).

A relevant example is the work of Healey et al. (1985, 1988) who review the role of plans in the implementation of planning policies in selected regions in the 1980s. This study found that planning was achieving containment at the urban fringe but not regeneration in the older urban core. In urban fringe areas, where demands to build on green fields are strong, planning is good at allocating land, mediating conflicts, and stabilizing the context for investment. Planning powers are marginal to (dis)investment in older urban areas, where the main problems relate to resources, the behaviour of those with direct interests in land, and co-ordination of public sector agencies (see also Goodchild 1978, Lichfield & Darin-Drabkin 1980, Pearce 1992). The context for this is a recognition of the predominant role of the private sector in development activity, including housing, especially since 1980. Planning has to rely mainly on responsive development control powers, waiting for private developers to put forward schemes and not being able to initiate or shape developments from the outset.

The Healey et al. study also highlights two distinct approaches to policy implementation: one stresses a tight framework of statutory plans, the other stresses discretion. British planning has shifted over time, towards giving more discretion until quite recently, but now back in the direction of a clearer "plan-led" approach (see Ch. 4). Local authorities often like to maintain plenty of discretion, but have to balance this with the greater bargaining power with developers and inspectors that a statutory plan would give. British planning, which allows local planning authorities much discretion in their decisions, is quite different from the type of planning found in North America and elsewhere, which relies more on rather legalistic zoning rules (Grant 1992). Our studies of the actual operation of planning for housing in Britain described later on indicate that the issue of the link between plans and implementation is a crucial one.

3.2 Broader views of the function of planning

It may seem to be stating the obvious to observe that the effects of planning on the housing market and private housebuilding depend upon what planning actually does: on the behaviour of the planners. But this is a fundamental issue, and one on which it is difficult to put forward neat and simple theories. It is not completely obvious what planners do and why.

In §3.1 we defined and described planning in outline. One of the points we made was that planning had several operational objectives (containment, zoning, conservation, etc.). It is easier to agree on the list of what these are than to decide what the relative importance of each objective is, either in general or for a particular planning authority at a particular time. Since some of these objectives may be partially in conflict with one another, so that they have to be traded off in some way, this is an important area of uncertainty. A second observation was that different groups and institutions are involved in planning: local and central government, professionals and politicians, counties and districts. Each may have a different set of key objectives, or a different weighting on each element in the common list of objectives. A third observation was that planning (especially British planning in the 1970s and 1980s) gave great scope to the exercise of discretion on individual cases, both by local authorities and by ministers.

For all these reasons, there is considerable uncertainty about the effective operational rules and objectives of planning. The planning system itself is complex, and it is trying to influence and shape a very complex and fast-changing development industry and market. Furthermore, it is doing so on the basis of inadequate information about current conditions and a general lack of certainty about future conditions. Planning textbooks will provide normative statements about what planning should try to achieve and how to go about it. But what goes on in practice may differ considerably from these prescriptions. As social scientists we should seek to provide an objective picture of the activities and impacts of planners.

However, it is not easy to provide any theoretical account that is both simple and adequate to the complex reality. One reason for this is that the different academic disciplines that address these questions tend to emphasize different issues. For example, economists would ask the question: What is the objective (or social welfare function) that planners try to maximize? Political scientists might ask: In whose interests do planners act? Lawyers might ask: What powers do planners possess and what were the intentions of Parliament in giving them these powers? The public administration analyst might ask: What are the structures of planning institutions and what procedures do they follow?

There is not space to discuss these issues at great length in this book (Hague 1991 provides a useful review of planning theory). Instead, mainly in order to illustrate the possibility of different accounts of the function and behaviour of the planning system, we simply offer sketches of four alternative views or perspectives on planning as a political and administrative process. Although these four views are not the only possibilities, they do capture many of the different perspectives and issues mentioned above. And although they are presented as alternative and rival accounts, in practice it may be found more helpful to draw on several of them in presenting a full picture.

The four views or approaches, which are discussed in turn, are labelled as follows:

- welfare economics
- pluralist politics
- structural political economy
- bureaucracy.

Table 3.1 summarizes the key features of each view and enables comparisons to be made at a glance.

Table 3.1 Four views of planning.

	Welfare economics	Pluralist politics	Structural political economy	Bureaucracy
Key characteristics				
Objective	Welfare maximize	Re-election	Corporate growth, profit	Max. staff, influence, prof. values
Constraints	Resources Information	Support Median voter	Resources Legitimacy	Resources Information Planners
Key interest group	All citizens	Pressure groups	Corporate business	Goals achievement
Decision criterion	Cost–benefit	House prices	GNP	
Operational policies				
Containment	Moderate	Strong	Weak	Strong
Zoning	Between uses	Strong	Weak	Less formal
Density	Indicative	Strong	Weak	Strong
Co-ordination	Strong	Weak	Moderate	Strong
Infrastructure	Important	Underprovision	Overprovision	Important
Design	Weak	Moderate	Weak	Strong
Conservation	Moderate	Strong	Weak	Strong
Outcomes				
Style	Mixed	Rules	Discretion	Discretion
Centre/local	Consensus	Conflict	Conflict	Consensus
Positive planning implementation	Sometimes	No	Sometimes	Yes
Efficiency	High	Low	Medium	Medium–low
Economic growth	Medium	Low	High	Medium
Inequality	Low	High	Medium	Medium–low

Welfare economics

The welfare economics perspective was introduced earlier as a framework within an underlying case for planning as an intervention in the market can be derived (Harrison 1977, Walker 1981). If planning operated according to the prescriptions of this theory, what would it look like?

Planning would be a comprehensive, rational approach to decision-making (Jenkins 1978, Simon 1945, March & Simon 1958) in which the guiding model would be cost–benefit analysis (Le Grand et al. 1992). Planners would seek to maximize, subject to the constraint of available resources, a social welfare function that embraced both efficiency, broadly defined, and equity towards different social and income groups – an efficient and fair city. Full account would be taken of externalities as well as market effects. The planners would seek to promote economic growth and the concomitant physical development, so long as the adverse external effects were minimized or compensated through broader economic benefits and the collective costs of infrastructure were kept within check and clearly justified.

This view is clearly at one end of the spectrum in the sense that it is highly idealized and normative, that is it is essentially a statement about what planners should do. Of all the views, this one has the most ambitious and unrealistic information requirements, and this is one key reason why planners do not live up to the ideal, even if they aspire to. However, the view has a very positive normative status. Recommendations about what planners should do, or arguments which they should take account of, are very often couched in the terms of this perspective.

Looking at the question of operational goals, this approach has the general characteristic of avoiding extreme emphasis on one goal rather than another, because welfare economics is all about trade-offs between goals. Under this view, planning is very strong on co-ordination and on making the most of infrastructure investment. It will not make a strong stand on containment if this threatens such goals as economic growth or fairness. It may tend to be weakest on goals that deal with more intangible values, design and conservation. The approach seeks more consensus, and is likely to generate less conflict between central and local government. On the other hand, there is a serious danger that it makes planning over-technocratic, weakening the relationship with and commitment of politicians.

Overall we would expect this approach to be good for efficiency in the broad sense, and good for equity too (low on inequality), but to achieve more moderate rates of economic growth because of its unwillingness to sacrifice the environment or the poor to single-minded pursuit of short-term measured GNP growth.

Pluralist politics

This view represents a rough marriage of both a mainstream tradition in political science (Dahl 1961, Lukes 1974, Ham & Hill 1984) and the more recent "public choice" approach favoured by some economists (Downs 1957, Buchanan 1978, Laver 1979, Mueller 1989). The view assumes a decentralized, democratic system of government (including planning). Decisions are governed by political calculations about winning or retaining votes, particularly in the centre ground of local politics (appealing to the so-called "median voter"). A range of single-issue and local pressure groups have to be appeased in order to maintain adequate levels of political support to remain in office.

Applying this approach to the issue of housing development - especially in a situation such as that of Britain, where most existing households are owner-occupiers with an investment stake in their home - leads to the conclusion that in many cases local decision-makers will resist development. In other words, containment and zoning restrictions will be strongly applied, as will conservation policies. Other goals (e.g. co-ordination) will receive less weight. This prediction seems to fit most clearly the relatively affluent suburban areas, where relaxation on containment, zoning and conservation can all be predicted to have an adverse impact on amenity and property prices (see discussion in last section of this chapter). American studies provide strong support for this picture of suburban policies on zoning (Downs 1974, 1991; Monk et al. 1991: 16–19).

In economically more depressed areas considerations of job-generation may take more precedence and lead to more relaxed policies for industry and commerce but not necessarily for housing. Where local government financial resources, including those required to cover infrastructure costs of development, are dependent upon local economic conditions and structure, and not subject to full equalization as in Britain (Foster et al. 1980, Bramley 1990), then again local planning authorities may act rather differently (but again mainly in relation to industrial and commercial development).

Although not couched formally in terms of this particular view, Evans's (1991) picture of the biases in the planning system is quite consistent with it. He argues that the system gives too much weight to the interests of existing suburban and rural residents, and that its adverse consequences include an overall shortage of housing land, higher house prices, excessive densities (especially on suburban sites), and concentration of housing on environmentally unsuitable sites.

The normative status of this view is quite high, because it appeals to the value of democracy. But, if this view describes the overall way the planning system operates at all accurately, it gives serious cause for concern about the final outcomes. These are likely to be inefficiency, low economic growth, and more inequality – for example, the existing suburban residents enjoy more amenity and wealth accumulation, while marginal new housebuyers are excluded from the market.

Structural political economy

The third view (or set of views) derives partly from neo-Marxist theories of the State which were popular with academics interested in urban issues in the 1980s (O'Connor 1973, Saunders 1981, Cawson 1982). However, they may also be related to versions of pluralism which highlight the disproportionate power of certain elites, and to the idea of corporatism (Winkler 1977, Dunleavy 1981) or "corporate bias" (Middlemas 1979). The essence of these theories is that certain interests have privileged access to and influence within the political process, whether this influence is exercised overtly or covertly (Lukes 1974). There have been several attempts to apply these ideas to the field of planning and housing (Ball 1983, Rydin 1986, Short et al. 1986). It is not clear *a priori* which particular set of interests will predominate, and this indeterminacy is crucial to the planning and housebuilding issue. Some argue that rural landed interests, housebuilders with strategically located land banks, and rich suburban residents, could be the decisively influential groups, in which case the outcomes would be very similar to our pluralist politics view. An alternative and more mainstream view would be that the corporate business sector, which includes the housebuilding and development industries, is the predominant influence on policy; and that this sector has a vested interest in economic growth, suburbanization (which promotes high-consumption lifestyles), and a relaxation of restrictions and regulations on the activities of business. The portrayal of this view in Table 3.1 assumes that this second group of interests prevails.

Under this view planning would tend to be weak in its effective policies on containment, zoning, density and conservation. It would probably still be strong on co-ordination and would ensure a high provision of infrastructure, possibly more than could be economically justified. The outcomes would be a high level of short-term measured economic growth, but less overall efficiency or equity than under the welfare economics approach.

Saunders (1984) suggested that the State might be best perceived as dualistic in nature, with more pluralistic processes operating at the local level at the same time as more corporatist or structural forces operated at national level. Although this view attracted considerable criticism, it may contain some useful insights, and could certainly help to account for some of the conflicts within the planning system between central and local levels of government.

Bureaucracy

One is tempted to say "last but not least" when introducing the bureaucracy view, because it comes closest to the most widespread caricature of planning. Planning is operated by the planning bureaucracy in its own interest, in pursuit of such goals as maximizing the staff and budgets of planning departments, as well as pursuing the particular professional values of planners. Hill & Bramley (1986: Ch. 9) show that this view can draw on classic, ideal views of Weberian bureaucracy, theories of urban managerialism stressing the importance of "gatekeepers", analyses of discretion and "street-level bureaucracy" (Lipsky 1980), and analyses that stress the importance of professions (Dunleavy 1981). The view can also reflect the crude but influential public choice or "economics of bureaucracy" approach that emphasizes self-interest and unequal access to information (Downs 1967, Niskanen 1971, Jackson 1982).

Under this view the key interest and decision-making group are the professional planners in local and central government. It is assumed that they seek to maximize their budget, staffing and sphere of influence as well as to promote certain professional values, for example those deriving from the garden cities movement. Like all bureaucracies, they operate on imperfect information and bounded rationality, being somewhat cautious and risk-averse and changing policy incrementally. "Standard operating procedures" provide one key strategy to cope with the volume and diversity of demands placed upon them, yet at the same time the scope to exercise discretion and negotiate with outside interests may be welcomed. Particular standard operating procedures used by planners to determine housing land requirements and availability are discussed in the next chapter.

This group will favour strong containment, as this increases their overall bargaining power and leverage. They will be less keen on rigid legalistic zoning, and much more in favour of a discretionary approach to individual planning applications, providing more scope for time-consuming investigation and negotiation. They will, however, try to influence the density and type mix of housing (as discussed further in Ch. 8), because they will have specific professional beliefs and norms to try to achieve and because they believe their estimates of "needs" should take precedence over the vagaries of developers' perceptions of short-term market demands. They will be more likely to intervene in matters of design and aesthetics, and will be quite strong conservationists except in some situations where comprehensive public-sector led redevelopment is favoured. They will try to co-ordinate the different sectors of development (e.g. industry, commerce, housing) to a greater degree than in the other views.

The overall effect of these behavioural assumptions is that a planning-bureaucracy dominated system would be autonomous from and unresponsive to market forces, discretionary rather than rule-bound, and more interventionist and interested in positive planning implementation activities. There would be little central–local government conflict because the same professional group would control policy at both levels.

The overall outcomes would probably be in the middle of the range on all of our criteria. Efficiency would be reduced by excessive or inappropriate intervention and delay, and the lack of sensitivity to market signals. The same factors, and the general stance that combines restrictiveness with discretion/uncertainty, would limit economic growth and urban development, although in some circumstances (e.g. urban regeneration) public-sector led initiatives might be a positive feature. To the extent that planners' ideology places weight on distributional considerations, this view might generate less inequality than some alternatives, but this might be weakened by the regressive distributional side effects of key aspects of policy (e.g. containment).

Overview

By comparing the likely outcomes of these different views of how the planning system behaves, we can gain some insights into the overall biases in the system and what lies behind them. Take first the key issue of containment. Both the pluralistic politics and the bureaucratic views predict that containment will be pursued beyond the optimal level (that produced by the first view, if one accepts the welfare economic paradigm). The structural political economy view predicts that containment will be weak, if mainstream corporate interests prevail (as in Table 3.1), but allows the possibility of strong containment if certain interests (rural landowners, some key developers) prevail.

On the issue of clarity/rigidity versus discretion/uncertainty, the pluralistic politics view seems to be the one that produces a tendency to rigidity, whereas other views (especially the bureaucratic one) go for more discretion. This would seem to be consistent with the contrast between the American system, where elected local governments set up zoning ordinances, and the British one, where a professional planning bureaucracy governs a system containing extensive discretion. Planning would be more responsive to market forces in the structural political economy view, on some assumptions, and the welfare economic view. It would be relatively autonomous and unresponsive under pluralistic politics and bureaucracy views. Central government intervention to override or modify local decisions in order to promote certain developments would be most likely under the structural view, reflecting corporate interests, but might also occur under the bureaucracy perspective.

Given the rather crude caricature views presented and the complexity of the reality, we are not suggesting that one can or should simply choose one view as the correct description of the British planning system. Rather, the views are devices to stimulate thinking about possible connections between broader social, economic and political forces in society, the structures and processes of planning, and the kinds of outcomes it delivers. They also help to encapsulate the essence of recent academic debates about the political economy of planning and housing. In constructing plausible stories about the development of particular policies (e.g. the mid-1980s debates about green belts; see Elson 1986, Rydin 1986), it may make more sense to draw elements from different views.

3.3 Housing supply in a world without planning

We now turn from the aims and functions of the planning system to consider the effects of that system on the housing market and the supply of housing. In developing an understanding of the possible effects of planning, it is helpful to proceed in two stages, dealing first with what would happen if there were no planning, and second with the impact of certain kinds of planning intervention. The approach in this section is mainly informed by the mainstream microeconomic approach to urban analysis, which involves a somewhat simplified or idealized model of the urban housing system.

The urban economic model

The starting point for any analysis of land supply for housing must be the standard urban economic model of urban spatial structure, generally attributed to Alonso (1964), although developed greatly by others (e.g. Mills 1972, Evans 1973); the overall approach is well described in Richardson (1977). This model envisages a monocentric city situated on an extensive plain with locational and development choices conditioned by a trading-off of accessibility to the jobs and

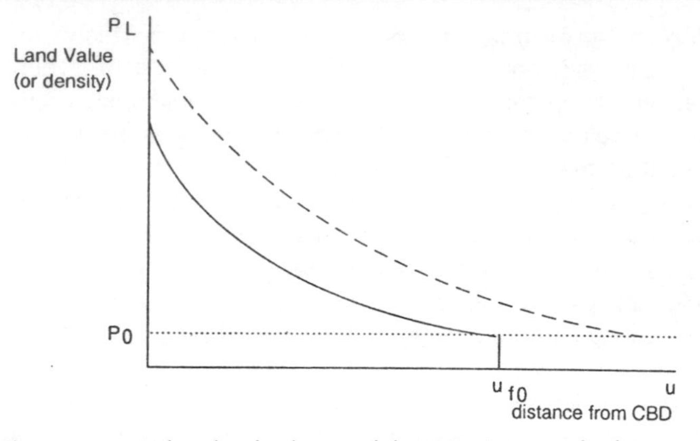

Figure 3.1 Urban land values and densities in a standard economic model.

services at the centre against the consumption of space. Competition generates a peak at the city centre of densities, high-value commercial uses, and rents/land values, with densities and rents declining with distance from the centre (see Fig. 3.1). At the periphery of the city, density is very low (space consumption high) but access costs are high, and this factor eventually reduces the rent/price that potential residents would be willing to pay (net of construction costs) to below the level of agricultural value. The urban fringe is the point (u_f) at which "greenfield" land is supplied for housing use. Land supply is assumed to be infinitely elastic once the rent/price rises above agricultural value (see Fig. 3.2).

Does this mean that there is no land supply constraint, or inelasticity, affecting housing? There are situations where this infinitely elastic supply would apply, for example the creation of a new city or after the opening of a new transport facility. However, in practice we are more typically dealing with cities that have already been substantially developed and transport infrastructure that is relatively fixed. In this case a rise in demand, caused by growth in population or incomes, may cause some slight outward movement of the city periphery, but the main effect is an increase in densities accompanied by an increase in rents/ prices (shown in Fig. 3.1 by the dashed line). This is essentially the process of long-run housing supply analyzed by Muth (1969) and others, as reviewed in Chapter 2.

So even in this theoretically "ideal" world without planning, land that is useful for housing and other urban purposes, by virtue of its location, is semi-permanently scarce and commands a corresponding rent. The main factor that can overcome this tendency is an improvement in the transport infrastructure increasing speed or reducing cost (Evans 1973). This reminds us that planning and housing policies should not be divorced from transport policies.

The theory of land prices and supply

Although this traditional theory is plausible as a very broad predictor of tendencies in unplanned cities, recognition has grown that some observed phenomena in real cities are anomalous and require some additional factors to be taken into account (Evans 1983, Neutze 1987). One of these anomalies is the tendency for development to take place in patches, rather than uniformly in the peripheral zone of unplanned cities. Instead of all land switching to housing as land values rise above the agricultural level, only some land does, in dribs and drabs over time.

The second anomaly is that in these peripheral locations the land values of the sites developed for housing are generally not the same as agricultural values, but significantly higher. The third notable anomaly is the tendency of past attempts at taxing development gains to appear to result in a drop in the supply of land for development. Under the traditional theory, development gain - the difference between development and existing use value (this time assuming some planning control) - can be taxed at high rates (short of 100%) without affecting the supply. This is because supply is supposed to be highly elastic for any small increase in realized price above existing use value.

Evans (1983) provides perhaps the clearest attempt to explain these anomalies, with similar arguments being developed by Wiltshaw (1985) and Neutze (1987). The explanation involves a significant break with the traditional economic view of land. Land at the urban fringe has an upward-sloping supply curve rather than a rectangular one (compare Figs 3.2 and 3.3). In a given period only a fraction of the stock of undeveloped urban fringe land would be offered for sale at agricultural value or a little above (say L1 per period at price P1). As the price rose significantly, progressively more land would be offered per period of time. The model now has a time dimension and focuses more on flows.

The main factor Evans points to is the fact that owners/occupiers have varying levels of "surplus" associated with particular pieces of land at particular locations. This means that they derive more benefit from occupation than the current

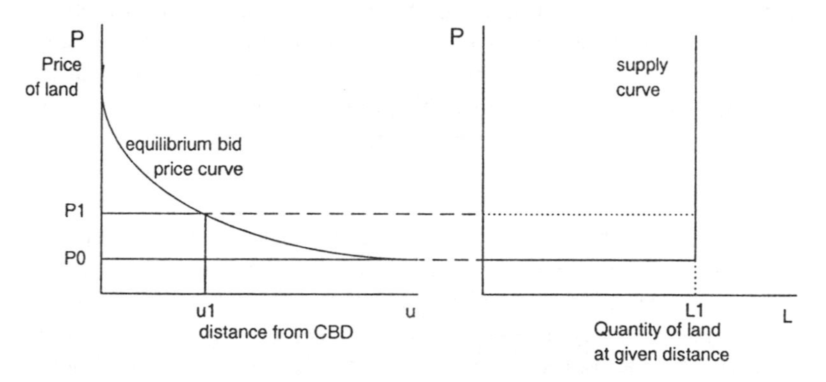

Figure 3.2 Urban land price and supply under traditional theory.

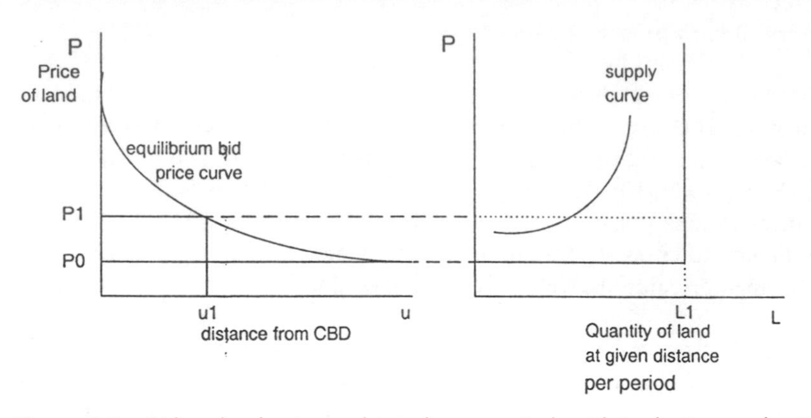

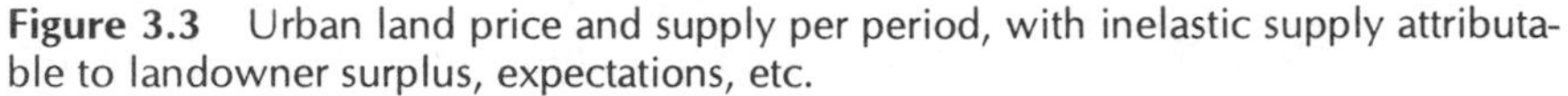
Figure 3.3 Urban land price and supply per period, with inelastic supply attributable to landowner surplus, expectations, etc.

market value and require varying levels of compensation to make them move. Underlying reasons include such factors as the goodwill of an established business, investment in the quality of the land, and sentimental and kinship attachments. There is a moderate rate of natural turnover, but many other owners/occupiers will be reluctant to move. And they know that the land value will be there for them to realize when it suits them to move later.

Expectations

This leads on to the second major factor, stressed more by Neutze and others, namely expectations about future land values. If, as is normally the case in growth economies and regions, the potential development value is likely to grow gradually in real terms, then little is lost and something may be gained by holding on to the land. The more rapid the expected increase in values, the more it pays to hold on, leading to a possible short-run perverse supply response.

Another version of this argument is the uncertainty about the form of development that will be most appropriate, and most profitable, at some future date; Will it be housing, warehouses or industry?; Will it be high density, down-market or low density, up-market housing? The highest value is retained by keeping your options open, that is by not actually developing the site (Brown & Achour 1984, Titman 1985). So uncertainty may deter development in this way, even though prices signal that development is profitable.

In other chapters we comment on the strongly cyclical character of the market for housebuilding and development, as one of the main problems facing the industry. Housing demand and prices can fluctuate sharply over short periods in response to changes in national economic and monetary conditions, particularly interest rates. Housebuilding takes time, and at the time a site is started there may be considerable uncertainty surrounding the likelihood and profitability of sales at the time, typically two years hence, when the houses will be ready. So this is another aspect of the connection between uncertainty about the future and a hesitancy of supply in response to current market prices.

Evans and the other authors mentioned argue that these factors create an inelastic land supply and explain the anomalies identified above, as well as other features such as differing behaviour with differing tenures. So in a competitive market system without planning, there will still be constraints on the flow of land offered for development, as well as a scarcity of the most accessible land, both of which will mean that increases in demand may push up rents/prices.

Monopoly

In addition, these authors note, but do not emphasize, the possibility of a lack of competition, that is a local monopoly of the supply of land. Local monopoly is possible insofar as particular groups of people or businesses may be tied to a particular locality by specific occupational skills, community ties, or unique amenities, while at the same time landholdings may be concentrated. With a captive market such a monopoly owner would find that it paid to release land slowly. More realistically, one could talk of monopolistic competition, with different sites/locations being partial substitutes.

This kind of local monopoly is less likely to the extent that the housebuilding development industry remains relatively unconcentrated. This seems to be the case in the Bristol area, for example, where the top five builders accounted for only 28% of output on larger sites in the period 1986–9; the top 10 accounted for 53% and the top 15 for 67%. Local competition is discussed further in Chapter 5. It is possible that landownership is more concentrated, but in England it is very difficult to obtain systematic data on this. However, a possible danger of planning controls is that they actually create more of a monopoly by restricting the sites on which development can take place.

Externalities and infrastructure

If there was no planning system the pervasive externalities associated with urban development would have a severe effect on the market and on supply. In general, because of the lack of certainty about future developments on adjacent land in this unplanned situation, individual investors could be less sure about the future value of their own particular housing investments. This could be a general deterrent to investment and development, and a particular deterrent to certain kinds of development, for example better quality housing. If planning succeeded in reducing such uncertainties, it could increase the supply of development.

Without some planning and co-ordination, infrastructure and services would present major problems. Much of the land in theory available for development would not be developable in practice because of the lack of services (a common situation in developing countries). The supply of infrastructure itself would be a risky investment, because of uncertainty about the extent and nature of development to be served in particular areas, and so urban services would be underprovided. The high capital cost of urban infrastructure required to provide transport, water, sewerage, energy and other services to new housing developments is probably the most fundamental limitation on the effective supply of land for housing, in most countries.

The seriousness of this last set of problems, in particular, would tend to lead to spontaneous attempts to create some of the advantages of planning within a basically market system. Examples, which can be found in the historical development of cities in Britain and elsewhere, include the use of such legal devices as covenants and leasehold tenure to impose common standards (e.g. of density, plot sizes, building lines and heights) and collective arrangements. These could then be reinforced by local legislation and by-laws. The modern system of local government has largely grown up out of this need to regulate development and provide supporting services, and its associated local taxation powers have often been closely related to property. Thus, even in a system that sought to avoid planning and rely upon the market, schemes of local taxation of development values would tend to emerge, in order to finance the necessary infrastructure and services. This effect can be clearly seen in market-dominated systems such as the USA.

3.4 The impact of planning

Containment

The standard urban economic model (Richardson 1977) can be used to examine the likely impact of planning controls on the urban housing market and housing supply. This analysis, which we only sketch in very informally and briefly here, is of course a very simplified picture of the longer-term tendencies of the system, other things being equal.

Let us take first the most important manifestation of British planning: containment of urban development at a particular boundary by means of a green belt or similar mechanism. Figure 3.4 shows the main effect on the housing and land market, with the solid line showing the relationship between rents/land values and distance from city centre with containment policies, and the broken line showing the relationship without containment. A very similar pair of lines could be drawn for density of development, assuming this had time to adjust to the planning control.

The main conclusion is that containment through planning would raise rents/values throughout the built-up part of the city up to the boundary, but beyond the boundary where development was not permitted, values would fall to a very low

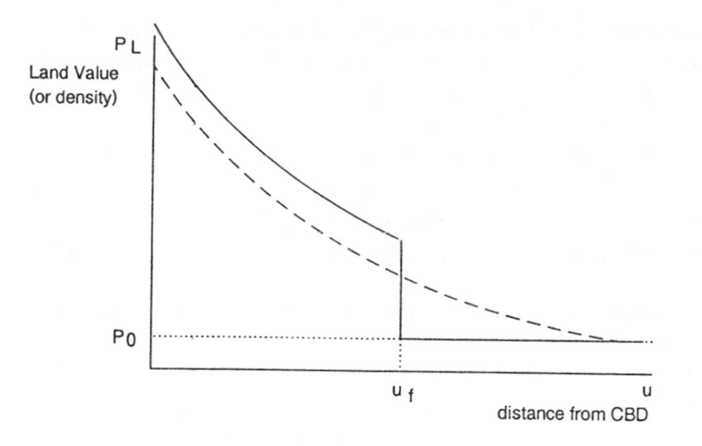

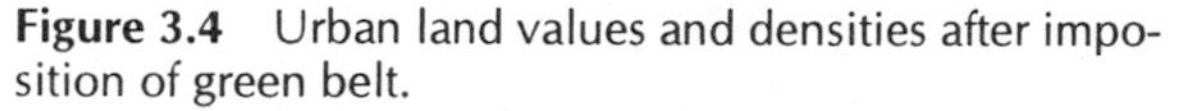

Figure 3.4 Urban land values and densities after imposition of green belt.

(agricultural) level. This assumes that the two hypothetical cities had the same population and income levels, and that demand would have been sufficient to push the natural market fringe of the city beyond the administratively determined green belt boundary. That density would be higher is intuitively clear from the constant population assumption; the same number of people would be squeezed into a smaller city. The exact extent of the response would depend on the processes of substitution of buildings for space in the production of housing, and possibly on the substitution of other forms of consumption for housing, as described in the discussion of the Muth model in Chapter 2. In practice, a very important part of the process would be the "infilling" of space between main roads, given the strong tendency toward "ribbon development" when there is no effective planning control, as in Britain in the 1930s.

Society is apparently somewhat worse off as a result of this planning intervention. The citizens of our model city have been obliged to consume less space, which reduces their welfare (Cheshire & Sheppard 1989, Evans 1991). How much worse off they are depends on the extent to which, by changing the building form or by consuming other things, the housing consumer can be compensated for loss of space. However, if planning control was introduced for a good reason connected with economic efficiency, there would presumably be some other benefit elsewhere in the system to offset the loss just described. For example, planning containment might significantly save in infrastructure costs, and this might be reflected in lower taxation or utility charges (Harrison 1977: ch. 11).

Residents appear to be worse off (Fig. 3.4) because of the higher rents or house prices they must pay. However, this is a transfer payment, from one set of people to another, which alters the distribution of income and wealth but does not correspond directly to the overall average loss or gain. Basically, the existing owners of land and property, at the time whenthe planning control was introduced, gain at the expense of the other people, for example the tenants or the people who buy houses later (the first group may include some owner-occupiers).

Part of the motive for containment policies may be concern about environmental externalities of the kind discussed earlier. People may value the amenity of the green belt, particularly if living close to it. This situation is reflected in Figure 3.5, which assumes that environmental amenity is reflected in what people are willing to pay for housing in a particular location; a technical term for this is to say that the amenity is "capitalized" in house prices or rents. Now, the rent gradient no longer falls smoothly to the city boundary, but tends to rise again close to the boundary, while being closer to the no-planning level in the middle ring suburbs. Developers will try to raise densities at the city fringe, if allowed to do so.

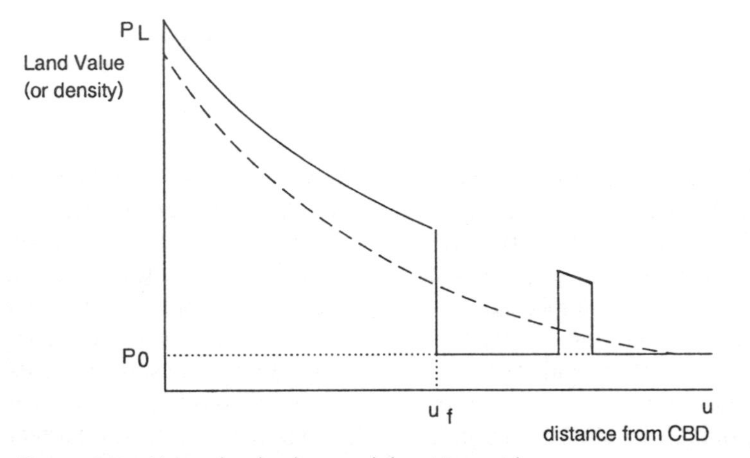

Figure 3.5 Urban land values and densities, with green belt satellite town and enhanced amenity values.

The figure also illustrates another likely consequence of green belts, which is that property values and densities may rise quite sharply in satellite towns and villages within or beyond the green belt but still within commuting distance of the city centre. Both of these phenomena are what we would predict in the British cases of green belts around high-demand cities, notably London. They are also more or less what we observe in practice.

Historical development process

A major limitation of the standard urban economic model is that it neglects the historical dimension of urban development. This is particularly important when it is recognized that buildings have a long life and that redevelopment is a costly process. Figure 3.6 illustrates the effects of introducing a plausible historical dimension to the model.

The city developed in three distinct phases, pre- First World War, inter-war

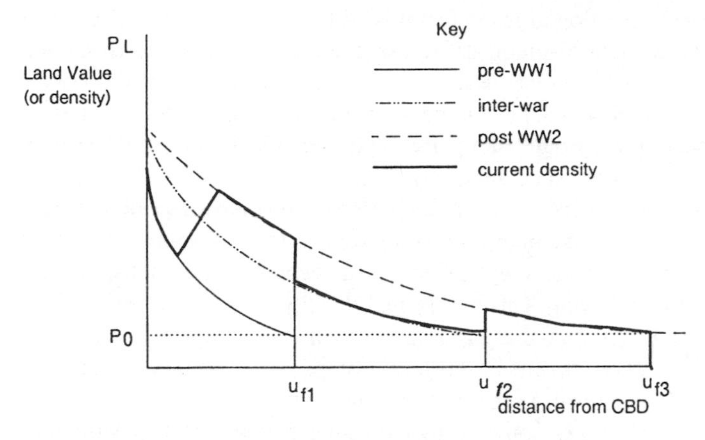

Figure 3.6
(a) Historical development of housing density in three phases, with redevelopment.
(b) House prices resulting from historical development process.

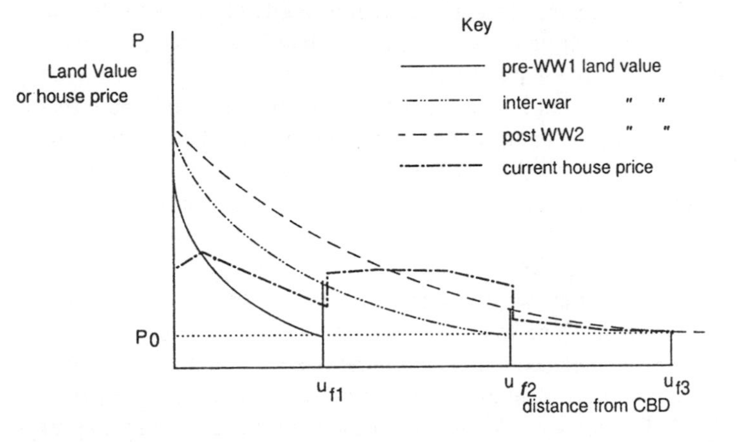

and post-war, in each of which different economic and technological conditions prevailed. In the first (pre-ww1) phase, incomes were low and transport technology limited, so that the market rent function fell steeply from a central city peak. Most development during this period was in an inner ring at high densities, although densities declined sharply moving away from the centre. In the middle period, incomes were higher and transport technology developed (electrified suburban railways, buses and some private car use), leading to a flattening of the rent gradient. Most housing development took place in the middle ring suburbs at moderate densities. Finally, in the post-war period with higher incomes and much wider car ownership, the rent gradient flattened further, reinforced by some decentralization of industrial and commercial activity. Most housing development took place on greenfield land in the third, outermost ring.

This model draws attention to some features of the development process that might emerge even without planning. If we assume that it is costly to redevelop existing built-up sites at different densities, to reflect changed demand conditions, it is likely that there would need to be a substantial price or rent differential before such redevelopment would take place. The thick black lines in Figure 3.6 represent the situation after such redevelopment had taken place. Within the inner ring, part is shown as having been redeveloped for housing at higher density, although this is in fact the outer part of the oldest ring. The innermost part of this ring might be vulnerable to extensions of the central business district, not shown here. In the middle ring, current optimal density exceeds the actual built density, but the price differential is not enough to induce change, In the outer ring, new greenfield development in the post-war period is at higher densities than the inter-war development in the middle ring.

Figure 3.6b also illustrates some further curious features of this situation. Price is expressed here per housing unit, rather than per square metre of land, so it reflects variations in average plot size in different parts of the city, as well as variations in price per unit of area. Prices rise to a local peak in the unredeveloped inner ring, and again in the middle ring, in both cases because the original density is lower than the current market-indicated density. Also, because in the earlier periods the rent gradient was steeper than it is today, the average house price rises with distance within these old sectors which have not been redeveloped. Such tendencies could then be reinforced by local neighbourhood effects and submarkets on the demand side of the housing market, with "gentrification" of the inner zone and an up-market move of the middle zone. This simple example serves to remind us that the urban housing market, however efficient, will not always generate completely smooth, downward-sloping profiles of house prices and densities.

How might planning interact with the market in this kind of model? The answer depends mainly on the balance between the different operational objectives of the planners, in particular between containment on the one hand and density zoning/conservation on the other. If planning intervention were solely concerned with containment, the likely effects would be to increase the redevelopment pressures in both the central areas and the low-density inter-war suburbs. Such pressures are very noticeable in South East England, and the term "towncramming" has come to be associated with these tendencies. However, if planning is equally or more concerned with conservation of existing urban environments, and with forms of zoning that tend to preserve existing density levels, then this market pressure for redevelopment would not be allowed to operate. Those aspects of change which are not subject to so much planning control, for example conversions of houses to flats or extensions to houses, may be even more likely to happen, as a more limited response to market pressures. Again, there is much evidence of these processes in the mature suburbs of outer London and the South East (Gosling et al. 1993). Housebuilders per se would be forced to seek other sites, on the green fields beyond the present built-up area or on former industrial land within it.

Density controls

This leads on to the question of what would be the general effects of planners trying to control housing density. Planning policies have quite often referred to density (Harrison 1977: ch. 11), sometimes trying to set minima (to economize on the use of land) and sometimes maxima (to maintain adequate standards of amenity). It is difficult to generalize about all such possible policies, but one specific hypothetical example can at least illustrate the potential effects. Figure 3.7 illustrates the effects of the application of a uniform residential density on a city within the standard urban economic model (i.e. reverting to the assumption that the built structure can flexibly adapt to market conditions).

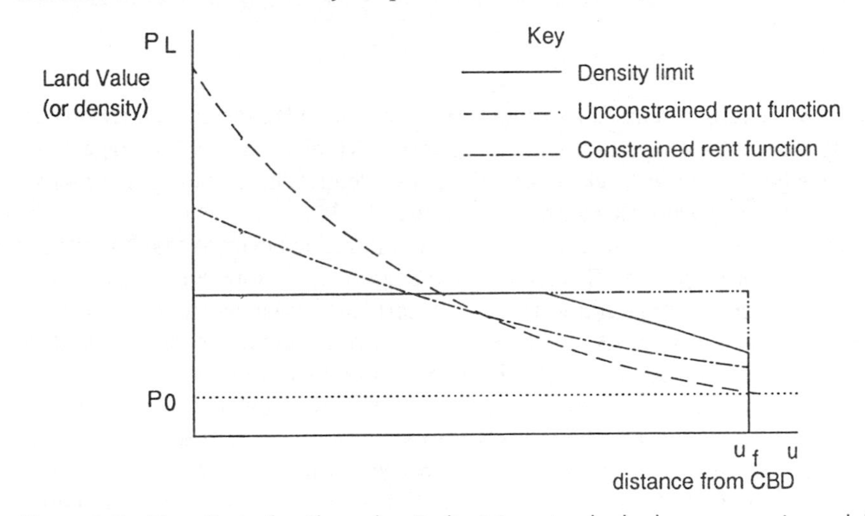

Figure 3.7 The effect of uniform density limit in a standard urban economic model.

The Figure shows that density would follow the policy-determined level, except possibly towards the urban fringe where some land might not be developed for housing at all, so reducing the effective gross density in this area. The rent function per unit of land area would be flatter, but the price per house would fall more steeply with distance. The central business district would tend to expand more, because of the low adjacent bid price for housing. More people would live in the suburbs, and fewer in the inner city, and this would be especially true of lower income groups; the inner residential areas might become gentrified. There would be an overall welfare loss, because of greater total travel costs and the loss of space in the suburbs.

In practice, density controls are unlikely to be as crude as this. There may be a wide band between upper and lower acceptable levels. The upper limits may only apply in certain inner-city areas. The lower limits may be invoked on fringe sites, partly to conserve land but also because of planners' views about the type and size mix of dwellings required. For example, developers may believe that large detached houses with double garages and two bathrooms may be most profitable, but the planners may be concerned about the demographic forecasts of ever-growing numbers of small single-person households, and about access and affordability for first-time buyers (see Ch. 8).

In general, density controls are likely to reduce the longer-term responsiveness of the overall housing supply to changes in demand. In Chapter 2 we showed that adjustment of density plays a central role in the theory of housing supply. In Chapter 8 we go on to examine empirical evidence on the relationship between density and market prices, which tends to support the contention that the British system (including planning) is associated with a low level of responsiveness.

Expectations

We have already discussed the significant role that both expectations and uncertainty play in housing and urban development. Monk et al. (1991) suggest that existing theory and research are particularly inadequate in relation to these topics and associated phenomena such as speculation.

One conclusion we can draw from the literature, however, is that uncertainty may deter development. This leads to the slightly surprising conclusion that, if land-use planning reduces the level of uncertainty about the future pattern of development, it may in fact increase the supply of development land and reduce prices. It is admitted that this may be an over-optimistic view of planning, especially the British system which contains substantial elements of discretion for both local authorities and ministers. However, it would be fair to say that planning must narrow the range and scope of uncertainty to some extent (as suggested by Healey et al. 1985). It is the externality effects, which link the price and profitability of one development to the type and timing of developments on other nearby sites, that provide the most important basis for planning to reduce uncertainty. Whether this effect is sufficient to offset its tendency to conservatism in the release of land is questionable, especially given planning's limited ability to determine the timing of developments (see below).

The most serious uncertainties facing housebuilders relate to the macroeconomic instability of demand. How they cope with this uncertainty is discussed further in Chapter 5.

Under a planning regime, builders also have to form expectations about the outcome of planning applications with which they are involved (and perhaps also about the outcome on other competing sites). Clearly, this is a qualitatively different kind of uncertainty, relating to a politico-administrative process. Resources may be employed to reduce it, which leads into the issue of "rent-seeking" discussed below. One view is that most large building companies can predict outcomes of planning applications fairly successfully, even in the discretionary British system. Whether the time required to obtain permission is so predictable may be more questionable, as local planning authorities can engage in protracted negotiations over detailed matters. Delay attributable to planning may not be too serious if it is predictable, although it is a further factor limiting the responsiveness of housebuilding output to short-term surges in demand.

Rent-seeking behaviour

"Economic rent" is a term used to describe income accruing to a fixed factor which exceeds the minimum supply price, and land with planning permission is the classic case of such a fixed factor. Owning such a factor is a very attractive position to be in, and it has been suggested that a good deal of social, economic and political behaviour may be motivated by a desire to get into a position to collect such a rent. If planning makes any difference to anything, it seems certain to create rent/price differentials between land with and without planning permission (as, for example, in Figs 3.4 and 3.5), although how far it increases the average rent level rather than its distribution may be debated. Rent-seeking is discussed by Cheshire & Leven (1982) as one of the "costs" of the planning system, other costs including delay and the direct costs of administration.

Developers engage in activities designed to maximize their chances of obtaining these rents by obtaining planning permission: retaining expensive consultants and lawyers, engaging in public relations, lodging appeals, offering "planning gain" amenities to local communities, entertaining councillors, etc. Some of these could be said to represent a deadweight loss to the economy, although another view might be that this is simply a different distribution of the rents. Others could be defended as leading to "better" decisions or, in the case of planning gain, the provision of facilities of a positive value. The latter could be an approximation to a development tax helping to finance infrastructure which, if it existed, might well lead to more efficient outcomes (Harrison 1977). Planning agreements are discussed more fully in the next chapter.

Evans (1991) suggests from data on land options pricing that this kind of behaviour is becoming more important, in the sense that developers seem to be incurring more costs. However, these could include planning gain costs. If these costs are correctly seen to be worth incurring, this may indicate that these activities do actually help to promote a supply response from an otherwise rather negative planning system. Although falling short of an ideal economically efficient system, this sort of second-best solution in the face of real political constraints may have some merit; it is rather in the same category as Evans' suggestion that planning permissions be auctioned.

Phasing

A fundamental characteristic and potential problem with a system such as this, where the public planning authority grants or withholds permission but private market actors initiate and implement housing development, is that there is no very direct link in the short term between plans and actual development on the ground. In practice, there are two different stages in the development process where different actors and considerations are important.

The first key stage is that of seeking outline planning permission on a particular site. This decision rests primarily with the landowner, although a developer with an option on the land may undertake it on the owner's behalf. As already explained, many landowners are under no financial pressure to see the land developed immediately, and can delay indefinitely or until what may be judged in market terms a most opportune moment. Whether a site is allocated in a local plan or not clearly makes a great difference to the chances of getting permission, but in the past two decades a large proportion of housing development was on unallocated land. In either case the timing of any application is not under the planners' control. There is a tendency for more applications to be made in times of boom; however, allowing for the lags from outline to detailed permission and start to completion, these sites are likely only to produce housing at the opposite end of the economic cycle, if at all.

A characteristic of the planning approach is that it is intentionally incapable of taking account of the identity, attributes and intentions of the *owners* of particular sites. This is understandable in one sense, that planning should be impartial in relation to specific interests, but unhelpful in another. Decisions to develop sites ultimately rest with owners, and allocating a site for housing is no guarantee that housing will be built there within a particular time period. Past policies, for example the 1976 Community Land Act and DoE Circular 44/78, gave more encouragement to positive intervention to secure development, including the use of compulsory purchase powers, but such approaches have not been favoured under the Conservative government since 1979.

Generally when outline permission is obtained, ownership and control passes to the housebuilder/developer. The actual new housing supply resulting from planning decisions depends on the phasing of output on individual sites, including the possibility of no completions in the immediate period or an extended phasing of development. Monk et al. (1991: 17) make the useful observation that once permission is obtained the overall level of uncertainty falls sharply and, consequently, the development decision may be re-evaluated at a different discount rate. They also observe that this perspective has not really been developed in the literature.

Bramley (1989: Appendix) presents a model of the behaviour of housebuilders who hold a given, limited stock of land on which they may build housing, utilizing a discounted cashflow projection to evaluate phasing options. With any positive real interest rate being used to discount costs and revenues, this simple model will generate the result that the whole of the site will be developed immediately, or not at all. Yet this flies in the face of much observed experience, documented in the land availability studies, that builders tend to space their output over a period of time and not exhaust their landholding immediately.

The model incorporates three factors that help to account for this. First, the demand curve facing the builder in any short period may be downward sloping. This assumes a degree of monopolistic competition, because of the unique attributes of each site's location and product differentiation between builders. It ties in with the evidence that builders frequently perceive a limit to the number of units they can sell on a particular site in a year. Secondly, the cost function contains an element of variable sales cost, including the risky costs of not selling all output immediately, as well as the costs of marketing. This element is an increasing function of the level of annual output.

Thirdly, expectations of future price levels (or demand schedules) have to be considered. If prices were completely uncertain, then an appropriate response could be to increase the discount rate, reinforcing the tendency to build immediately. But if expectations were that demand prices would tend to rise in real terms, then there would be a tendency to extend the phasing or even defer development. Price expectations can also be modelled as some function of recent past price levels or changes ("adaptive expectations") or on the basis of some model of the housing market (so-called "rational expectations").

Once these elements are built into the model, the normal predictions are likely to be of phasing over several years. Increased demand does increase output from given sites, even under these assumptions, and price-supply elasticities of the order of 0.5–1.5 are generated. In fact, at local market level, the elasticity would be greater as marginal sites came on stream (especially important in low demand areas). Higher real interest rates increase output, but this ignores any indirect effects via demand or via reduced profitability and land values. Increased land supply in the form of larger sites also increases output, but by a less-than-proportional amount (additional sites could have a proportional effect, but there would be a demand feedback to consider here). Some assumptions about expectations behaviour (the future will continue recent trends) can generate zero supply elasticity, whereas others increase supply response (prices will return to an expected norm).

3.5 Conclusion

In this chapter we have examined land-use planning and its potential impact on housing supply in a broad but informal theoretical way. First we looked at what land-use planning is, in terms of its component activities, operational goals and implementation. Some of these goals, particularly containment, are especially important for housing, not least because they have been the most successfully implemented. We went on to reflect on some broader views on the political economy of planning, addressing the function of planning in a broader social and political context. Some of the issues thrown up here, for example on the responsiveness of planning to the housing market, are picked up empirically later on, particularly in Chapter 7.

We then turned to the impact of planning, first considering with the aid of the standard urban economic model what housing supply might be like in a world without planning. For various reasons we conclude that housing supply would still face certain limitations and problems in this situation, but that typical planning policies such as containment would tend to restrict supply and raise prices and densities further. Important issues raised in this discussion include the expectations of developers and how they phase development.

CHAPTER 4
Planning and land availability in practice

4.1 Recent debate

Debates about the supply of land for housing are a longstanding issue of contention in the British planning system and certainly dominated debate in the 1980s, when the policy context emphasized the role of the market in meeting housing needs. The debate concerned not only the quantity of land supplied through the planning system but also its location and real availability in terms of ownership, quality, development costs and the effective demand for housing. Structure plans were the main arena for these debates, with the housebuilding industry effectively voicing its concerns via the Examination in Public (EIP) process. A key target of these campaigns was to break the increasingly tight restraint policies consolidated in structure plans in the early 1980s (Ball 1983). At the heart of the debate is the extent to which the supply of land should be determined by the market, or should be based on planned assessments of future requirements, balanced by other objectives of the planning system, in particular policies for urban containment and the protection of green belts (Healey 1992).

As a consequence of controversy and lobbying there have been a succession of studies of land availability for housing in the past twenty years, reviewed below, together with exhortations by central government that planning authorities should release a sufficient supply of land, particularly in the three housing market boom periods since 1972. The guidance has tended to become increasingly strong and specific (see DoE Circulars 9/80, 22/80 and 15/84), and in the 1980s particular mechanisms were introduced which gave the housebuilders and developers a role in the process of agreeing joint statements of land availability. In the view of some commentators this advice gave pre-eminence to market criteria in determining the meaning of availability, and encouraged the planning system to be more sensitive to the priorities of housebuilders with respect to the location and choice of sites in terms of marketability and market segments. (Hooper 1985, Rydin 1986).

The studies of land availability for housing reviewed here are a consequence of the controversy surrounding land supply, and the related issue of delay.

Although some are now quite out-of-date and even pre-date the effective operation of the newer style of (post-1968) planning system, they nevertheless shed considerable light on the process by which land is released and how this impinges on the development process.

An important early study was that carried out by the Economist Intelligence Unit (EIU 1975), which dealt with housing land availability in the South East in the period 1971–4. The main focus was on the relationship between "land available in planning terms" as identified by local planning authorities and "land actually available" in the sense of having housing actually under construction or with a definite commitment to build. There was also a detailed analysis of the extent and causes of "delay".

It was found that the relationship between "land available in planning terms" and "land actually available" was complex and indirect. More than half the planning permissions granted for housing were on sites not previously allocated or included in development plans. This made up for the shortfall in land allocated through the planning system and was the main means by which authorities maintained the flow of land into development. Although this finding casts doubt on the adequacy of operation of the forward planning process, it does relate to a period preceding the preparation of new-style structure plans. A subsequent national study found that 70% of land with outstanding permission had been started two years later, with a further 13% likely to start, so availability figures for this stage of the process were reasonably accurate (Byrne 1978, EIU 1978). The non-take-up or delay of the remaining sites was attributable to a variety of factors, including planning, the market downturn, builders' financial difficulties, and aspects of landholding practice and ownership.

More than half the sites studied by EIU in 1975 experienced delay. Sites without delay averaged under three years from outline planning application to completion, but the delayed sites averaged 7.5 years. The study confirmed that delays could be significant, and that some were attributable to planning and related procedures; but it also pointed to a range of factors relating to developers and owners, such as site assembly, revisions to schemes and changes of ownership. The report also argued that the elimination of delay and the speeding up of the development process is not necessarily either desirable or achievable, and that builders expect delay and aim to build to market demand allowing for it. As far as planning procedures are concerned, negotiated changes to a scheme may be better and quicker than a series of refusals.

The report concluded that the process was more influenced by strongly cyclical demand than by land supply, and that housebuilders concurred with this view. However, it recommended better monitoring of land flows, including unallocated land.

A second major study, by JURUE (1977) provided many similar messages. This was a study of housing land availability and release in the southwest sector of the West Midlands region between 1968 and 1973. It stressed that pipeline times were such that the system could not respond within the timescale of the boom in demand, and that the greater part of the pipeline time was in the hands of developers. The planning system was characterized as procedurally rigid, but was also under intense pressure at the time of the boom in the housing market, and speculative applications on non-conforming land were bound to experience high rates of delay and refusal. Again, a large proportion (40%) of land supply was on sites not previously allocated in development plans (so-called "white land"), and the existing allocation of land in parts of the study area was very tight, partly attributable to the outdated, old-style planning framework. Inevitably the report recommended that the stock of land allocated and with permission should be increased to allow a better response to demand. But it also argued that output may still not rise in step with demand because of the distribution of ownership of the stock and to shortages of other inputs during a construction boom. Because large sites held by large builders dominate supply, these builders effectively control the rate of development. Again, local authorities were urged to monitor both stocks and flows of land and market trends.

The third major study was the joint DoE/Housebuilders Federation study of Greater Manchester (DoE 1980). This had a different focus and represented an attempt to reconcile the views of planning authorities and the development industry concerning land supply. The study looked at land available in 1978 for development in the period 1978–81 in the Greater Manchester metropolitan area, and related this to local authority and builders' estimates of "need" and "demand" respectively and to past performance. Separate surveys were completed by local authorities and the majority of builders operating in the area, the latter survey covering landownership and acquisition/sales as well as output and intentions. Agreement was reached between planning authorities and builders on the availability or otherwise of all sites initially identified, taking into account such factors as services, access and ownership constraints, as well as planning permission. The study also attempted to disaggregate land supply in recognition of the structure of the industry (large vs small builders and sites), the structure of demand (three market segments) and location.

The findings of this study paint a picture rather different from that of previous ones. There was not a major shortage of allocated and available land, although there were imbalances once the analysis was disaggregated by segment and location. Recourse to unallocated land was not required on the same scale, and builders' land banks were increasingly orientated to land with planning permission and services. In parts of the county available land exceeded forecasts of demand. These results are perhaps not surprising given the timing of the work, at the end of a pronounced recession in housebuilding, and the location, a region of relatively low demand. However, the approach adopted did provide the model for similar joint studies undertaken in other areas.

Studies of land supply for housing carried out in the 1980s (Tym 1987, 1991) relate to a different context. Full structure plan coverage and the adoption of the joint study approach piloted in the Manchester study could be expected to have improved the relationship between forecast housing needs, planned land allocations and actual construction. In most of the South East counties included in the 1987 study, land availability reports demonstrated an adequate supply of land to meet structure plan targets, although localized shortfalls at the level of districts were more common. In most cases the local authorities took action to make good shortfalls by revising targets, releasing additional land through local plan reviews, releasing public sector land for development or granting additional planning consents. The 1991 study was primarily orientated to evaluating methods of assessing land availability against planned provision in a sample of districts in the South East. The major finding of this study was that not all sites identified in land availability studies are developed within the anticipated development programme. However, the shortfall is not that dramatic, with 77% of sites identified in 1981 being developed by the end of the decade. The most important constraint was ownership, with doubts about marketability also being significant. On a third of the identified sites which had not been developed, there was no obvious explanation for the non-implementation of planning consents. These findings underline the point, developed theoretically in Chapter 3 and empirically in Chapter 7, that planners do not directly control the rate of development of land, and that there is a potential implementation problem here.

Only 35% of the sample sites developed in the 1980s included in this study had been identified in local plans, although only 11% of completions were on sites that had at no time been identified. From this they draw the conclusion that planning could not and should not seek to identify every single housing site, and find broad agreement among both planners and developers for this view. Although certainty regarding large housing sites is desirable, there is a need for flexibility for builders to bring forward small and medium-size sites in order to meet changing market demand. In line with earlier studies, housing construction and the rate of implementation is determined in large measure by demand conditions in the housing market. As well as the usual call for better monitoring of land supply, the Tym study recommends that local authorities should take more account of ownership and marketing constraints through the medium of joint studies, or else apply a discount to their land assessments to allow for uncertainty.

4.2 Constraints on land supply

The studies reviewed do reveal some of the ways in which supply of land is constrained, with planning as one but not the only factor. In addition we need to consider physical constraints, and more fundamentally, the behaviour of landowners and developers.

Planning constraints

As we saw in the previous chapter, there is a longstanding commitment within the British system to the objective of urban containment (Hall et al. 1973) and this is probably the most important constraint on the supply of land for housing in areas where potential demand is highest. Restraint is backed up by statutory designations - green belts and AONBs - an by a variety of local protective designations - green buffers, green wedges, areas of landscape value. Despite strong decentralizing pressures throughout the 1970s and 1980s (Champion 1989) restraint policies have proved remarkably resilient, and moreover, the management and control of growth on the urban fringe is a planning policy objective that has been implemented with a degree of success (Healey et al. 1988).

Density controls will affect the way land released for housing translates into numbers of units, and may affect the extent of redevelopment within existing urban areas. Infrastructure constraints, hitherto mainly related to public expenditure decisions, also lie behind many cases of refusal to allow residential development, although increasingly developers are required to make contributions to the costs of infrastructure. Conservation concerns may restrict the scope for redevelopment and infill within urban areas and new development in attractive rural settings.

The corollary of restraint on the urban fringe is the encouragement of development within urban areas, utilizing vacant and derelict land. As we shall see, this particular policy objective has been given a boost both by the post-1977 inner cities policy and by the emerging "green" agenda within planning. Such inner-city sites can pose particular difficulties in terms of assembling land, higher development costs and uncertain market conditions (Brisbane 1985). Nonetheless, during the 1980s the use of recycled urban land for private sector housing increased. In 1983 the Housebuilders Federation reported that 30% of housebuilding took place on recycled urban land (DoE 1984) and more recent estimates suggest a figure nearer 45% for the whole decade (DoE 1990). This trend relates to the changes in urban structure discussed in Chapter 3, as well as to planning policies. Industrial decline in inner cities has released significant amounts of land for redevelopment, and changing demand stemming from demographic and social change underlies the redevelopment and conversion of the existing residential stock.

Policies for land release in plans are not immutable, however, and the British planning system continues to be characterized by a good deal of flexibility. The earlier studies of land availability (EIU and JURUE) confirmed the "leakiness" of the planning system. We might expect the advent of full structure plan coverage from the early 1980s to have reduced this, but a high degree of flexibility is still evident (Tym 1991). Throughout the 1980s central government advice emphasized that the development plan was only one consideration in the making of decisions on land use and development, and could be outweighed by other factors, notably government policy (DoE 1985). Circulars 9/80 and 22/80 emphasized that, even if planning authorities could demonstrate a five-year supply of housing land, this did not preclude development on other, unallocated sites. Such "windfall" sites appear to have become more important during the decade (CPRE 1988), so final housing output may be higher than the level indicated in the development plan. Our own research indirectly supports this (see Ch. 7).

A further feature of the system that builds in flexibility to changing economic circumstances and shifting political priorities is the ability of the Secretary of State to adjust housing targets included in regional guidance and in structure plans. Again, throughout the 1980s adjustments to structure plans via EIPs provide evidence of responsiveness to market demand, and government policy throughout the period encouraged the planning system to be responsive to the market (Brindley et al. 1989, Thornley 1991).

Appeals against the refusal of planning permission are also a means by which developers can challenge local restraint policies and central government can influence decisions. DoE data quoted by Monk et al. (1991) shows the number of appeals increasing throughout the 1980s, particularly towards the end of the period. There is an apparent relationship between the number of appeals and peaks in house prices, although the rate of success on appeal is also an influence. Success rates again increased during the decade, reaching a peak of 40% in 1986, and then falling back.

In a discussion of the effect of the land-use planning system on land supply, Monk et al. (1991) conclude that the evidence suggests that planning does not operate as an absolute constraint. However, the system is likely to have an effect on the locations where land is allocated, and as suggested above, supply in greenfield locations where potential demand is strongest is likely to be lower than demanded by the market. And constraint is likely to bite harder during a boom when pressure is greatest to release more land. Such short-term pressures can have an impact over the longer term, as land scarcity during a boom encourages builders to bid up the price of land beyond a residual valuation (see Ch. 5), and in the longer term may affect costs and rates of return in a way that damages viability and hence restricts output (Monk et al. 1991). Whether the scarcity costs of restrictive planning control are necessarily very large or avoidable, however, are questions we discuss elsewhere. And as others have pointed out (Smyth 1982), for builders holding land banks, scarcity can enhance profits by adding to the value of land held. Planning may also enhance values by protecting the environmental qualities of particular areas.

Physical constraints

Other factors that constrain land supply include physical constraints: topography, access, service and infrastructure provision, ground conditions and contamination. Although these present problems that can be overcome, cost is a major factor that can deter development, especially in combination with other factors such as uncertain demand and the availability of easier or more profitable sites in greenfield locations. Planning policies and physical constraints are interrelated, in the sense that planning may favour sites that are "difficult" in these terms. Planning can also facilitate development by finding solutions to problems of access or infrastructure (although increasingly the costs of this are being loaded onto developers) and by accessing government grants to pay for reclamation and make redevelopment more attractive. A wide variety of measures have been introduced in the 1970s and 1980s to deal with problems of degraded urban land, in acknowledgement that public sector intervention is required to restore land and underwrite investment risk (Kivell 1993). Derelict Land Grant, City Grant and the Urban Programme have been the main grant regimes in the 1980s, and more comprehensively the Urban Development Corporations have been set up to manage the reconstruction of areas where industry has declined, leaving a legacy of derelict and degraded land.

An evaluation of Derelict Land Grant schemes suggests a degree of success in terms of environmental and safety objectives, although success in terms of the provision of development land is more difficult to demonstrate (DoE 1987). Development takes a long time to achieve, and many reclaimed sites remained vacant in the face of low levels of commercial demand (Kivell 1993). Such findings are perhaps not surprising given that the greatest extent of the problem of dereliction is likely to be in the declining industrial regions, where development pressures are weakest. New housing development may be additionally difficult as a result of safety concerns relating for example to contaminated sites.

The behaviour of landowners and developers

The land availability studies reviewed above provide examples of aspects of developer and landowner behaviour that affect land and housing supply. As planning is a largely negative or responsive instrument, the decision of landowners to sell or of developers to undertake development has a crucial influence on patterns of development, although planning will alter the situation facing landowners and developers and hence affect their behaviour.

The issues can be grouped into:

- owners' and developers' expectations about land release and the market
- forward land acquisition and land banking
- phasing of development.

Expectations

Chapter 3 introduced the general idea that expectations can play an important part in affecting housing supply. The structure and behaviour of the housebuilding industry is discussed more fully in Chapter 5. Here we introduce some of the main practical issues that are likely to affect landowners' and developers' expectations of planning and the market.

Some authors argue that speculative withholding of land from development may occur if there is an expectation that house prices, and hence the returns from development, will continue to rise in real terms (Neutze 1987, Bramley 1989). As discussed in Chapter 3, in conditions of uncertainty, there may be value in keeping one's options open and restricting the supply of land onto the market. Neutze draws from this the conclusion that planning may even reduce the level of uncertainty about the future pattern of development and may thereby increase the supply of land. However, the substantial element of local authority discretion in the planning system, and the potential intervention of the Secretary of State, to grant permission on unallocated sites both add to uncertainty. Despite this, some still argue that planning does narrow the range and scope of uncertainty (Healey et al. 1988). The recent changes to the status of development plans discussed later in this chapter can be expected to strengthen further the capacity of planning to promote certainty.

A more extreme form of this argument is the possibility of local monopoly control of land, which allows particular landowners or developers to control the market. Our own study in the Bristol area suggested that the supply side of the new housebuilding market, in terms of the number of active developers in one market area, was rather competitive (Lambert 1990). It has also been argued that landowners are a diverse group with different aims and strategies, and that monopolistic behaviour cannot be proved in practice (Goodchild & Munton 1985). Indeed, their analysis suggests a wide variety of unpredictable and even perverse behaviour, within which personal reasons and motivations can be important. However, one could still talk of monopolistic competition, because of the extent to which each site has unique locational and environmental attributes. As the practice of holding options on potential development land has become more common (and it is the larger developers who are most able to do this), so the future supply of housing land in a particular locality may be concentrated in relatively few hands. There was a suggestion that this was happening in the Avon area in the late 1980s, but, as in other studies in England, information on the ownership of development land was very sketchy.

Given lead times for the construction of housing of at least two years, housebuilders themselves also have to form expectations about the demand for housing. Although builders may have a good appreciation of demand in different segments of the market and different localities, they face in Britain a highly volatile market over time (see Fig. 5.1). There is evidence that, even over the short term (under two years) rates of construction and the product mix can be varied to cope with fluctuations in the market, but this is after the decision to begin construction has been taken. Interviews with builders in the Bristol area (Lambert 1990) suggest that most do not engage in sophisticated forecasting, that the sudden downturn of the market in the late 1980s was unexpected and that production levels then overshot the demand. It would be unsurprising if such experiences led to conservatism and a reluctance to expand production when demand is increasing.

Landowners and builders also have to form expectations about the outcome of planning applications. As discussed above, comprehensive development plan coverage should reduce uncertainty, although sufficient discretion remains to make speculative applications worthwhile in conditions of high demand.

Landowners and developers are also not just passive recipients of decisions handed out by the planning system. Some studies of landowner and developer behaviour in relation to the planning system suggest that they engage in sophisticated lobbying activities that seek to influence policy in general terms and to have their sites included in development plans. Research by Adams & May (1990) found that "active" landowners making representations in local plans could achieve a degree of success, with a quarter of all representations by landowners resulting in a subsequent change in the plan. Other work on landowner involvement in planning (Farthing 1993) suggests that this understates the influence of landowners, whose relationships with planning authorities extend beyond the formal consultation stages of local plans and demonstrate a degree of incorporation within the planning process. In Berkshire, research by Short et al. (1986) examined interaction and negotiation at several levels. The Housebuilders Federation maintained regular contact with the DoE and achieved some success in increasing the total county allocation of 8000 houses in response to complaints of land scarcity. In the process of identifying sites for the additional allocation the planners received many offers of land, usually in areas broadly acceptable, and backed up by highly detailed cases. Again, at the level of development control, pre-application discussions are common in order to test the acceptability of proposals. Interviews with builders in and around Bristol suggested that some developers could package proposals, including offers of supporting infrastructure and services, that were influential in determining the pattern of land release. It was further suggested that most could predict the outcome of outline applications fairly successfully, although outcomes at the detailed application stage were more uncertain and variable between planning authorities.

A broad general result of uncertainty may be to strengthen the dominance of large housebuilding companies. This is discussed in the next chapter. Large housebuilders can spread their operations between many sites in different regional and local submarkets, where demand conditions vary, and where different unpredictable planning outcomes will tend to average out. The trend to consolidation in the industry into national companies operating in different regions has been widely noted. Larger firms are also able to engage in land banking, and a land bank is another strategic response to uncertainty. In addition, large firms are likely to be better able to employ the specialist expertise required to maximize the chances and improve the prediction of success in planning applications and negotiations.

Land banking

The issue of land banking is relevant in this context because development of land with a low historic value or land trading activities can be an important source of profit to housebuilders, in addition to profit from construction (Smyth 1982, Ball

1983). MacDonald (1978) provides a summary of the reasons for holding land banks. They are mainly necessary to cope with the uncertain flow of suitable sites, and they help to ensure continuity, flexibility of response, cushioning for delays on specific sites, a spread of development between areas, economies of scale in relation to infrastructure, and an influence over planning decisions through the assembly of sites, to achieve a partial local monopoly and to benefit from enhanced land values.

These advantages might appear overwhelming were it not for cost considerations. If land in the bank has to be bought with full development or substantial hope value, the working capital tied up in the site could be very substantial and, depending on interest rates, unattractive. One of the features of the 1980s has been a move to consortia of builders operating on very large sites; this approach achieves some of the above advantages, although at the expense of local monopoly. However, the consortium may function as a cartel and/or be a way of exploiting preferences for diversity in consumption, so that monopolistic competition prevails.

It would appear that the policies of the larger builders with respect to land banking vary. Some hold the minimum necessary, two to three years supply, whereas others hold considerably more. Again, the mix varies of land allocated and with planning permission, and unallocated land. Company strategies with respect to obtaining profit of land gains or land trading, or on high volume turnover therefore differ (Smyth 1982). Land acquisition and banking strategies may also be expected to vary with fluctuations in demand and conditions in the market.

A relatively cheap and lower-risk way of augmenting effective land banks for reasons of continuity and flexibility is to purchase options. These involve a small down-payment, typically 10% of current market value, in exchange for the right to purchase for development with a modest discount when planning permission is granted. The cost and risk are small, but so is the scope for development gain. However, the signs are that this practice is increasingly adopted by developers; in the Bristol area in the late 1980s it was thought that most potential development land was spoken for in this way.

Phasing

As pointed out in Chapter 3, the phasing of development on sites with planning permission determines the actual new housing supply, and decisions on phasing may result in no development in the immediate period or an extended phasing of development. Again, previous work (JURUE 1977, Ball 1983) emphasizes the influence of housing demand fluctuations and predictions of the sales rates of houses in different market segments on the time taken to carry out development. Also during boom conditions it was apparent in the Bristol study that supply constraints on labour and other inputs could limit output below forecast sale rates, a finding that echoes the EIU study in the previous decade. Rationing of land stocks to ensure continuity of production over a longer period may also limit output in the short term.

4.3 Policies and procedures for land release and monitoring

Regional guidance, structure plans and unitary development plans in the metropolitan and London areas form the main mechanisms for the forward planning of land for housing. Local plans provide the detailed land allocations to meet structure plan assessments of housing land requirements, together with the criteria that will govern the release of unidentified sites. In addition central government has responded to controversy and lobbying about housing land release, particularly in the three boom periods since 1972, by issuing increasingly strong and specific guidance on monitoring and the quantitative provision of land available for housing (see DoE Circulars 102/72, 44/78, 9/80, 15/84, and PPG3 1992).

The starting point for most projections of the need for housing land is an essentially demographic approach to forecasting the future population of an area, allowing for natural change and migration, and the extent to which that population will form separate households in the light of population structure and trends in household formation. In general, plans are expected to allocate sufficient land for housing to accommodate the projected net increase in households.

The location and phasing of these land allocations will be the outcome of the balancing of these requirements with competing uses and available infrastructure, while seeking simultaneously to meet the wider policy objectives of the planning system. Whereas development plans look forward 10–15 years, the DoE's guidance on housing land availability requires that local authorities identify land already available or likely to become available to meet projected needs in the immediate five-year period.

An important feature of this approach is that economic considerations, particularly the demand for and price of housing, are subsumed and concealed within a demographic calculation. In an area of high demand, subject to strong policies of containment, prices will be high and the demographic forecasts, which project forward from recent experience, will build in the consequences of this tight market. In-migration and household formation will both be suppressed by the high prices and lack of available accommodation, so that the household projections will be lower that they might otherwise have been. In Chapters 6–7 we provide some empirical evidence to support this contention. There is therefore a fundamental circularity in the process (Chiddick & Dobson 1986). This will be reinforced by the tendency, in assessing short-term land requirements, to look at recent rates of building as well as "need" estimates, although recent DoE advice has urged local authorities not to do this, but to relay on the plan. Where building rates have been depressed by previous, inadequate land release, as well as by such factors as land banking, speculative withholding, or market fluctuations and uncertainty, then the subsequent release of land would be further depressed by this approach. On the other hand, practitioners express concerns about what a five-year supply means towards the end of the plan period, especially where performance deviates markedly from the plan. For example in areas of high demand where the whole of a ten-year allocation is taken up in the early years of the plan period, should plan targets be increased to reflect recent build rates or should the authority release no further land?

Research carried out by Coopers & Lybrand (1985) examined the methodologies actually used in structure plans in the South East, and found a variety of approaches. Some counties started from an overriding land supply constraint stemming from green belts and very strong policies of containment. Several planned for accommodating additional households equal to the projected growth of existing households, with zero net migration. A third group planned to meet local needs for employment generation. Other counties planned for a continuation of past migration trends, while yet others followed mixed strategies. Market demand tended not to be included in any direct way, through, for example, the use of house and land price variables.

There is further evidence of the importance of policy considerations in the latest set of land supply estimates for the South East (SERPLAN 1992). A comparison of the allocation of the region's total housing need for the period 1991–2006 between counties in the South East with the DoE household projections for counties (the starting point of the exercise) reveals large disparities from county to county (Breheny 1993). Essentially London is allocated a substantially larger share of growth than would be expected on the basis of household projections or the continuation of past trends. The restraint counties to the west and south are given sizeable reductions on trend allocations.

DoE Circulars 9/80 and 15/84 required local authorities: to prepare joint land availability studies, together with representatives of the housebuilding industry; to make available a five-year supply of housing sites; and to take account of market/demand criteria when making their allocations. By 1987 joint land availability studies had been completed for 33 structure plan areas. While controversy continued, it tended to focus on calculating principles rather than general criteria (see Hooper et al. 1988).

The most recently available information on the joint land studies undertaken shows the number completed declining in the latter half of the 1980s (from 34 in the period 1980–85 to 26 in the period 1986–91), with a marked North/South divide. Counties in the South and the South East carried out few joint studies in the late 1980s, although local authorities continued to carry out their own land availability assessments (Lease 1992). This research suggests that the more buoyant demand conditions and the higher level of controversy in the South make the development industry reluctant to engage in the process. Participation in a joint study may imply agreement with a disputed structure-plan housing target, and may necessitate revealing information on landownership and development intentions to competitors in the region. In such circumstances developers may find it more effective to put their resources into promoting increased planning targets, submitting speculative planning applications and testing sites at appeal.

These joint studies have been criticized on several grounds (Hooper 1985, Rydin 1986), but mainly for failing to take account of the lessons of the 1970s studies, in particular by concentrating on the stock of land at a point in time rather than analyzing flows through the stages of the pipeline. Factors on the demand side are considered, but in a rather partial way, and the assignment of individual sites to distinct market bands is criticized. Although most studies have shown aggregate stocks to be adequate this could still conceal local shortages, timing problems, and a system that may be unable to respond to short-term demand surges.

At the time of writing, a deep recession in the housing market has rather taken the edge off the land availability controversy. There seems to be agreement though that DoE guidance following Circular 9/80, backed up by central government intervention via structure plan approval and appeals, has forced planning authorities to modify their approach. On the one hand, there is said to be an increased awareness and understanding of the development industry and an absorption by planning authorities of market criteria into its decision-making (Healey 1992). On the other hand the crisis of over-building, relative to short-term demand, in the late 1980s may have had a sobering effect on the housebuilding industry and reinforced the value of a strategic agreement on the allocation of housing land. Additionally, the political strength of anti-development interests in the South East, apparent in the political climb-down over the attempt to loosen green belt restrictions, may have been taken on board by the industry. Nevertheless, there is an emerging conflict regarding land supply for housing in the context of current structure plan reviews (Coates 1992) and the housebuilders continue to contest the most restrictive policies in parts of the South East.

4.4 Planning and the market in the 1990s

Despite the rhetoric of the 1980s the planning system escaped fundamental reform. Selected areas were removed from local authority planning control (the urban development corporations) and the regulatory regime was relaxed in others (Enterprise Zones, Simplified Planning Zones). Otherwise the system of development plans and development control established in the 1968 Act remained intact. Nevertheless, it has been argued that styles of planning in different areas were fragmenting (Brindley et al. 1989) and that the dominant approaches ("trend planning", "leverage planning") were primarily concerned to facilitate market-led development. Others have argued that the 1980s saw a reorientation of the system away from one concerned with social and community need to one emphasizing the interests of business and property development (Ambrose 1986, Thornley 1991). The mechanisms were a disaggregation of the system into different regimes for different areas, a centralization of power, and repeated advice to local authorities to incorporate policies and operate procedures in a way sensitive to the needs of the market. As Healey (1992) points out, the peculiar procedural flexibility of the British planning system allows for this adaptation to shifting central government agendas. Plans have always been advisory only, and, in making decisions on development planning, authorities are required to take account of "other material considerations".

However, by the end of the 1980s several forces seemed to push government policy back towards emphasizing the importance of plans. The housebuilders in particular were arguing for a system of regional guidance that could provide a strategic agreement on land required for housing, and override local political opposition to development. Repeated appeals against the refusal of planning permission, particularly for development on the urban fringe, were proving costly for developers and politically difficult for central government. Throughout the decade environmental interests represented by bodies such as the CPRE were seeking to maintain the longstanding objective of the British planning system to protect rural landscapes, especially green belts. However, by 1990 "environmental" considerations were broadened to encompass an ecological analysis of global issues such as climate change and the loss of biodiversity, "the environment became an issue of planet survival rather than of local amenity" (Rydin 1993). The issue of "sustainability" began to influence the planning agenda.

A plan-led system

The 1991 Planning and Compensation Act is one outcome of these pressures. All districts are now required to prepare a district-wide local plan, providing comprehensive plan coverage for the first time since 1968. Although structure plans were retained by the Act, strategic planning is currently threatened by the proposed reorganization of local government. The Act also gives added legislative force to the development plan by requiring that decisions on development should be made "in accordance with the plan unless material considerations indicate otherwise". Although continuing the tradition of flexibility, current advice emphasizes the "primacy" of the development plan (PPG12).

As a result of these changes there is much plan-making activity under way. A system of regional guidance and advice is evolving, although uncertainties remain about the status of this advice and the degree to which essentially voluntary arrangements can command conformity from the local authority participants in the process, particularly over the sensitive issue of housing land allocation (Breheny 1993). Similar concerns surround proposals to replace the county-prepared structure plans with jointly prepared strategic plans in areas where local government is reorganized into unitary authorities. In the metropolitan areas and London, Unitary Development Plans (UDPs) are in preparation, combining the functions of structure and local plans. In the remainder of the country, district-wide local plans are underway. By March 1993 81 out of 297 non-metropolitan districts were fully covered by local plans. In the metropolitan districts and London boroughs only three UDPs were adopted, although 21 of the 33 London Boroughs were fully covered by pre-existing local plans. However, most districts expect to have full local plan or UDP coverage by the end of 1996.

This shift to comprehensive plan coverage and the primacy of development plans has potential implications for the relationship between planning and the market. On the one hand, plans that designate specific sites for development provide much more certainty, which we argued earlier should promote supply. In addition, there should be less costly appeals, and economies in the provision of infrastructure. On the other hand these changes may reduce the adaptive flexibility of the system, particularly in the face of market pressure to release more land during periods of high demand, a feature that was noted during the 1970s and 1980s. It may also strengthen the local monopoly position of certain landowners in some situations. It also places a higher premium on plans as a guide to decision-making and provides additional incentives for landowners and developers to become involved in the process of plan preparation, rather than appeals. The practice of landowners and developers lobbying local authorities to include particular sites in their local plans is likely to become more widespread and intense, with perhaps a greater emphasis on proposing an attractive package of community benefits. A key issue here is likely to be the extent to which developers can be persuaded, or offer, to provide community facilities and to meet housing needs for which the public sector will no longer provide the resources.

4.5 Planning agreements

The use of planning agreements to obtain from landowners and developers contributions to the cost of infrastructure and community facilities has a long history. Section 52 of the 1971 Planning Act lays the basis of practice in the recent past, now replaced by section 106 of the 1991 Planning and Compensation Act. Although there have been periodic controversies about the legality and ethics of the practice (e.g. Property Advisory Group 1981), the practice continues with the implicit acquiesence of developers and the government.The rationale for the use of planning agreements is that they can:

- facilitate the development process by overcoming constraints in terms of infrastructure and supporting services for development
- that they compensate to some extent for the costs imposed on a community by new development
- that they redistribute some of the gains arising from development to the wider community, in the absence of a more formal development tax (Healey et al. 1993).

In other words planning agreements can provide a flexible mechanism to overcome some of the problems, such as externalities and infrastructure, which, as we saw in Chapter 3, provide the basic rationale for planning, while tackling the longstanding and unresolved problem of development gains.

The most recent legislation introduces the possibility of "unilateral undertakings" that allow developers to offer contributions, where negotiations are protracted or benefits sought are considered unreasonable, and these can be taken into consideration at appeal. It also provides developers with rights of discharge and modification. This gives somewhat more power to landowners and developers in their negotiations with planning authorities. DoE Circular 16/91 provides the current policy guidance relating to the reasonableness of planning agreements, the gist of which is that benefits should be related to the development and be necessary for the grant of planning permission. More broadly, the guidance gives the green light to agreements designed to secure the implementation of local plan policies for a particular area or type of development, which would seem to give planning authorities considerable discretion to negotiate on a wide range of items. Illustrations of acceptable matters include social housing, nature conservation and a wide range of social, community and educational provision that arise as a result of development. Central government therefore seems to have discovered the benefits of planning agreements as a way of getting the private sector to bear some of the costs of infrastructure provision (Healey et al. 1993).

Throughout the late 1970s and the 1980s public expenditure constraints were forcing more of the cost of infrastructure and other services onto developers. Research on large residential development sites in the South of England in 1988 found that most authorities were negotiating open space, landscaping and play areas, the provision of sites (and sometimes the buildings) for schools, community buildings, health facilities, and shops and public houses (Farthing et al. 1993). On the largest schemes in this research the total cost of the agreements could be as much £1.5 million. Research in Berkshire suggested that the costs of providing infrastructure for new development were becoming the focus of conflict between planners, developers and central government; however, this was not a major financial problem for developers, who tend to reduce the price offered for land (Barlow 1990). Similar findings emerged in the study of Bristol, where in 1988–9 contributions averaged £3000 to £5000 per home, and were generally reflected in lower land bids. There were, nevertheless, concerns expressed in both areas about the uncertainty and delay surrounding the use of planning agreements.

Again, following a period during which allegations of the misuse of planning agreements were common, the DoE commissioned research into the subject in 1991 (Grimley 1992). The research examined the use of local authority powers to enter into agreement with developers, the content and terms of these agreements, and the impact of agreements on developers. Agreements entered into by a sample of 28 authorities over the period 1987 to 1990 were examined. In some respects the findings expose myths about the practice. Only a very small proportion of developments are covered by agreements, and the highest proportion related to residential development. More than half of these related to occupancy restrictions, e.g. use by agricultural workers. Only 5% contained a requirement relating to wider community or planning benefits – typically contributions to park & ride schemes, environmental or recycling measures – although this 5%

is likely to represent a far higher percentage of residential completions, as the most wide-ranging agreements will be attached to the largest developments. Most highway agreements related closely to the development site and only 12% involved a financial payment, mainly relating to legal costs and fees, which were considered modest in the context of total development costs. Generally the findings are that authorities are adhering to government advice (then provided in Circular 22/83) and that a very small proportion relate to wider planning objectives extraneous of development. However, delay was found to be more of a factor, with 95% of agreements taking more than three months and many much longer.

Further evidence on the use of planning agreements is provided in a study by Healey et al. (1993). Here the findings were that the content of agreements did frequently exceed the guidance given in Circular 22/83, as local authorities were seeking to alleviate a wide range of social, economic and environmental impacts, but that there was "little evidence of the outrageously extraneous obligations that are often the stuff of anecdotes" (Healey et al. 1993: 26). The study also confirms that developers are willing to enter into agreements as long as this is a means of obtaining planning permission and does not make a development unprofitable. However, the authors recommend that a more systematic and accountable process needs to be introduced, through clearer plan policies on the circumstances in which planning obligations will be sought, and the scope of the agreements.

Planning and affordable housing

Another significant feature of change in the planning system is a new emphasis on the role of the planning system in "enabling" the provision of social housing. The concept of local needs for housing has long been a popular one, and structure and local plans have included some reference to local needs throughout the 1970s and 1980s. In practice, however, the policies were a rather weak declaration of intent as the means of implementing them were absent. Many were in any case rejected by the Secretary of State on the grounds that planning control should deal only with the physical characteristics of development and not the characteristics of occupants, or the price or tenure of housing.

In February 1989, in an apparent reversal of previous policy, the Secretary of State announced that the planning system could be used to secure the provision of low-cost housing for local needs in rural areas. Here a combination of strict planning controls on new development, a strong market for more expensive housing and a limited rented supply (reinforced by the Right to Buy) brought the issue of access to affordable housing into particular prominence. As the policy has evolved in DoE Circular 7/91 and most recently PPG3 (DoE 1992) the underlying principle has been extended to all areas, not just rural.

There are two sorts of mechanism available. In rural areas, small "exception" sites, typically on the edge of villages where housing would not otherwise be allowed, can be released for affordable housing to meet identified local needs. Subsidy comes through the land being made available at a low cost, reflecting the restriction of development to low-cost housing. Mixed private/social schemes, providing cross subsidy are explicitly excluded. More generally, PPG3 makes clear that a community's need for affordable housing is now a material planning consideration and should be taken into account in formulating development plan policies. It allows local authorities to negotiate with developers seeking planning permission for market housing on "substantial sites" for inclusion of an element of affordable social housing. However, "rigid quotas", regardless of local circumstances, are ruled out, although policies in local plans may indicate targets for affordable housing provision, justified by evidence of needs. In both cases the implementation of the social housing package is ensured through the use of planning agreements under Section 106 of the Planning Act and the involvement of Housing Associations or equivalent agencies.

These approaches pose difficulties for the planning system. In rural areas the exceptions policy poses a particular dilemma in the relative weight to be attached to the need for housing versus environmental considerations. These conflicts are likely to be most intense in areas of green belt, where problems of access to housing will be most evident. The government has made it clear that exception schemes are additional to housing targets agreed as part of the development plan, and the process is largely reactive and opportunistic in nature, something that runs counter to the declared primacy of the development plan set out in the Planning and Compensation Act. The policy has also been criticized for confusing "local" with "need", and giving local authorities limited scope to control either price or tenure, which are fundamental to the issue (Bishop & Hooper 1991).

Early evaluations (Williams et al. 1991) show that the rural exceptions policy has been widely adopted, but progress on implementation is slow. There is evidence that schemes take a long time to get going, as the development process has distinctive characteristics and requirements: identifying appropriate land and willing landowners, providing evidence of needs, drawing up planning agreements and establishing appropriate management to ensure long-term affordability. By mid-1991 some 60 exception sites involving just over 750 units across the country were on site; in total around 3000 units would be provided by schemes in the pipeline at that time. Often schemes still required public subsidy to make them affordable.

Of more potential significance in numerical terms is the provision of social housing, negotiated as part of large and medium-size private housing schemes. However, the extent to which local authorities can require developers to provide social housing has yet to be tested through the appeal system. Barlow & Chambers (1992) estimate that around 1500–2000 units of social housing may be generated by planning agreements in the early 1990s, with an average target of around 25%. Current conditions may be quite favourable with the uncertain market for private-sale housing, but on the other hand this means that land values and the potential for cross-subsidy are significantly diminished.

Again, there are constraints that limit the potential contribution of social housing from this source. Research on planning agreements negotiated in the past has found that the earlier in the process the planners attempted to influence the nature of the development and the expectations of landowners and developers, the greater is the opportunity to negotiate gains (Farthing et al. 1993). Clearly, the leverage of local authorities on sites that are already allocated or have planning permission, which may amount to five or more years' worth of supply in accordance with DoE advice, is limited. The timescale of planning and development on large housing sites also affects the timescale of provision of affordable housing. On large and complicated developments, timescales of ten years or more are not untypical.

The ability to deliver affordable housing will also depend on the scale and nature of overall land release in a particular locality. In areas where the planning strategy relies extensively on recycling of land within existing built-up areas, the ability to negotiate affordable housing will be constrained by high urban land values and the smaller size of schemes. For example, in 1991 almost two-thirds of the short-term supply of housing land in the South East, outside London, lay within the built-up area of existing settlements (Feasey 1992). There is also a strong North/South divide in the ability of the planning system to deliver social housing. The Barlow & Chambers study shows a preponderance of schemes in the South where land values are much higher, and implicit subsidies therefore greater, and planning controls are stronger, increasing the bargaining power of local authorities.

Negotiations over the provision of affordable housing will also add a new and potentially costly element into an existing structure of negotiation on large housing sites. Planners have routinely been negotiating with developers for the provision of infrastructure and community facilities on large housing sites. Successful negotiation of affordable housing quotas would either have to be traded off against other facilities, or imply lower returns to landowners. As far as developers are concerned, contributions to infrastructure, open space and community facilities at least have the advantage of facilitating development and improving marketing, whereas inclusion of social housing may be viewed as a marketing disadvantage.

However, with a new set of district-wide plans now in preparation, the opportunity exists for social housing policies to be given more legitimacy. By 1993 70% of local authorities had developed affordable housing policies, and more recent research suggests that the practice of negotiating social housing as part of market schemes will build up into the 1990s (Barlow et al. 1993). As the housing market revives and output and profitability pick up, the scope for more social housing provision is greater, although more profitable conditions will also harden the attitude of landowners and developers.

However, a degree of confusion still prevails over the relationship between the planning system and the question of housing need. Plan policies expressed in favour of a particular form of tenure are still outlawed. Strategic policy in structure plans or UDPs provides guidance on total housing provision, but without differentiation between market and social housing. Local plans apply these provisions to particular sites, with an indication of an overall target for affordable housing. Quite separate assessments of housing needs may emerge from local housing strategies prepared by local housing authorities. Suggestions to clarify the current uncertainty include better corporate working between housing and planning departments, the application of more prescriptive quotas, or more far reaching, the creation of a separate "use class" for social housing, to allow the separate identification of land for social as distinct from market housing (Bishop & Hooper 1991). Although, for planners, the social housing use class has the attraction of being an integral part of the planning system, it does have significant practical disadvantages. The differential designation of land would be bound to raise issues of equity between landowners, there are problems of enforcement, and perhaps most significantly a social housing designation could result in land being withheld from development in the hope that a market housing designation would eventually be given. From a housing point of view, a separate use class would perpetuate the much criticized tendency for social housing to be developed in spatially segregated ghettos. For all of these reasons this line of approach has been rejected.

4.6 Other key policy issues

New settlements

One outcome of the 1980s controversies concerning the supply of land for housing were a series of proposals led by the private sector for free-standing new settlements, primarily located in the London Green Belt or elsewhere in the South East. The initial proposals were led by Consortium Developments, a consortium of volume housebuilders formed in 1983. The arguments mounted by the developers in favour of such proposals were that new settlements provided a way of meeting the need for new housing land in a few locations, avoiding the political controversies arising from more piecemeal peripheral expansions or infill developments and, moreover, generating sufficient development gain to pay for substantial infrastructure and service requirements. Although the recent attempts to promote new settlements do not stem from a regional strategy, as was the case with the post-war new towns, some central government statements during the 1980s suggest a role for new settlements in the redirection of growth in the South East towards the east Thames corridor.

Since 1983 around 60 separate proposals for new settlements have been made, reaching the planning application stage (Amos 1988). Central government guidance developed from the early 1980s onwards. Circular 15/84 states that there may be some scope for the five-year housing land supply to be met through the identification of new settlements. And, despite the rejection of the first proposal (Tillingham Hall), the Secretary of State's decision letter stated that "well conceived schemes of this kind in appropriate locations may have a part to play in meeting the demand for new housing" (DoE 1987). The most recent PPG3 sets out fuller guidance in the form of criteria that schemes should meet. The list includes:

- proposals should be supported by the local plan
- they should command local support
- a clear demonstration that alternative infill is less desirable
- proposals should result in positive environmental improvement, e.g. through reclamation of derelict land
- proposals should take account of the need to minimize travel and vehicle emissions; and
- proposals should fall outside recognized areas of constraint, such as green belt, AONBs and national parks.

This forms a very restrictive set of criteria and the suspicion must be that central government is maintaining a public image of not ruling out the option, while adopting an unofficial position of resistance (Moore 1992). The nearest that any scheme has come to realization is in Cambridgeshire, where the structure plan incorporated policies concerning the development of new settlements, and a series of applications were submitted for different sites. Again, central government resisted the proposals during the latest stage, despite a favourable Inspector's report. The recent depressed state of the housing market, together with political pressures, and the unresolved problem of bringing forward new settlement proposals through the local plan process, eventually led to the demise of the major promoters, Consortium Developments, in 1991.

The new environmental agenda

A major objective of the planning system has traditionally been the conservation and protection of the environment. This has traditionally been equated with landscape and agricultural land resources, and, since the 1970s, with conservation of the more attractive/historic urban areas. In the 1980s when market-led principles seemed predominant, the planning system was used by certain interests (e.g. the CPRE) to challenge both the need for and the location of new development. These campaigns are sometimes characterized by the rather pejorative acronym of NIMBY ("not in my back yard"), although in the South East in particular the concerns expressed over the location and extent of new development (e.g. proposals to loosen green belt restrictions or to build new settlements) enjoyed a degree of success.

By the late 1980s the planning system was increasingly used by environmental interests to introduce a new set of global environmental concerns into the system. This is also an area where the European Commission has become a major policy actor. In the White Paper, *Our common inheritance* (DoE 1990) the government set out its policy commitments in the environmental field, including a substantial section on town & country planning. This emphasizes four themes:

- the need to locate new development to conserve energy, with particular reference to transport infrastructure
- the role of environmental impact assessment as an adjunct to development control procedures
- the need to consider pollution effects in relation to planning applications
- and the use of planning agreements to compensate for resources or amenities damaged by construction.

PPG12 adds further weight to this with a substantial section on environmental considerations in plans, again focusing on the need for the location of new development to take account of the need to minimize travel, and hence CO_2 emissions, and the use of non-renewable resources. As far as new housing development is concerned, this guidance, backed up by PPG3 and by the EC Green Paper on the Environment, emphasizes the use of derelict and vacant land within existing built-up areas and the avoidance of large-scale development peripheral to urban areas.

Although there is still a good way to go in terms of understanding and operationalizing the concept of sustainability in development plans, the key issue that land-use patterns are important determinants of travel patterns and energy consumption seems to be having an effect (see for example PPGs 6 and 13). Moreover, the influence of the EC is significant here, particularly in respect of the introduction of environmental impact assessments, which current British policy anticipates will be incorporated in the practice of development control. Under pressure from the EC the British planning system may shift towards a more precise specification of the criteria to be used in making decisions on development. Combined with the greater weight to be given to plans, and the increasing interest in ensuring that environmental costs are reduced, the nature and effects of the system could change substantially in the medium term.

CHAPTER 5

The housebuilding industry and the development process

5.1 Introduction

This chapter considers the nature of the housebuilding industry and the role of housebuilding firms as the key decision-makers in the process of new housing supply. Later chapters in this book apply a statistical approach to modelling the supply of housing and how this responds to a range of economic, planning policy and fiscal variables. This chapter uses a more qualitative approach in examining the structure and behaviour of the industry, how it forms expectations and makes decisions, and how it relates to the planning system. The data includes an interview survey with a sample of housebuilding firms active in the Bristol area in the late 1980s, and a variety of secondary sources, which have been comprehensively reviewed by Monk (1991).

5.2 The structure of the industry

New owner-occupied housing is primarily supplied by the speculative housebuilding industry, although firms that build to contract on behalf of a client are growing in importance in the supply of new housing association dwellings for rent. Speculative builders generally control all of the development functions involved in the land conversion process, and this means that they have to be concerned with land acquisition and assembly, obtaining planning permission, and marketing the final product, whereas for the contractor land assembly and marketing are the client's concerns (Fig. 7.1 provides an overview of the development process). Although firms generally concentrate on one kind of development, in a growing number of cases speculative and contracting subsidiaries are owned by one parent company, often together with a range of other construction activities.

Much of the distinctive character of the housing market and the supply of new-build housing stems from the key characteristics described in Chapter 1, including durability, high cost and immobility. The long lead-times involved in the production of new houses, coupled with the dominance of supply by second-hand houses, means that short-term economic and financial factors affecting demand largely determine the state of the market; this point is developed further in Chapter 6. Hence, in England in the mid-1980s, rising real incomes and low interest rates led to increased demand, which because of the slowness of supply response translated into rapid growth in house prices. Together with increased interest rates, in due course these exaggerated price increases severely depressed effective demand, leading to falling house prices in many regions from 1990 onwards. Since the early 1970s this experience of boom and slump in the housing market has been repeated three times (see Fig. 5.1).

Housebuilders have the difficult task of forecasting this "cycle" of demand, with typical pipeline times for new housing construction of two years or more. Therefore, a house started at the beginning of a boom may not be completed for sale until market conditions have deteriorated, and this is even more true of whole sites or estates. Speculative housebuilding is also distinctive in the large amount of capital that needs to be invested in land and development prior to production. Together with the volatility of the market, this makes the industry exceptionally risky. The volatility of the market also affects the character of the housebuilding industry, which has undergone a long process of restructuring so that production is now dominated by a moderate number of volume producers.

The housebuilding industry nationally has an unusual structure, which is summarized in Table 5.1. In 1992 there were more than 23000 firms registered with the National Housebuilding Council (NHBC); most were very small enterprises producing a few units annually, many were inactive, and the industry is dominated by several large players. In 1992 the top 32 companies supplied almost half of total production, each building 500 units or more; the largest 25 companies held a 42% market share. At the other extreme there are more than 6000 companies building fewer than ten houses a year.

A major restructuring of the industry took place during the 1970s following the 1972/73 boom and slump in the housing market, which saw a significant decline in small and medium-size firms and a marked increase in the market share of firms producing 500+ units each year. The numbers of firms in the different size categories has varied since then, as firms shift between size categories or move in and out of housebuilding according to the building cycle, but the greatest losses in the most recent period of housing market recession remain the smallest producers. Also, concentration in the industry has continued to take place; for example the market share of firms producing more than 500 units increased from 35% in 1977 to 45% in 1987 (see Table 5.2)

This degree of concentration reflects a variety of factors: the impact of large public sector contracts in the 1960s, the economies of scale available from large-scale land buying and constructing "standard" house types, and the restructuring of the industry that took place following the sharp downturn in housebuilding in the early 1970s, when many small and medium-size companies were bought up

Table 5.1 Size and output of housebuilders in different size categories, 1992.

Size of firm (units)	Number of firms	Total starts (%)
0	16150	0
1–10	6527	12
11–30	696	9
31–100	329	13
101–500	128	21
501–2000	22	18
2000+	10	26

Source: NHBC quarterly returns.

Table 5.2 Structure of housebuilding industry over time: starts by size of output (%).

Units	1977	1982	1987	1992
0	0	0	0	0
1–10	16	14	13	12
11–30	13	10	11	9
31–100	14	12	13	13
101–500	22	18	18	21
501–2000	35	17	16	18
2000+	incl. above	25	25	26

Source: NHBC quarterly returns.

by larger builders. As Ball (1983) points out, volume production allows the effects of market fluctuations to be minimized through a strategy of diversification of sites and house types. Other advantages include being able to achieve a higher turnover of capital, and the ability to trim margins on individual schemes and consequently to make higher bids for land than can be contemplated by smaller producers.

The largest companies have traditionally pursued a strategy of achieving growth by acquiring smaller housebuilders, where the motivation is to diversify into new regions and to add to land banks. Also, throughout the 1980s some companies with other property and construction interests established or bought up housebuilding arms, reflecting the profitability of housebuilding during this period (Ball 1988). Some housebuilders diversified out of housebuilding into industrial and commercial development activities. Therefore, part of the restructuring of the industry involves a shift from medium-size regionally based firms, specializing mainly in housing, to multi-region specialist subsidiaries of large conglomerates or more broadly based construction sector companies.

The ownership of housebuilders by corporations with a wider range of diverse interests also allows the industry to limit its vulnerability to short-term shifts in demand by switching investment into other subsidiaries, regions or countries. Whereas the collapse of the mid-1980s boom in the housing market resulted in a dramatic decline in housebuilding activity (Fig. 5.1, Table 5.3), the spate of bankruptcies that occurred following a similar collapse in the 1970s seems not to have occurred again, at least among the larger companies. Although some companies with a very specialized product were early victims of the recession, most of the larger firms have survived, albeit with much lower levels of production. This is partly because the larger developers have increased their use of contracting-out production to many subcontracting firms in the 1970s and 1980s. These large developers have therefore been able to pass on the costs of recession to the smaller subcontractors.

The investment strategies of the companies will therefore depend on the whole range of activities in which they are involved, rather than just the short-term profitability of housebuilding. Output of new housing may be influenced by the wider strategies of these companies, although demand for new houses and the profitability of construction continue to exert a major influence on the level of output, as shown in Chapter 6.

Figure 5.1 shows that the 1980s saw an unusually long period of sustained acceleration in both house prices and housebuilding activity. As demand increased as a result of rising real incomes and falling interest rates, house prices and house sales also increased. Housebuilders responded by increasing production, especially from 1985 onwards, and output reached levels not experienced since the early 1970s (around 200000 new houses completed in 1988). The market downturn associated with a series of rapid interest rate rises from mid-1988 has resulted in a reduction of housing market activity as manifested by house sales, and new housebuilding has fallen dramatically (Table 5.3). The recent experience of boom and slump in the housing market illustrates very well the volatility of new-build supply in response to short-term market changes.

The national trend towards concentration in the industry is confirmed in studies of particular localities. In Berkshire in the 1980s the increasing dominance of the large-volume builders was noted by Short et al. (1986) and Barlow (1990).

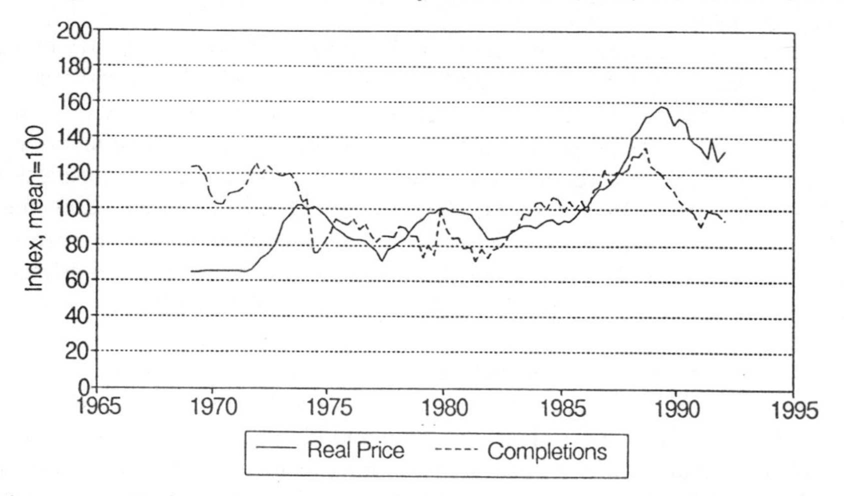

Figure 5.1 Real new house prices and private completions, Great Britain 1969–93.

Table 5.3 Private sector starts and completions, 1982–92.

Year	Starts	Completions
1982	140 790	125 398
1983	172 405	148 050
1984	158 335	159 416
1985	165 682	156 507
1986	180 006	170 427
1987	196 814	183 731
1988	221 404	199 331
1989	170 122	179 536
1990	135 252	156 388
1991	134 920	148 248
1992	121 010	137 200

Source: DoE housing and construction statistics.

Most of the large companies were recent (post-1975) entrants to the market, attracted by the county's growth and prosperity. Our research in Avon in the late 1980s also demonstrated the dominance of a modest number of large housebuilding companies in one particular market area. Just nine companies (all regional subsidiaries of the major volume builders) built more than half of all new houses in a three-year period from 1986 to 1989. Similarly, eight developers owned more than half the undeveloped land with planning permission. Interviews with a sample of these firms revealed that most of the larger firms were relatively new to the area, established for between two and six years, attracted by a growing and buoyant housing market during the 1980s. So although this particular market mirrors the national picture of a high degree of concentration of production, competition between the largest producers was intense and becoming more so as more companies moved into the area.

Competition was however tempered by a certain amount of co-operation between the largest firms in the development of some very large housing sites. A significant proportion of housebuilding in Avon is taking place on three large sites, which together account for around 20000 of the total structure plan target of 35000 new houses in the period 1986–95. Large site development is also increasingly common in other parts of the country, particularly in southern England (Short et al. 1986, Farthing 1993). For the planning authorities this has benefits in minimizing the political opposition to housing land allocations and in allowing the negotiation of substantial "planning gain" packages, hence passing on infrastructure costs to the private sector. For the volume developers, large sites provide some guarantee of production over a longer period and allow for economies of scale. A mix of house types and styles also facilitates marketing. Development of such sites often involves the formation of consortia, which co-ordinate contributions to infrastructure and the phasing of development. However, small and medium-size firms are squeezed out of such developments because the financial commitment required to purchase land and make contributions to infrastructure is generally beyond them. The practice of large site release may also allow the members of the consortium controlling the land to function as a cartel within a particular housing market area.

Nationally there is evidence of growing concentration in the housebuilding industry, but this is not the experience of all regions. Couch (1988) found that in the Wirral the share of the market of large national companies fell during the 1980s, and the total output and market share of local firms rose. Couch suggests that the national trend to concentration is weaker in the Wirral, and possibly in other similar "depressed" areas, because of weaker demand and a diminishing supply of land. These differences in the structure of the housebuilding industry in different areas will have implications for the relative power of developers, landowners and the planning system. The discussion in Chapter 3 of the broader power relationships governing the planning of new housing indicated that the balance of influences was not necessarily easy to predict. In areas of high demand and growing concentration in the South, an intensive struggle over land release has taken place (although tempered in the current recession) and the large builders may have been able to exert considerable influence over the quantity and form of land release (Short et al. 1986). In areas of low demand Couch suggests that "the relative lack of interest shown by larger firms and the weaker market power and limited political influence of smaller firms are likely to enable the local authorities to maintain strong restraint policies".

5.3 The economics of housebuilding

Profitability

Large profits can be made from speculative housebuilding, but over the building cycle profits are extremely volatile. Using estimates based on a comparison of total development costs and the average prices of new houses, Barlow & King (1992) show gross margins averaging 18.1% in the 1980s, but with a high degree of short-term variability; profit margins fell from a peak of near 30% in 1981 to around 10% in 1984, climbed to near 30% again in 1986/87 and fell to below 5% in 1989. Their comparative analysis with France and Sweden suggests that average gross margins are not that dissimilar, but that volatility is a much more important feature of the UK housebuilding industry. They conclude that one outcome of this is an industry that is highly unstable and prone to high levels of bankruptcy and financial crisis.

Profit margins are a function of the relationship between input costs – land, labour, materials, fixed costs, marketing and the costs of capital – and the selling prices of houses. The determination of profit margins is however complicated by their sensitivity to the timing of land purchase in relation to the sale of the product and the impact of this on the cost of the land element and the turnover time of capital. So although strong cyclical trends are apparent in the aggregate trends for the industry, the fortunes of individual companies can diverge widely from the overall average (Ball 1983). Variations will reflect the investment and marketing strategies of the firms, i.e. the form and location of development and their land banking strategies.

Employment and production methods

It can be argued that the volatility of the housing market has heightened the need for flexibility in the industry. Part of this flexibility has been achieved through the almost universal use by the large housebuilding companies of subcontracted labour to carry out production, with direct employment limited to site management. Thus, although the major volume housebuilders dominate the industry in terms of market share (measured by the number of houses built) many very small firms are actually involved in the production of houses, often firms specializing in particular aspects of the construction process.

This system of subcontracting may have advantages of cost and flexibility to the employing firm, but it has also been argued (Ball 1983, 1988) to have negative consequences in terms of the inadequacy of training, shortages of skilled workers during market upturns, and a low level of technical innovation. The argument is that the system of subcontracting removes incentives to improve the efficiency of production processes through investing in training or new techniques. The volume housebuilders can to some extent pass on the costs of falling profits by squeezing the prices of subcontracted labour, while for the smaller subcontractors intense competition on the basis of price eliminates the possibility of such investment. One outcome of this may be problems of quality control and a poor-quality product, as demonstrated by the much publicized failings of timber frame construction during the early 1980s. A further result is an industry characterized by very poor working conditions and extreme instability in employment.

Land banking and valuation

In Chapter 4 we discussed the practice of land banking as a strategic response to uncertainty. All companies will land bank to some extent as land will need to be held for a minimum of around two years for operational reasons. For companies that maintain the minimum land bank (say two years) the major source of profit will be on construction, and profits will be amassed on the volume of turnover. For companies who maintain longer-term strategic land banks, the profit margin on each house may be substantially enhanced because land with a low historic value is being used to build houses priced at current market values. Even companies that rely mainly on profit from volume will benefit from inflationary gain during periods of high house-price inflation, as in 1987/88, when profit margins increased substantially. And the development of land with low historic value may allow some companies to reduce prices and maintain sales in a downturn in the market (Ball 1983).

Previous work has discussed the variety of land banking strategies that can be pursued (Smyth 1982, 1984, Ball 1983,). A variety of sources (EIU 1975, Bather 1976, Short et al. 1986) suggest that size of firm is a crucial influence on land banking activity, with small firms constrained from much advance land purchase because of credit constraints, and large firms having the financial flexibility to invest in land, often buying counter-cyclically. However, Smyth (1982) suggests that there are also considerable differences in the land banking strategies of the larger companies. This was confirmed in the research in Avon, where some volume producers bought mainly land with outline planning permission or allocated for residential development, held land for the minimum period only, and relied mainly on turnover for profits. Others placed greater emphasis on development profits, held a mixture of land with and without planning permission, and engaged in land trading to some extent. It was however increasingly common for land to be acquired under conditional contract or option as a way of ensuring future land supply with minimum risk. This involves payment of a deposit (typically 10% of the market value) for the right to buy the land for development when planning permission is granted, normally at a discount of 10% or more of its new value with planning permission.

Land banking strategies will also vary over the course of the building cycle. During the boom of the late 1980s, some firms in Avon claimed to be making few strategic land purchases because of the rising cost of land relative to house prices, although the practice of taking out options continued. With lower land prices in the early 1990s, some firms are beginning to build up land banks (*Building*, February 1993: 15), although many of the largest producers still burdened by debts from the previous collapse in the market were continuing to shed land.

The research in Avon also confirmed that land bids were typically made on the basis of a "residual valuation". This means that a site is valued at the difference between the market-determined selling price of the completed homes and the total cost of development and construction, including a target level of profit. Hence the prices bid by the housebuilders depended on their forecasts of the overall profitability of housebuilding. This is in line with other research (e.g. Drewett 1973) and confirms the view put forward by Ball (1983) that land prices do not cause house price rises, but are a residual consequence of the level of house prices relative to construction costs. It was also apparent that the share of house prices attributable to the land element varied according to the building cycle. During the boom period 1985–8, in the South of England land increased from around 30% of total development costs to near 50%. In a buoyant market housebuilders were pushing new house prices ahead of the second-hand market by between 10–15%, allowing them to outbid competitors for land. The housebuilders were also prepared to trim margins where high turnover and volume guaranteed profits, again allowing them to bid more for land. Perceptions of landowners' expectations were an important factor in land-bidding behaviour. And there were indications that in a relatively constrained planning context, where, as we have seen, much of the available land is already in the hands of the larger developers, landowners were able to appropriate some of the increasing profit from housebuilding.

5.4 Forecasting demand and planning output

All housebuilders must to some extent be responsive to demand shifts in a highly volatile market. Adjustments to output can be achieved by reducing or increasing starts on existing sites, by adjusting the phasing of sites under construction, or by delaying or bringing forward building on new sites. In addition, the mix of house types and density can be adjusted, subject to some planning constraints. Over a longer time period, land acquisition policies are the key to output plans.

All of the companies we interviewed engaged in some kind of medium-term forecasting. For some, growth of output was projected, mainly through geographic spread in the region. For the dominant volume builders the medium-term strategy was more likely to be to stabilize production at levels near to current levels of output. Although the interviews were carried out at the beginning of the most recent recession in the housing market, the industry continued to display a degree of (misplaced) optimism about the prospects for continued growth.

Some larger companies with long-term strategic land banks made systematic efforts to examine demographic trends, employment and income growth, and future public investment in transport infrastructure. However, these firms were in the minority. The overwhelming impression derived from the Bristol research was of an industry that relied substantially on short-term planning, emphasizing flexibility. Demand forecasting was orientated to short-term land acquisition decisions, research was mainly market research in a small area, and plans were at most looking 12 months ahead. As other research has shown (Ball 1983), output is extremely sensitive to current changes in profitability. Other factors affecting expectations seemed to have only a secondary influence on output, although a greater effect on land acquisition.

The need to operate in an opportunistic fashion and to respond to short-term market shifts was emphasized, particularly as the industry is so affected by government policy on interest rates. Interest rate changes are of significance on both the demand and the supply side of the housing market. On the demand side, rising interest rates both depress demand and create uncertainty over sales rates. On the supply side, rising interest rates push up borrowing costs and increase the importance of fast capital turnover, but this is difficult when sales rates are also unpredictable.

One response to shifts in demand, and in the speed at which houses are selling, is to vary the completion times of developments already under way. There is considerable evidence that completion times can vary widely (Ball 1983) and that larger housebuilders generally gear their completion times to maintain house prices and avoid oversupply in a local market (Rydin 1985). Forecasting sales rates on particular sites is something that most companies in our survey could do with confidence in "normal" market conditions; it was evident that the rapid interest rate changes in the late 1980s introduced an unusual degree of uncertainty. Desirable sales rates on a site varied between two and twelve a month, depending on whether companies were geared to volume production or not, and reasonably accurate predictions could be made up to nine months ahead. Assessments of sales rates then governed the phasing of development on a site. However, there were variations in the response to market shifts; some of the largest volume builders were more likely to be production-driven, seeking to achieve a particular rate of sales through adjusting pricing and marketing, including offering a variety of incentives to potential buyers.

There were also indications that adjustments to production levels could be constrained by several factors, including the availability and price of inputs such as land, labour and materials. Companies' own plans for output and profit growth were also a constraint, as they affected shareholders' perceptions of corporate viability. So, for some of the companies we interviewed, planned targets for output and profit were an important influence on their activities, regardless of short-term demand shifts. In a period of rising house prices and increasing margins, it was possible to increase profit levels while restraining output. This had the advantage of not depleting land banks and of avoiding the risk of overexposure when the market turns down. Forward selling was also used as an alternative to expanding output, again offering some protection against sudden changes in the market. These tactics imply that the responsiveness of supply to demand and price changes may be somewhat muted, or inelastic. Similarly, some companies claimed they were planning to maintain production, even though prices and demand were declining at the time of the research, and were hopeful that sales rates could be maintained through price adjustments and a variety of incentives. This suggests that the severity of the recession was seriously underestimated.

It has been suggested that the degree of risk in the UK housebuilding industry, and the volatility of profits, encourage a conservatism in operational behaviour (Barlow & King 1992). This is apparent in the widespread use of a few standard house types and the reluctance to innovate in design and production techniques, although conservatism on the part of consumers and lenders may also play a part here. It may also encourage a cautious stance in relation to the level of output; certainly the instability of the market seems to make long-term planning difficult.

Labour shortages (particularly some skill shortages) were identified by all of the companies as a constraint on increasing output during the boom conditions of the late 1980s. Conversely, a motivation for trying to maintain production when the market turns down is to retain labour for the future. However, the almost universal reliance on subcontracted labour to carry out construction allows the industry to respond very flexibly to downturns in demand. Nevertheless, a desire to maintain good relationships with some subcontractors, valued for their quality of work, moderated the extent to which some housebuilding firms sought to exploit these relationships.

Land supply constraints are given a high profile in the public pronouncements of the housebuilding industry, and most of the companies we interviewed reiterated these complaints about land availability in the Avon area. However, most companies held land banks of at least two years and the issue seemed to be more about the competition between housebuilders for the land that was available and the price of the land. As we have seen, there were many new entrants to the market during the 1980s and, for companies that were new to the area, building up a land bank may have been difficult. For smaller companies, who were excluded from developing on the large sites allocated for housing by virtue of their scale and the nature of their product, and who depended on relatively expensive bank borrowing, land availability was a more serious issue. Often the smaller sites sought by these companies were judged to be too expensive to be able to ensure profitable development.

An alternative response to changing demand conditions is to change the mix of house types produced. A variety of sources describe how housebuilders adjust the nature of their product as the market changes, typically moving production up-market as conditions improve, to take advantage of a buoyant trade-up market and the higher profit margins on more expensive houses, and moving down market to serve first-time buyers as the market slackens (Ball 1983, Barlow 1990). There is also evidence that large builders have diversified their product range over time, including seeking new market niches such as sheltered housing and low-cost partnership schemes with local authorities, to provide some protection against fluctuations in demand for different house types.

Part of adjusting the mix of production is to change the density of development. Research on this suggests that developers will frequently try to increase the density of development in order to maximize profits. In Berkshire the research by Short et al. (1986) found that builders who acquired land with outline planning permission would often seek to increase the density in order to extract further profit on a site. Some sources suggest that densities have been increasing over a long period and that space standards of new housing are consequently deteriorating (Ball 1983, Barlow 1990, Evans 1991). In Ball's view this reflects the inability of the industry to keep prices at an affordable level without sacrificing quality, whereas in Barlow's work the trend to higher density reflected demographic factors and the demand for smaller properties, as well as land scarcity in an area of high development pressure. In Evans' work the increasing density of new housing development is interpreted as an effect of restrictions on land supplied through the planning system. However, it is clear that density of development may be an important area of negotiation between developers and the planning system. In Berkshire Short et al. (op. cit.) found that planners' attempts to resist increases in density were not always successful, whereas our work in Avon suggested that density was less of an issue: often planners and housebuilders were seeking the same thing in higher densities. We discuss density further in Chapter 8.

Partnership and low-cost housing

As the housing market moved into recession in the late 1980s, so partnership developments for "affordable" or social rented housing were becoming attractive to housebuilders. These schemes were seen as a way of maintaining production in a slack period and providing a cushion against cyclical fluctuations in the private new-build market. Also the late 1980s saw an increase in funding for housing associations and plans for a substantial growth in social housing production, together with changes in the planning system to allow "exception" schemes on unallocated land, as described in the previous chapter. Although the latter are probably too small scale for the majority of the largest builders, smaller producers perceive benefits in being able to access unallocated sites.

Some major housebuilders have established specialist partnership divisions that undertake design/build contracts for housing associations or joint ventures with local authorities on land owned by the local authority. The housebuilders in our survey were projecting that partnership and low-cost housing would reach 20% of their output over a five-year period. Currently in 1993 social housing starts make up more than a quarter of total housing starts. The 1992–3 Housing Market Package also involved Housing Associations in acquiring dwellings directly from private developers. Moves into partnership and low-cost housing are part of a more general diversification strategy for some companies, but it is likely that the lower profitability of such schemes will dampen enthusiasm when the market recovers. Most housebuilders remain principally concerned with managing the whole of the development process, and the skills emphasized are those of the timing of land purchase, cash flow management and marketing. Although profits from speculative building are volatile, they can be substantial in a rising market.

However, the changes to the planning system that allow the negotiation of an element of social housing as part of market housing development mean that all private sector developers, not just traditional partnership developers, will have to become involved in social housing provision to some extent. The financial implications of social housing provision can also be significant; in the absence of public subsidy then subsidy in the form of reduced land values or smaller development profits is implied. We discuss further the implications of these issues for the housebuilding industry in Chapters 7 and 10. However, the growing expectation that developers will make a significant contribution both to infrastructure to support new residential development and to meeting social housing needs does suggest that large development profits will be less easy to come by in the 1990s.

5.5 Perceptions of the planning system

As we discussed in the previous chapter, land availability for housing has become an issue of some contention between housebuilders and the planning system. Complaints by housebuilders regarding the failure of planning to identify sufficient land for housing are frequently voiced in the trade press, and political lobbying and campaigns orchestrated by the Housebuilders Federation have focused on the issue of land supply at various times in the period since 1979. The perception that the planning system imposes constraints on land supply, and hence constrains output below what it would be in a less regulated market, is reported in studies of the housebuilding industry. In some cases there is an impression that planning imposes an overall quantitative constraint, at least in particular areas (Short et al. 1986, Tym 1990). In others there are indications that planning imposes constraints on development in favoured greenfield locations, and shifts development towards less favoured brownfield sites (Barlow 1990). In other studies the impression is that land availability is more crucially affected by the demand for houses at different points in the housing market cycle than by changes in allocations by the planning system (EIU 1975). In the Avon work, which coincided with the end of a boom period in the housing market, complaints regarding planning constraints on land supply were commonly ex-pressed, but these were mainly concerned with the location and form of land release policies, essentially the emphasis on a few large development sites in fringe locations, that tended to exclude all but the largest volume producers.

The need to obtain planning permission is variously perceived as imposing unacceptable delays on development (Tym 1989) or as an essential part of the process. In terms of the development pipeline, it is seen as less significant than factors relating to land assembly and scheme design (EIU 1975). In our work in Avon, delay was perceived as a problem at the detailed planning permission stage, when more and unpredictable political intervention by planning committees occurred. At outline planning permission stage, delay was not perceived as a problem, and outcomes could be more confidently predicted as there were often extensive pre-application negotiations. It seemed therefore that some developers accept the need to negotiate schemes through the planning system and build this into their plans. Most of the larger developers expressed a willingness to negotiate the details of schemes and to trade off the costs of delay against the profitability of schemes.

The extent of negotiation between housebuilders and the planning system is discussed at some length by Short et al. (1986). In Berkshire the quantity and quality of interaction with the planning system depended on the characteristics of individual firms. Firms were categorized as: (a) cautious, restricting themselves to safe sites with existing planning permissions; (b) naïve, with a tendency to submit unacceptable applications that are generally refused; (c) negotiators, probing the limits of planning control, with extensive interaction with the planning system and a high application success rate; and (d) aggressors, again testing the limits of planning, but with a tendency to forsake negotiation for the appeal route. The cautious and naïve builders had minimal contact with the planning system, and rarely employed planning consultants or agents. Among the cautious firms were many that emphasized production rather than land dealing. The negotiators and aggressors invested more resources in tackling the planning system and had a high level of contact. The negotiators in particular were more likely to employ planning expertise, often former local authority planners, to handle negotiations and "their interaction with the planning system is such that they have virtually become incorporated within it" (Short et al. 1986: 111).

5.6 Conclusions

The impact of firm concentration

Concentration in the housebuilding industry is, as we have seen, a consequence of the peculiar characteristics of the market for new housing, and broader change in the economy. An increased scale of operations allows firms to minimize risks by diversifying production over more sites, regions and house types to cope with fluctuations in demand in the market, and may also allow the effects of unpredictable planning decisions in different areas to be averaged out. Access to credit, either internally or externally generated, is an advantage in land acquisition and the larger firms have the ability to land bank, and to considerably enhance their profits through land dealing or the development of land with low historic cost. They can afford to take a longer-term view of the market and to take advantage of adverse market conditions to buy land when prices are depressed. Ball (1983) suggests that the increasing dominance of large development capital in the housebuilding industry alters the reaction of the industry to economic pressures; where housebuilders are part of larger diversified property and construction holding companies, such firms are relatively immune to the housebuilding cycle and can ride out slumps in the market. It also has implications for the relations between developers and landowners, and developers and the planning system, enhancing the power of the developers in negotiations over the price and availability of land.

Others, however, emphasize the damaging consequences of risk and volatility in the industry (Barlow & King 1992). This makes the industry relatively conservative, as evidenced by low technical and product innovation, makes long-term planning difficult, and leads to a high rate of bankruptcy and financial crisis. Large stocks of unsold houses at the end of the late 1980s boom are evidence that many housebuilders failed to predict the inevitable downturn in the market, and many building firms have gone out of business; the total number of firms on the NHBC register declining from 29000 in 1989 to 23000 in 1992. However, most of the casualties have been the smallest, producing fewer than 10 units each year.

It is also worth emphasizing that, although relatively few large players dominate the industry in terms of output, production is a very fragmented process because of the system of subcontracting. A greater reliance on subcontracted labour has become the norm during the 1970s and 1980s because of the advantages of flexibility and cost that it offers in a market subject to major fluctuations in demand. However, it is a system that has been criticized for engendering low levels of training and technical innovation, problems of quality control, and poor working conditions in the industry.

Local studies of housing markets during the 1980s found that the national trend to concentration was a feature of change in the structure of the housebuilding industry, particularly in areas of high demand such as Berkshire and Avon. But there is also evidence that the focus of much research on high demand areas in the South may be misleading; in areas where demand is weaker, small and medium-size local companies may be more important. This has implications for the relative power of landowners, developers and the planning system. The increased politicization and professionalism of the housebuilding industry have been noted in studies such as those in Berkshire, and have led to a sustained and in some ways successful attack on structure plan policies to reduce housing land allocations. Some sections of the industry (Short's negotiators and aggressors) were also adept at manipulating the planning system and they invested significant resources in this.

Competition remains intense, however, between the volume builders, particularly over the acquisition of land, although there are indications that smaller and larger firms compete less with one another and may operate in different segments of the land market.

Supply response

Output of new houses is responsive to house price changes in general terms, but the relationship is not straightforward, and there are indications that the supply response to changes in demand and price may be somewhat muted. Output may be constrained below achievable sales rates during an upturn in the housing market because of skill shortages in the construction industry. In the face of recession, some companies planned to maintain production levels, through changing market segment in an attempt to sustain sales. Company policy and business strategy may be an important influence on a firm's activities as well as short-term demand changes, and the trend to concentration of production among large, diversified firms enables companies to take a longer-term and more strategic view of their activities. Nevertheless, our own interview survey gave the impression of an industry that was predominantly short term in planning and outlook.

Finally, there were indications that housing production was becoming more diversified during the 1980s, with more emphasis on maintaining a broad portfolio of house types and the exploitation of niche markets, such as the retirement market and social housing construction. Within this trend to greater diversification, however, the housebuilding industry remains rather conservative, with a continued reliance on a few standard house types and a reluctance to innovate with respect to construction methods and design, perhaps reinforced by the conservatism of consumers and lenders. The quality of new housing construction is a related issue, and quality improvements in materials, standards of workmanship and design may require a less conservative approach to the product. Part of the explanation for the reluctance of the industry to innovate lies in the broader context of housing production, which is volatile and risky as we have seen. Part relates to the significance of land development gains in the overall profits of the industry, which diminish the emphasis that firms need to place on the production process. A final factor that affects the quality of the product is the system of subcontracting that again places little emphasis on a workforce with adequate skills and motivation.

CHAPTER 6

Modelling housebuilding and house prices

6.1 The modelling approach

Aims of the research

This chapter describes a new approach to building quantitative economic models of the supply of new private housing at local level in Britain. This approach was developed by the authors as part of a continuing programme of research, growing out of wider concerns with the impact of the housing finance system in Britain (Bramley et al. 1990, Joseph Rowntree Foundation 1991, Maclennan et al. 1991). Subsequently, findings from this research have fed into an inquiry into the relationships between planning and housing and between planning and the national economy (Joseph Rowntree Foundation 1994). The research was also motivated by our dissatisfaction with the paucity of systematic economic research into housing supply in Britain and the crucial role of planning and land supply in this.

The research aimed to quantify the local supply response of private housebuilding to market demands in the context provided by the British land-use planning system. More specifically, our aims included:

(a) to measure the elasticity of supply of new private housing construction with respect to house prices
(b) to assess the variation in this supply elasticity between different localities with very different planning policies and constraints on land supply
(c) to measure the feedback effects from land and housing supply onto house prices
(d) to assess the responsiveness of planning to housing market demand
(e) to predict the impact of changes in planning policies for land release on the housing market
(f) to predict the impact of changes in tax and subsidy arrangements on housing supply and prices.

This chapter is mainly concerned with the way in which we constructed models to meet the first three of these aims. These models then provide a basis for further analysis dealing with aims (d), (e) and (f), which we discuss in further detail in Chapters 7 and 9.

Building on theory and qualitative research

The modelling approach builds on the insights derived in earlier chapters from both economic theory and empirical research. Chapter 2 reviewed the state of the art with regard to general economic theories of housing supply and their application to empirical studies that attempt to measure supply elasticities. This literature was found to be overwhelmingly North American and as such suffers from several limitations from a British policy perspective. Not only is the policy and land supply context very different in North America, but there is also in much of this literature a preoccupation with long-run equilibrium market outcomes. For practical policy-makers there is a need to examine what is likely to happen in the short and medium term in the particular context of a system characterized by comprehensive planning control and a limited supply of suitable land. Macroeconomic models based on national time-series data provide further insights into the effects of economic and monetary variables on housebuilding activity, but again fail to deal with land supply.

Chapter 3 considered the nature of planning in terms of its operational objectives and broader policy functions, and went on to analyze its likely effects on the urban housing market. It showed how supply might be less than fully elastic, even without a planning system, but that planning constraints could further limit response and alter the behaviour of developers.

Chapter 4 reviewed the way land availability for housing has been assessed and planned in practice in Britain over the past two decades. This has been a major arena for conflicting views between the planning profession and the housebuilding industry, and government has attempted to intervene in order to promote procedures that deliver land supply more effectively. Information on land availability generated as a result provides part of the database for the models described below.

Chapter 5 reviewed the structure of the housebuilding industry and examined some more qualitative evidence about its behaviour. This again provides certain pointers to how we should conceptualize and model supply, in relation to such issues as time-lags, expectations, flexibility, phasing, land prices and bidding, and how developers deal with the planning system.

The models described in this chapter fall into the general class of econometric models. Chapter 1 introduced these models and provided a general description of their main features. Such models quantify the relationships between several economic variables (house prices, completions, land supply, etc.) on the basis of systematic statistical data on the values of these variables across manycases. The models described in this chapter are cross-sectional. The units of observation are local housing market areas defined approximately by district authority boundaries.

Demand and supply

The housing market is like any market in the sense that it brings together a demand side and a supply side. The most elementary economic textbooks deal with this situation by showing how the outcome of a market process, the prices set and the quantities of the commodity bought and sold, are determined by the interaction of supply and demand. Thus, there is not a single behavioural relationship to be captured in the model, but two or three: the determinants of the behaviour of the households demanding housing, the determinants of the behaviour of housebuilders supplying housing, and the way the market reconciles these two sets of behaviour. There are different ways of handling this in econometric modelling. One approach is to assume that the relationships all operate "simultaneously", and to construct a consistent set of simultaneous equations that must be satisfied if the market is to clear. Another approach is to assume that the market does not clear, that is that there is some "disequilibrium" between demand and supply. A third approach is to recognize that there may be time-lags in some of the relationships, so that the market functions in a sequential way. Given the importance of lags in housing construction (documented in Ch. 5), we have found the third of these approaches most fruitful, although we have also explored the alternatives.

Level of analysis

The cross-sectional approach used here focuses attention upon differences between local areas (districts) in house prices and housebuilding output. It tries to explain these by reference to differences in demand-side factors (locational advantages, employment, social structure, demography) and in supply-side factors (construction costs, land availability, planning policies and constraints). We chose this "inter-urban" level of analysis because it best captures the significant differences that can arise in these factors, especially land- and planning-related factors. Land is a unique factor of production because it is spatially fixed, and its availability varies dramatically between different localities. Other factors in the model are not quite so fixed, but are still tied to varying degrees to particular localities, especially in the short run, as well as being quite variable between localities.

The underlying assumption of this approach is that there are such things as local housing markets, or at least submarkets within an overall national system. We do not assume that local markets are completely closed and insulated from one another, merely that they are not perfect substitutes for one another (Monk et al. 1991: 1–2). On the supply side, land is fixed but construction industry resources may have some mobility, albeit limited by the costs of moving away from organizational bases with local labour and supplier linkages and local market knowledge. On the demand side, different local markets may be effective substitutes for some more mobile consumers, which may make local markets more open. This is a major reason why house price movements tend to be replicated across the country, subject to various lags and ripple effects (Giussani & Hadjimatheou 1990, Coombes & Raybould 1991). Nevertheless, job and family/social ties are very strong for many households, and most movement is very local (Forrest et al. 1991).

We use local authority districts as our unit of analysis primarily for practical reasons to do with data availability. In theory, a superior unit of analysis might be the travel to work area (TTWA) or similar local labour market area (LLMA). These are determined by the analysis of past Census data at ward level on employment concentrations and travel-to-work patterns. But such units are still somewhat arbitrary, dependent on the algorithm used, and not necessarily stable over time. There are some positive arguments for using districts, which may be closer to the natural communities within which people have social and family ties. Lower income groups are less spatially mobile (Forrest et al. 1991), and the social rented housing they may depend upon is organized at the district level. The district is also the local planning authority, so that this makes it the natural unit to use when analyzing planning policies. Nevertheless, in discussing the demand side below we do give particular attention to the issue of the openness of local markets.

The assumptions underlying the models

The preceding discussion has begun to spell out some of the assumptions that underlie our approach to modelling, so it might be appropriate to set these out more formally at this stage. This study adopts a distinct framework, which is internally consistent and which distinguishes it from some other models of the housing market. The core assumptions are as follows:

(a) Local housing markets may be approximated by districts, and are sufficiently separate for differential local demand and supply conditions to affect prices and output, but also sufficiently open for national and structural factors to have a strong influence on prices.

(b) Local markets are relatively integrated internally, so that second-hand and new housing are close substitutes with closely related prices.

(c) The owner-occupier housing market may be modelled as the flow of housing units bought and sold each year ("a house is a house is a house"); the number of completions is the measure of new-build output.

(d) The model is of medium-term flow equilibrium with lags.

(e) Output is systematically influenced by the current and expected availability of land with planning permission for housing, as well as by prices and profitability.

(f) Planning policies are in part autonomous, but planning decisions are also in part responsive to market demand.

(g) The land market is endogenous, with land prices being determined by the current and expected profitability of housebuilding, that is the residual difference between house prices and construction costs.

These assumptions are quite restrictive, but may be seen as a consistent interconnected set that (a) renders the analysis tractable and (b) fits in with the types of data available. Thus, at the local level at which land supply operates, we have consistent data only on flows of units and for a few years at district level. However, it is also argued that these assumptions are reasonable on the basis of existing knowledge about the operation of the planning system, the private housebuilding industry and the land market (as reviewed in Chs 3–5; see also Bramley 1989, Lambert 1990, Monk 1991, Monk et al. 1991).

The first assumption simply restates what was said about the level of analysis in the previous section. The second assumption is arguably reasonable in British conditions but would not necessarily apply in other countries, because of different institutional arrangements governing finance, taxation and subsidies for new as opposed to second-hand housing. Past evidence on the existence of "submarkets" within local owner-occupier markets in Britain has been at best ambiguous (Ball & Kirwan 1977, DoE 1992b). Our own finding that local markets are relatively open on the demand side, when taken in conjunction with the tendency of most moves to be short distance (Forrest et al. 1991, Forrest & Murie 1993), supports the reasonableness of this assumption. Moves towards more credit liberalization and away from traditional practices such as "redlining" (Boddy 1980) were a prominent feature of mortgage finance in Britain in the 1980s (Diamond & Lea 1993). We are not assuming that all consumers are indifferent between different neighbourhoods, ages or types of house; simply that sufficient consumers are willing to consider alternatives to ensure that market forces ripple across the boundaries between submarkets. As we show below, with the data available on new house prices there are some signs that these do not behave in quite the same way as second-hand prices, but these data are themselves questionable.

Assumption (c) implies that we have chosen to model the housing market in terms of flows rather than stocks, and there are several reasons for this choice. Flows are more relevant to policy questions in the short and medium term, as argued by Merrett (1989). For example, questions about the number of social housing units to be provided, or about land availability, relate to such flows. From a common-sense point of view, flows are more relevant to the operation of the market, because it is only houses that are offered for sale, and buyers who enter the market in a given period, that constitute the market. Although some national time-series models (Tsoukis & Westaway 1991, Meen 1992) purport to include stock variables, in practice it is only changes in these variables, which equate essentially to flows of completions, that matter.

Another aspect of assumption (c) may be more questionable, namely the counting of all housing units as being of equal value. It is convenient to do this, for both data and policy reasons, and it avoids the difficulties of operationalizing the concept of housing services introduced in Chapter 2. A partial defence of this assumption lies in the aggregated level of analysis; for a local housing market area there will always be a spectrum of housing types available. Building regulations and voluntary codes guarantee minimum standards of new-build output in Britain. The house price measures used in the models are at least approximately standardized. In fact, we relax this assumption in Chapter 8, when we go on to consider variations in density, house type, size and value.

Assumption (d) says that the market can clear at the going price in one year, but that new construction supply is a "lagged response" to prices and conditions 1–2 years earlier. The second part of this assumption seems justified on the basis of past literature and our own studies of housebuilding (see Ch. 5; also Whitehead 1974: ch.8; Mayes 1979: 88–90; Lambert 1990: 3–4, 20; Monk 1991). The first part is rather more questionable, but in part relates to the limitation of data availability mainly to annual values and our focus on cross-sectional relationships that are more medium term than short term. There are various adjustment mechanisms other than price in the owner-occupier markets; households queue by waiting longer in unsatisfactory accommodation, while vacancy rates can vary. These are explored further in Chapter 9. We do not have good data on short-term variations in these phenomena, although this is an area for further research.

Assumption (e) is perhaps the core element in this piece of research. We are assuming first that developers operate systematically in a way that makes sense in terms of conventional microeconomic theory. They seek to maximize profits, and therefore will be more likely to develop housing when and where profits are larger. We are also tending to accept the Evans (1983) view of land supply, discussed in Chapter 3, as a flow with a price elasticity well below infinity. But we go beyond most existing supply models by assuming that supply is also systematically related to the land made available for development by the planning system. If no land is available with planning permission in a locality, no construction can take place. The more land is available, the more construction could take place, but whether and how quickly it will happen depends upon profitability and other factors. Other factors that may affect supply, relating to construction resource availability and cost, can be taken account of through an appropriate model of development profit.

The wording of assumption (e) also refers to expectations of future land availability, the significance of which was discussed in Chapter 3. Developers' expectations here may be influenced by both planning policies and real constraints on potential land supply (e.g. existing built-up areas). We test the hypothesis that rates of development are positively related to indicators of expected future land supply. If housebuilders with limited supplies of existing land with permission expect little further land to be released, they will reduce output to maintain an even workload into the coming years, and exploit the probable rise in price/profit that would result from land shortage. If the land supply is expected to increase, the reverse may be expected to happen. Developers' expectations of future house price changes are also clearly important.

Assumption (f) says that we expect planning to be in some degree autonomous and not highly responsive to market forces, and it would be rather surprising if this were not the case. The nature, goals and functions of planning were discussed at length in Chapter 3, where it was concluded that the degree of autonomy would depend upon the view taken on the broader function of planning. For example, some versions of a Marxian structural political economy view would see planning as catering to the corporate interests of the development industry and other major sectors of business, and as such very responsive to market forces. By contrast, views based on pluralistic politics or bureaucratic process see planning as very unresponsive to market forces. One benefit of our modelling approach is that it allows this question to be tested empirically, one of the issues examined in Chapter 7. However, it should be noted that, if we find that the flow of new planning permissions is in some degree responsive to the market, the supply of new building is going to be enhanced indirectly, through an induced land supply effect, as well as directly through profitability.

Our final assumption, that land values are determined by the "residual" difference between house prices and construction/development costs (including so-called "normal profits"), is a commonplace in both economic literature and professional valuation practice. It also accords with qualitative evidence from housebuilders themselves (see Ch. 5). It is hard to collect reliable land price data at local level in England, partly because of confidentiality of transactions and partly because there are very few transactions and each one has very different particular site attributes. Land values may of course diverge somewhat from residual values in particular situations, and this may be important in the short-term dynamics of the market. Developers may for example overbid for land in booms, and their expectations of future development profits may not be realized.

Model structure

The overall structure of the model may be described in various different ways. Box 6.1 contains formal algebraic equations, and Appendix 1 provides details on the data used. Figure 6.1 below provides a more accessible view of the model as a whole. Exogenous factors are shown on the left-hand side of the diagram. These break down into three broad groups: (a) demand factors, including demography, incomes, employment, and locational attractiveness; (b) construction sector supply/cost factors, including some overlapping ones such as unemployment, wages, and some geographical characteristics such as density/sparsity of settlement; (c) land supply factors, including planning policies and constraints. The solid lines with arrows show the way these then interact with each other in the determination of the endogenous variables in the model: house prices, development profit (land value), completions output and new planning permissions. The broken line shows one feedback effect, from new permissions and completions to the existing stock of outstanding planning permission.

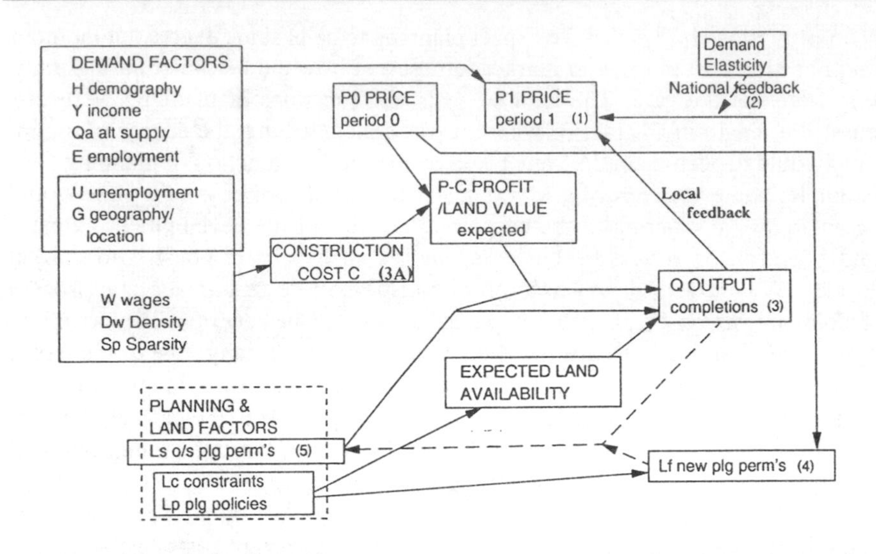

Figure 6.1 Lagged response supply & demand model (equation numbers in parentheses).

In Box 1 this model is described by five equations, and these are indicated on the diagram in the relevant box. So, for example, the house price in the current period (P_1) is determined primarily by Equation 1, although this is modified by the effect of Equation 2. Of the five equations, three are genuine behavioural equations whose parameters are estimated by fitting regression models to statistical data. These are the equations for house prices (1), completions output (3), and new planning permissions (4). Equation 5 is a definitional identity (it must be true by definition), linking the change in outstanding planning permissions to the using up of previous permissions and the supply of new ones. Equation 2 involves the importation of a key parameter, the overall national price elasticity of demand, into the model from other research results reported in the literature. This is discussed further below. While this structure may appear a little complicated, it is in fact driven by a desire to keep it as simple as possible while still making it possible to shed light on our basic aims.

One step in this direction is to refrain from treating the whole system as a set of simultaneous equations, which would require somewhat more complicated econometric treatment (Maddala 1988: ch. 9). The simultaneous equation approach has also been explored, but demand-side models for quantity work much less well than demand-side models for price. Instead, we resolve the supply–demand interaction problem by taking account of the time-lags inherent in the supply side of the process (assumption (d)). New-build output and new planning permissions are affected not by current prices but by prices prevailing one or two years ago (P_0). But current demand factors and current supply jointly affect prices immediately. This lagged adjustment process can be illustrated using a

Box 6.1 Formal equations for model

Demand

The first is a demand equation with price (standardized) as the dependent variable:

$$P_j = P(Q_j, D_s(Y_j, G_j, Z_j), D_L(H_j, E_j, Q_{aj}, T_L)) \quad (1)$$

where j subscripts denote local market areas

- Q = output (private completions per year)
- D_s = "structural" demand function
- D_L = "locally variable" demand function
- H = vector or index of demographic variable
- E = vector of employment variables
- Y = average household income index
- Q_a = measure(s) of alternative social rented housing supply
- G = vector of geographical/locational attributes
- Z = vector of social characteristics
- T_L = local tax bills or fiscal measures.

The exogenous demand-side variables are grouped into two categories: "structural" (D_s) are those that reflect relatively permanent features (e.g. location) determining an area's position in the national price structure; "locally variable" (D_L) are those that can vary significantly both from one (adjacent) district to another and over time. The effect of Q_j on P_j is related to the "local" prices elasticity of demand. The overall national effect of output on price is captured by an aggregate mechanism as follows:

$$\frac{\Delta P_N}{P} = \frac{\Sigma \Delta Q}{\varepsilon \Sigma (Q_N + Q_s)} - \frac{\Delta P_L}{P} \quad (2)$$

This is simply a rearrangement of the identity defining the price elasticity of demand, splitting the price change into two components: a local component (ΔP_L) (from (1) above) and a national component ΔP_N. Supply in the market includes both new build (Q_N) and second hand (Q_s), the latter being assumed to be invariant with price. The overall price elasticity of demand ε is imposed (see main text) with a central value of –0.7. In simulations, this national price adjustment mechanism is assumed for convenience to operate with a one-year lag.

Supply

The preferred supply function expresses output as a lagged function of profitability (price minus construction cost), land with planning permission for housing, and expected future land supply based on policies and constraints:

$$Q_j = S_{-1}((P_j - C(W_j, U_j, E_{cj}, N_j/A_j)), L_{sj}, L_{cj}, L_{pj}) \quad (3)$$

where S_{-1} refers to a function of suitably (1–2 year) lagged values of the relevant data and C is a function for construction cost per unit, and

- W = wage rates relevant to construction
- U = unemployment rate
- E_c = construction employment
- N/A = density of population
- L_s = stock of land with outstanding planning permission for housing
- L_c = constraints on future land supply
- L_p = planning policy for land release for private housing.

Planning

In Equation 4, the planning permission flow L_f is modelled as a function of: (a) the amount of potentially available unconstrained land, (b) local planning policy stance and targets, and (c) the demand in the local market, proxied by lagged price or price change:

$$L_{fj} = L_{f-1}(L_{cj}, L_{pj}, L_{sj}, P_j, P_{j-1}) \quad (4)$$

The stocks and flows of planning permissions are linked by the identity:

$$L_{sj} \equiv L_{sj-1} + L_{fj-1} - Q_{j-1} \quad (5)$$

conventional economic supply and demand diagram, as in Figure 6.2. An increase in demand attributable to higher tax relief (for example) is represented by an upward shift in the demand schedule, from D_0 to D_1. This has no immediate effect on supply, so the entire effect falls at first on prices, which rise from P_0 to P_1. After a year or two, supply adjusts upwards from Q_0 to Q_2, in response to the higher price. But this supply now cuts the demand curve at a lower price, P_2, which is the level the price now falls to. After a further adjustment lag, supply falls back to a lower level. This adjustment cycle is a classic feature in economics textbooks, sometimes referred to as the "hog cycle" or the "cobweb theory". Given our well founded assumption about lagged supply response, we believe this situation clearly applies to the housing sector as much as it applies to pigs. Its exact form may be modified if developers adopt more sophisticated bases for expectations about future prices than simply assuming prices to remain the same as at present, although the evidence in Chapter 5 did not indicate great sophistication.

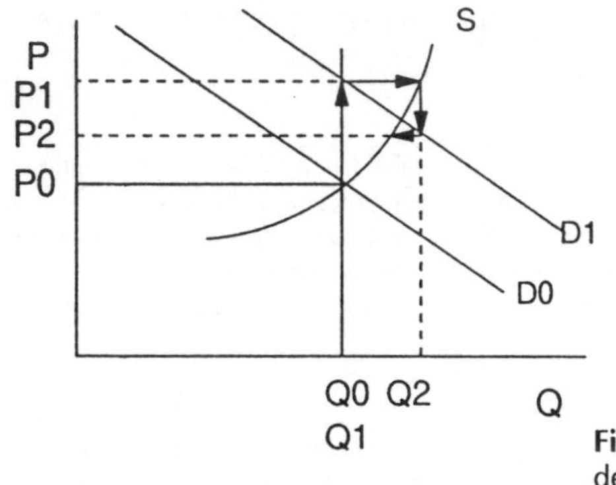

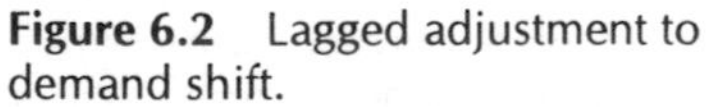
Figure 6.2 Lagged adjustment to demand shift.

The assumption that price responds quickly to current demand conditions is consistent with a common understanding of how the housing market operates. The supply curve in the short term is vertical, and demand variations feed directly into prices. This is why the main regression equation for the demand side has house price as the dependent variable. The factors included in our model are those that vary between localities, because we are developing a cross-sectional model, not those factors such as interest rates which are uniform nationally but which vary over time. We are modelling the demand for new private housing, not the total demand for housing. Therefore, factors that affect alternative supplies to potential buyers, including social rented supply and turnover supply from household dissolutions, are included in the demand model, with predicted negative effects. We subdivide demand-side factors into three broad categories: structural factors reflecting relatively permanent features determining a district's position in the national price structure (e.g. locational variables); locally and temporally variable factors such as employment; supply feedback effects.

Two features of the demand side relate to our view, reinforced by our findings, that local housing markets are rather open on the demand side. First, locational attractiveness factors are quite important, because some people may shop around for attractive places to live and because major attractors, such as central London, exert a wide influence over the market. Secondly, the feedback effect from supply changes to prices (such as from P_1 to P_2 in Fig. 6.2) are only partly effected at local level; a substantial part of this feedback happens at a wider regional or national level, as shown in Figure 6.1.

The key parameter in this national feedback is the price elasticity of demand; from a review of an extensive literature on this topic - including Whitehead (1974), Mayo (1981), Maclennan (1982: 54), Follain & Jiminez (1983), Ermisch (1984: 56) and Olsen (1987) - we concluded that a reasonable middle estimate would be -0.7. This means that a 10% price rise leads to a 7% fall in supply; conversely, a 10% rise in supply leads to a 14.3% fall in price. It should be noted that supply here refers to the overall net flow supply of units for sale in the owner-occupier market. The issue of turnover is discussed later in this chapter.

The design of the supply Equation 3 is determined mainly by assumption (e), as discussed above. New-build output is driven mainly by the interaction of development profit (i.e. residual land value, based on lagged prices) and the amount of land with outstanding planning permission, together with expected future land supply which is related to planning policies and constraints. This equation in fact contains a subequation 3A relating to construction costs. This is discussed further below. Comparing with other supply models (Whitehead 1974, Mayes 1979, Tsoukis & Westaway 1991, Meen 1992), the use of price and cost, or profit, is a common feature; financial variables are not relevant in a cross-sectional model, while the inclusion of land and planning variables is the main innovation, based on ideas originally sketched out in Bramley (1989). We feel confident in the robustness of the supply model, which lies at the heart of the overall system. The new planning permissions model, described in Chapter 7, is less satisfactory.

6.2 The data

A sample of districts

The choice of districts as the basic spatial unit, an approximation to a local housing market area, was discussed earlier. The feasibility of collecting the wide variety of data required for this study was a major factor in this choice. Although some of the data could be obtained relatively easily, from a variety of official and other sources, for all districts in England, certain crucial data on planning and land required a special enquiry through the local (county) authorities, and other data would have been costly to obtain for all districts.

It was therefore decided to collect data for a large sample of districts, enough to give sufficient observations for the statistical work, while concentrating the data collection. Ninety districts, about a quarter of the total in England, were selected. The sampling strategy was not random; all districts were chosen from 13 counties, the counties themselves representing a solid wedge of territory running north and west from the boundary of London. As can be seen from Figure 6.3, the sample falls within three standard regions, the South East, South West and West Midlands. The primary reason for choosing a sample in this way was to exploit at least cost the opportunities for using the county planning departments as a vehicle for data collection, supplemented in some cases by regional contacts.

The area sample resulting has some disadvantages, but some advantages too. It does not represent areas at two extremes of the housing market very well; London, and declining/depressed/northern urban areas. One substantive advantage of sampling a solid wedge is that underlying spatial trends in the data may be identified and taken account of. The sample also represents a particular time-period, also dictated in part by data availability. Most data refer to the period 1986–8. This time-period represents one of relative boom conditions in the housing market in these regions. On the whole this is useful because it enables us to identify the responsiveness of the supply side when it is under most pressure. However, our results may not be quite such a good guide to the impact of recession and low demand on the system, such as are being experienced at the time of writing. The research is now being updated, partly to overcome these limitations.

Data

Appendix 1 provides a list of the variables used and referred to in this chapter and the following ones, together with sources and summary statistics. These data fall into broad categories as identified below, with the algebraic symbols given in brackets.

- *demographic* data (usually prefixed N or H) which measure the overall scale of the market, potential demand flows, and alternative supply flows (especially household dissolutions), derived from official annual estimates, the 1981 Census, and some district-level household projections;
- *economic data* comprising employment (E) indicators, unemployment (U), earnings (W), indirect proxy-based indicators of household income (Y) from Bramley (1991), and some socioeconomic indicators such as class (Z); these economic variables play an important role in the demand Equation 1, but also feature in the construction costs submodel;
- *geographical variables* (G) include attractiveness factors such as distances from London, regional capitals, and North/South, and tourism measures; and measures of the land potentially available for housing or constrained (L_C), including built-up areas, green belts and Areas of Outstanding Natural Beauty;

Figure 6.3 Standard Regions and Counties of England and Wales, showing the study area boundary.

- *planning policies (L_P) and land availability (L_S)* were obtained mainly from County Planning Departments but cross-checked against official returns and corrected for consistency (a labour-intensive task); some subjective dummy variables for policy stance were assigned on the basis of planning documents, as discussed further in Chapter 7;
- *housing output (completions) (Q)* data were obtained mainly from official

returns, with cross-checking against another source (NHBC data) for one year (1988); apart from new private completions, other indicators of alternative tenures supply, vacancies, and poor-quality dwellings were tested, some of uncertain accuracy or rather dated (1981);
- *house prices* were based on two separate sources, a major lender (Nationwide) covering mainly second-hand sales and the registration agency NHBC covering new sales, with approximate standardization for age, type and size in both cases; assumption (9) relieves us of the need for direct data on land values, which are unavailable or unreliable at local level.

Where appropriate, variables that measure absolute quantities are expressed as a ratio per 1000 existing owner-occupiers; for example, the average value of completions output in 1988 was 17.6 units per 1000 owners, a net addition to the stock of 1.76%. The rationale for this is to discount for differences in the basic scale of local markets, and we use the number of owners as this basic scale measure. There are also good statistical grounds for transforming the data in this way in cross-sectional modelling. One consequence is that the apparent performance of the statistical models for output (most commonly measured by the r^2 statistic) is depressed, because the effect of size of market has already been accounted for.

Demographic variables were derived in part from Census and official population estimates, and partly from a special set of household projections undertaken at district level, using broadly the same methodology as official projections. These were based on trend data for migration between 1981 and 1986. The projections enable estimates to be made of gross new household formation and household dissolutions. Gross household formation is the number of separate households existing at the end of a year which did not exist, in some form, at the beginning of the year. Dissolutions are the converse, and mainly relate to ageing and death. These variables are of some importance in a net flow supply framework for the analysis of housing demand and market interactions.

The geographical variables mainly represent factors affecting the attractiveness of districts as locations for residence (and economic activity), such as distance from London and other major regional centres (Bristol and Birmingham). National and regional markets may have some tendency to follow the pattern of intra-urban markets described in Chapter 3, with declining rent/price gradients with distance from the dominant central business district, given that some people commute across considerable distances. Since we would expect these distance effects to decline with distance, we express these variables in logarithms. Recognizing the pronounced North/South economic divide in 1980s Britain, we also include a simple distance north (latitude) variable. Other locational attraction proxy indicators tested include tourist visitor nights and a measure of coastline.

Variables relating to land-use constraints were the most difficult to measure, because of the poorly developed state of land-use data in Britain. Three kinds of constraints were defined:

- urban (built-up) areas as defined by OPCS in 1981
- approved green belts

- Areas of Outstanding Natural Beauty (AONB), including small parts of relevant national parks.

The derivation and interpretation of these measures is discussed further in Chapter 7.

New data are being compiled on land use change, which in due course may become available for incorporation in models of this kind. In the 1980s a large share of housing development took place on recycled urban land, or "brown land", over 40% according to a DoE (1991a) study. We cannot at present measure this directly at district level, but we can use proxy indicators. In addition to the built-up area measure, we use the population-weighted average of ward population densities as a measure of the intensity of existing urban residential land use. The higher this figure, the more difficult it is expected to be to recycle urban land. It must be admitted that this indicator might also affect demand/prices.

Data on land available with outstanding planning permission was obtained in a consistent way for all districts. This was a laborious task, involving cross-checking local and national sources. Our measure was so far as possible consistent, referring to the capacity in units of all private sites, large and small, with outline or detailed consents and not yet completed, for April of 1986, 1987 and 1988. Changes in this stock of permissions, plus new completions, measures the annual flow of new permissions, although we also have an alternative cruder measure from another statistical return. New completions are measured using official local authority returns, cross-checked against the records of the National House Building Council (NHBC) for one year (there are some inconsistencies).

Planning policy is measured by the operative structure plan target for new private housing. The success rate of planning applications for housing was also computed. Simple dummy variables reflecting the overall policy stance were also assigned, based on a subjective interpretation of planning documents supplied by the counties. This was probably the least satisfactory aspect of the data compilation exercise, and is discussed further in the next chapter.

House price measurement can be tricky because of the extreme variability of house prices and heterogeneity within and between samples of transactions recorded. Our primary measure is standardized, representing the price of an average size (900 sq. ft) modern semi-detached or terraced house, derived from data compiled by the Nationwide Building Society, for the years 1982 and 1986–90. An alternative measure of the price of a typical new house, averaging three common types, was obtained from the NHBC for 1988. These two series are not very closely correlated (the correlation coefficient is 0.8), which casts some doubt either on our assumption (b) (integrated new and second-hand markets) or on the accuracy and standardization of the NHBC data.

For all its shortcomings, this dataset is unique in a British context and it offers a range of possibilities for analysis of housing supply and the housing market.

6.3 Demand and house prices

We can now turn to the results of our modelling exercise, starting with the demand side. The preferred "lagged response' model sketched out earlier is one where current demand factors, along with current output, determine price (Eq. 1).

Spatial patterns

District-level standardized second-hand prices range between £80000 near London to £22300 near the Welsh border in 1988, with a coefficient of variation of 24%. New prices seem to vary slightly more ($CV = 29\%$). At county level, prices fall progressively as you move from Berkshire, just west of London, to Staffordshire in the north of the West Midlands region (see Fig. 6.3). This pattern is consistent with other studies of house prices in this period (Hamnett 1989, Bramley 1990, Brundson et al. 1990).

Exploratory work shows that care is needed to ensure an adequate specification of the demand model, including appropriate geographical variables, because of the strong spatial trends in the data. Models specified in too narrow a range of types of variables may be misleading (for example, the Brunsdon et al. 1990 study, which emphasizes economic variables). For example, a set of economic and employment variables can apparently explain 80% of the variance in prices, whereas a different set of geographical variables can explain 85%. Clearly, it is difficult to separate the influences of these two sets of variables, because some of the economic variables (e.g. income, unemployment) show a common spatial pattern and are highly correlated with the geographical set. In technical terms, there is a problem of spatial autocorrelation in the data. The best solution to this problem is to include a wide range of variables, including the key spatial ones.

The determinants of local prices

Table 6.1 shows demand models for both second-hand and new house prices using a broad range of variables, selecting those from the various categories that seem to have a significant effect in one or other case. These models conform with the lagged response framework by containing current completions (QDN8) as an explanatory variable, for which the hypothesized effect is of course negative and is related to the local price-elasticity of demand. The table shows the coefficients measuring the effect of each variable on price (in £ thousands) and in parentheses the *t*-statistics showing the statistical significance of each coefficient (values above about 1.7 are significant at the 90% level). For example, an extra one new completion per 1000 existing owner-occupiers reduces second-hand prices by £58, or new prices by £524; only the second of these effects (coefficients) is statistically significant.

In general the results confirm that prices are determined by locational, eco-

Table 6.1 Regression models for second-hand and new house prices in lagged response framework (regression coefficients, with t-statistics in parentheses).

	PS8 second-hand (NABS)	PN8 new (NHBC)
Explanatory variables		
Constant	192.3	230.1
	(8.33)	(3.75)
Supply		
QDN8 private completions	−0.0583	−0.524
	(−0.94)	(−3.1)
Geographical		
G7LN ln(distance London)	−17.6	−24.1
	(−7.1)	(−3.7)
G8LN ln(distance Bristol–Birmingham)	−2.20	−0.43
	(−2.9)	(−0.2)
G9 distance north	−0.0648	−0.107
	(−8.2)	(−5.0)
DW ward density	−0.019	0.286
	(−0.3)	(−1.5)
Economic		
E1 jobs/workers	11.74	13.2
	(2.23)	(0.94)
E3 job growth 1984–7 %	0.509	0.549
	(2.88)	(1.15)
E10 manufacturing jobs	−0.166	−0.204
	(−3.0)	(−1.38)
U8 unemployment rate %	−0.729	−0.68
	(−2.05)	(−0.7)
Y1 household income £pw	0.036	−0.0905
	(1.12)	(−1.0)
z3 high social class	0.166	0.825
	(1.69)	(3.1)
Demographic		
H3A gross household formation	−0.24	−0.59
	(−1.36)	(−1.24)
H4 household dissolutions	−2.74	−12.23
	(−1.77)	(−2.97)
Alternative supply/quality		
QA1 social lettings	−0.0502	0.259
	(−0.53)	(1.0)
N7 private renting	0.079	0.726
	(0.58)	(1.98)
LSBATH lack/share bath	−0.63	−0.219
	(−1.22)	(−0.16)
Fiscal		
DOMRB7 domestic rate bill	−0.255	0.0099
	(−2.41)	(0.35)
Adjusted r^2	0.908	0.763
F ratio	50.5	17.2
Number of cases	85	85

Note: Dependent variable PS8 and PN8 are second-hand and new house prices for 1988 in £000, standardized for type and age.

nomic, demographic, supply and other variables in ways that are consistent with an *a priori* conception of demand within the flow of units framework. The geographical location factors, particularly distance from London and how far north, are still powerful influences even after allowing for other variables. Three employment variables have significant effects in the direction expected, as does unemployment, in the case of second-hand prices; with new prices these effects are weaker. Of the two demographic variables included, an estimate of household dissolutions (H4) has the predicted negative effect, while gross household formation has the "wrong" effect but is not statistically significant at the 90% level. Vacancies have also been tested as an additional indicator of alternative supply from the existing stock, but with inconclusive results.

The impact of social rented lettings seems to be inconsistent in direction and not statistically significant, whereas private renting tends to have a positive effect. Private renting may be a proxy for high demand, more centrally located areas, or a measure of competing demand for residential property from groups such as students willing to share. The quality of the older stock is reflected in the variable LSBATH which has the expected negative effect on second-hand prices, although again this is barely significant. Finally, the fiscal variable DOMRB7 (average domestic rate bill in 1987) has the expected negative effect on second-hand (but not new) prices. This is discussed further in Chapter 9.

An overall impression from comparing the new and second-hand models is that there may be significant and systematic differences in the determination of prices in the two subsectors. As a generalization, demand factors seem to have less effect on new than on second-hand prices, whereas the supply factor is more important in the case of new house prices.

The results are particularly interesting in relation to the output (completions) variable, QDN8. Higher output has only a very small effect on local second-hand prices and this is not statistically very significant (the chances of the coefficient differing from zero are only 65%). By contrast, the coefficient on new prices is much larger and clearly statistically significant; this result holds across several variant model specifications. A slightly stronger coefficient on second-hand prices emerges when we use a more restricted approach to the specification of the rest of the model, based on prior knowledge/judgement.

There is a case for grouping demand-side variables together into composite measures. First, this can clarify the overall shape of the model in terms of the basic structure proposed in Equation 1. Secondly, with considerable intercorrelation between variables, coefficients on individual variables may display some instability which can distract from the overall picture. Demand variables are divided into two classes: those that reflect relatively permanent features (e.g. location) determining an area's position in the national price structure (D_S); and those such as employment that represent influences that can vary significantly from district to district and over time (D_L). Appendix 1 shows how the variables are grouped; the versions reported here (DEMANDS1 and DEMANDL1) use equal weightings on each variable in standardized form. The demand model conforming with Equation 1 can now be estimated using three explanatory variables, as follows (t statistics in brackets):

$$PS8 = 54.77 + \underset{(14.1)}{17.55.D_S} + \underset{(5.2)}{8.91.D_L} - \underset{(1.8)}{0.121.Q} + u$$

$$\text{adj } r^2 = 0.844$$

and for new house prices

$$PN8 = 88.45 + \underset{(9.41)}{29.22.D_S} + \underset{(3.2)}{13.73.D_L} - \underset{(-4.83)}{0.81.Q} + u$$

$$\text{adj } r^2 = 0.657$$

These models have somewhat lower r^2 but have the advantage of parsimony and a very clear theoretical framework, with fewer dubious or spurious relationships included. The coefficients on the two composite demand indicators may be compared because they are in standardized units. This, together with the t statistics, shows that the effect of the structural demand factors is about double the effect of the local factors, but both clearly operate in a significant way. Alternative formulations of the composite indicators, separating out stock supply (including vacancies) suggest that local demand factors may be weaker.

The output-price feedback

The negative coefficient on output in the second-hand price model is now significant at the 93% level, while that in the new price equation is again much larger and highly significant. But the basic conclusion remains: the *local* impact of supply on second-hand prices is small. This is consistent with the view that local markets are very open, which in turn is consistent with the evidence that the spatial factors are very powerful (i.e. prices are mainly determined by position in a national system). By contrast, the local negative impact of output levels on the prices of those new houses seems to be quite substantial. This result may be partially spurious, if there are systematic quality biases in the new price data that we are unable to standardize for. Insofar as this result is genuine, it suggests that the assumption (b) of integrated local markets with closely related new and second-hand prices may not be fully justified.

An attempt was made to incorporate measures of the "openness" of local markets interacting with D_L and Q in these models, but so far unsuccessfully in terms of improving the specification. Further exploration of possible subregional feedback effects has also so far failed to indicate clearer supply-price feedback at either county or travel-to-work area levels. However, attempts to model migration have been more successful (see below), and Chapter 9 discusses how this and other information can be used to model local and regional price feedback.

The estimated coefficient for second-hand prices using composite demand indices shown above (–0.121) implies that ten extra completions per 1000 existing owner-occupiers (i.e. 1% on the stock) reduces prices by £1210, which is about 2.3%. This very low local price response to output corresponds to a very high local price-elasticity of demand of -24. This is a very high figure compared with most general estimates of this parameter, which tend to lie in the range -0.5 to -0.9. But a low response/high elasticity is expected, because we are measuring here the local effect and all local markets are open, as emphasized by the importance of our structural demand variable (D_S). Much of the price feedback effect is diffused into a wider regional and national market, and is captured in this model through Equation 2.

The effect on new prices is a good deal stronger at the local level, assuming the NHBC price data are not biased. The elasticity is -5.3 (-8.3 from Table 6.1), which is much lower than the second-hand price elasticity, but still relatively high (housebuilders are still mainly price-takers). One standard deviation in output would alter new prices by £18400 or about 25%, and the difference between maximum and minimum output levels is equivalent to £30700 or 41%.

The evidence from these models of a rather different pattern of price determination for new houses, including a stronger supply-price feedback, suggests that more attention needs to be given to the possible segmentation of new and second-hand markets and the mechanisms of adjustment within and between them at the local level. A partial test of the hypothesis, that second-hand prices adapt to output over a longer period (three years), was not supported by the data. Regressing new prices on lagged or predicted second-hand prices plus the other demand variables does not support the segmentation hypothesis, since new prices seem to be mainly determined by second-hand prices.

Migration

Further evidence of the openness of local markets is provided by exploratory regression models to explain local variations in net migration in the 1980s. Table 6.2 shows the results of using regression models for migration; a range of sets of variables were tested and those shown are the most plausible. Higher prices have a relatively small but significant negative or deterrent effect on migration. General locational attractiveness factors seem to be more significant than employment factors, at district level. However, the strongest influence on migration is supply, particularly household dissolutions (turnover supply) but also new private house completions. Social housing supply has a negligible effect, which is not surprising given that most local authorities and housing associations concentrate on meeting local needs. The coefficient on the private completions supply variable (QD3YA) seems to be around 0.7, implying that for every ten completions there are seven extra in-migrant households (or seven fewer out-migrants). These results confirm that local markets are very open.

In the general housing market model described earlier, and summarized in Figure 6.1, the effects of land and housing supply on house prices are estimated through two mechanisms, one local and one national. The national feedback

Table 6.2 Regression models for net migration (net migrant household per 1000 owner-occupiers, mid-1980s).

	(1)	(2)
Constant	−25.35	−31.52
Locational attractors	(−3.3)	(−5.5)
DW ward density	−0.018	−0.041
	(−0.2)	(−0.6)
G2 coastline	0.696	0.615
	(2.2)	(2.0)
Z3 high social classs	0.417	0.440
	(3.4)	(3.6)
Economic factors		
E3 employment growth	−0.226	
	(0.9)	
U8 unemployment	−0.466	
	(−1.1)	
Price	−0.312	−0.237
PAH8 average price	(−3.0)	(−2.8)
Supply		
HDIS3 household dissolutions	1.14	1.15
	(8.9)	(9.2)
QD3YA new private supply	0.685	0.718
	(7.4)	(8.1)
QA1 social lettings	0.073	0.0019
	(0.6)	(0.02)
Adjusted r^2	0.825	0.725
F ratio	46.0	59.0
Number of cases	86	86

mechanisms are much the more important, and involve the imposition of a key parameter from outside. Because this is not entirely satisfactory, we are exploring a more sophisticated feedback mechanism within the model. This takes account of migration, using the results just described above, and evidence from parallel research on the relationship between house prices and affordability (Bramley 1991a). In addition, account is taken of other aspects of the adjustment process, including vacancies and time-lags. The results of this work so far indicate that, in some localities, prices might be more sensitive to supply, and possibly even unstable. The policy implications of these refinements to the models are discussed further in the next chapter.

6.4 Supply models

The central feature of the overall model as set out earlier in Figure 6.1, and Box 1 is an equation predicting the rate of new private housebuilding completions for each district. This incorporates a submodel for construction costs, which is discussed first. We then describe the main model for output (completions). To compute supply elasticities, we also need to take account of induced supply of additional planning permissions, using a model described in more detail in Chapter 7, together with estimates of turnover in the housing market.

Construction costs and land values

The RICS (1991) Building Cost Information Service publish an annual *Guide to house rebuilding costs*, which provides the basis for a construction cost submodel. A set of rebuilding cost figures per unit of floor area for different house types can be used to estimate baseline cost for standard house types. A regional cost index available down to county level (DCOSTIND) is used as the dependent variable in a regression equation including relevant indicators of location (distance from London, G7LN), difficulty (simple and ward density, N/A and D_w), and labour supply and cost (unemployment U8 and manual earnings W1). The regression-based formula is intended to interpolate values for districts and is:

$$\text{DCOSTIND} = 1.234 + 0.00161.(N/A) - 0.000043.D_w - 0.0718.G7LN + 0.000747.W1 - 0.00923.U8$$

The adjusted r^2 was 0.76 and all variables were significant at the 10% level except D_w. This index is then multiplied by the rebuilding cost for each standard house type. Subtracting construction cost from price gives a figure for gross profit or residual land bid value per unit (PCN8 for new, PCS8 for second-hand).

Construction costs do not vary dramatically, the range being from 0.874 to 1.13 at district level. Thus, the main influence on differences in profitability or land value between districts is prices. The land share or gross profit percentages for 1988 (the peak of the market) vary from 12% to 73% of the price of new houses at district level, whereas the residual price per hectare of land ranges from £76000 to £3669450.

These estimates of residual land value or gross development profit may be misleading as far as some of the increasingly common recycled urban sites are concerned. In these cases land may have established use rights for other urban uses such as industry, in which case the base value is significantly higher than agricultural value. Furthermore, many brownfield sites require considerable expenditure on site reclamation and infrastructure provision before they are usable for housing, and again this could erode the apparent residual value.

Completions output

Within the basic lagged response framework, variant supply models (Eq. 3) were tested, involving the use of individual variables or composites and the use of interaction terms. Table 6.3 shows a basic linear model with nine individual variables giving a reasonable fit (adjusted r^2 of 57%) and most individual variables significant with the expected sign.

The model shows clearly that land supply and planning variables make an important contribution to explaining local levels of output, as expected. The land with planning permissions variable (LSF7) is in fact the sum of outstanding permissions and new permissions in the year, since in earlier tests the separate variables had similar coefficients. The significant role of variables reflecting land constraints and planning policies seems to support the hypothesis that expectations of future land supply influence current output. Developers' decisions are not solely influenced by the current stock of permissions. The only variable whose sign is not as expected is unconstrained land (LTRLN), and the negative coefficient here is not statistically significant at the 75% level.

For further work on the supply model it is convenient to adopt the same expedient as was used in the demand model, and group some of these variables together into composite factors, for the same sorts of reasons (clarity, parsimony, avoidance of spurious relationships, use of interactions). Two composites are constructed. The first (CONST1) represents the general constraints on development in an area, and comprises the sum of the three variables under the Constraints heading in Table 6.2 (DW, G18 and LTR2LN), standardized and with equal weight (but negative, so that the index should be positively associated with output). Green belt is put in this category, rather than policy, because experience suggests that green belts are rather permanent features (Elson 1986). The second composite (PPS1) represents planning policy stance, and comprises the equally weighted sum of the standardized values of the four variables under the policy heading in Table 6.3 (PPD1, PPD2, LP, PPRAT) the first two having negative weights so that the index is again positively associated with expected land supply and output.

The effect of applying the restriction on the model that these groups of variables should have equal (standardized) coefficients, which results from substituting the composites in the regression, is no loss of explanatory power; indeed, the resulting equation shows a slight improvement in the adjusted r^2 and F ratios.

One of the key underlying objectives of this research is to measure the *local* supply response (elasticity), which brings a presumption that the elasticity of supply varies between one locality, or type of locality, and another. Models such as those in columns 1 and 2 of Table 6.3 assume a constant effect of price on output. It is necessary to adopt a more complex functional form to allow for varying local response, and so interactions between some or all of the explanatory variables are tested. Since developers cannot build any houses if they have no land with planning permission on which to build, we would in particular expect the market demand forces, expressed mainly through the price or profit variable (PCS6), to interact with the land supply variable (LSF7). The model in column 3 of Table 6.3 includes such an interaction term and is a significant improvement on the simple linear models. Thus, the hypothesis of locally variable supply

Table 6.3 Regression models for output of completions in 1988: lagged response models.

	(1)	(2)	(3)
Explanatory variables			
Constant	12.00	12.89	12.27
Price/profit			
PCS6 second-hand price–cost 1986	0.433	0.381	
	(4.0)	(4.0)	
Land			
LSF7 land with planning permission for housing 1987	0.0412	0.0358	0.0414
	(2.94)	(3.0)	(3.9)
PCS6*LSF7 price–land interaction			0.00571
			(4.2)
Constraints			
DW ward density	−0.267		
	(−3.2)		
G18 Green Belt	−0.054		
	(−1.83)		
LTRLN log unconstrained land	−0.393		
	(−0.8)		
CONST1 composite (lack of constraints)		5.34	4.48
		(4.9)	(4.4)
Planning policy			
PPD1 very restrictive dummy	−7.38		
	(−3.1)		
PPD2 restrictive dummy	−3.93		
	(−2.5)		
LP structure plan provision	0.122		
	(1.12)		
PPRAT permissions % of applications	0.134		
	(1.58)		
PPS1 composite policy		6.36	5.12
		(3.6)	(3.4)
Adjusted r^2	0.572	0.579	0.658
F	12.5	27.5	30.6
N	77	77	77

Note: Dependent variables: QDN8 completions per 1000 owners, 1988; average of DoE and NHBC data. The following variables are expressed per 1000 owner-occupier households: LSF7, LTR(LN), LP; G18 and PPRAT are percentages. CONST1 and PPS1 are standardized sums of the relevant variables, with positive values indicating fewer constraints or restrictions.

response seems to be supported. Price may also interact with planning and constraint variables, or have non-linear effects, although tests suggested these were not very significant. Overall, we can explain two-thirds of the variance in the rate of new-build supply (per thousand stock).

Once the price–land interaction is included, the price variable on its own ceases to operate in the same way. The sign becomes negative and the statistical significance is marginal (barely significant at the 75% level). It is difficult to know how to interpret this, although one possibility might be a tendency to speculative withholding of land from development in high price areas. Because of uncertainty in the interpretation of this coefficient and its low level of statistical significance, it seems preferable to exclude this in the final preferred model (column 3 of Table 6.3). This is consistent with the assumption that houses can only be built on land with planning permission.

One of the debates in modelling the housing market is over whether the demand factors that affect output decisions are adequately captured by price (or profit in our formulation), or whether other direct quantities on the demand side directly influence output decisions as well (Tsoukis & Westaway 1991). Without going into details, our results suggest that price adequately captures demand.

The models described in this chapter take supply as a flow of units concept, rather than as a "housing services" concept as discussed in Chapter 2. Nevertheless, it is possible to use our data to test an alternative formulation of new-build output as a flow of *investment*. We can use our NHBC data on prices of new output in 1988 to construct a measure of the value of new-build as a proportional addition to the stock. Applying the same form of models to this different supply measure gives similar results, which we do not report in detail. This suggests that the model structure is fairly robust. The model does not fit quite so well, which may reflect weaknesses in the new price data or quality aspects of supply that the model captures less well. The price effect (elasticity) is rather smaller and the effect of planning policies and constraints seems to be if anything stronger.

Turnover in the market

Turnover is relevant to an assessment of the contribution of new-build supply to the overall supply in the market. Within the flow-of-units framework (assumption (c)), total housing supply on the market in a period (one year) comprises the sum of new building, conversions, transfers from other tenures or vacancies, and sales of properties released by death and household dissolution, by moves out of owner-occupation, and by moves within owner-occupation. However, since in this framework "a house is a house is a house", moves within the tenure and within the market area have an equal impact on the supply and demand side, and can be netted out. This means that at local level we can subtract (ignore) all intra-local owner-occupier moves; only out-migration adds to the net local supply. "Trading up" is discounted by the assumption of homogeneity of stock in this model.

To calculate the effective elasticities in the market (that is, those that will determine the interaction of supply and demand) we need to allow for these other sources of supply apart from new-build, particularly those (like dissolutions) which do contribute to net supply. There is very little relevant evidence on the responsiveness of these components to market conditions, but it is clear that the fundamental causes of most of the other net supply components are essentially demographic rather than economic (death, frailty associated with ageing, divorce and relationship breakdown). Therefore, it seems justifiable as a first approximation to assume that these components are not responsive to price. The effect of this assumption is that the supply elasticity is reduced in the same proportion that new-build represents in total net supply.

We can put some flesh on this outline by attempting to estimate the average magnitude of the various sources of supply of housing units for sale at the national level. Table 6.4 provides some estimates for 1987. These have been built-up by the author from a variety of sources, influenced by two previous attempts to make such estimates at local/regional level (Merrett 1989; Bramley et al. 1990: ch. 4).

The detailed sources and assumptions used in deriving these figures are not discussed here. The main conclusions are as follows. New-build represents less than one-quarter of net flow supply (22.5% in a good year such as 1987). It could be argued that certain other elements of supply, particularly conversions and former private rented units, might move in step with new-build in response to price changes, raising the responsive supply to 26–30%. This means that estimates of supply elasticity from new-build models should be divided by a factor of between 3 and 4 to obtain the effective elasticity of supply in the market.

These are national averages. At local level, the various components of net flow supply will in fact represent very different shares. It is possible to make an attempt to estimate values for local supply components, using relevant demographic, tenure and other variables and controlling the totals to be consistent with Table 6.4. As a proportion of estimated net flow supply, new-build ranges

Table 6.4 Estimates of gross and net flow of units supply of housing for owner occupation in Great Britain, 1987.

	Number p.a. (thousands)	Percent net supply
New build	180	23
Conversions	28	14
Void ex-private rented	47	6
Dissolutions		
– death & related	180	23
– divorce	40	5
– marriage	30	4
– other	30	4
Subtotal dissolutions	(280)	35
Moves into renting	65	8
Moving owners		
– inter-local migrants	200	25
– local movers	800	
Subtotal moving owners	(1000)	
Total gross supply	1600	
Total net supply	800	100

from 3.9% (Oxford) to 34.9% (Basingstoke). This range helps to explain the rather extreme elasticity figures reported below. These variations indicate that the "market" supply elasticity will not be a simple mapping of the new-build elasticity.

Local supply elasticities

A basic objective of this research is to estimate the magnitude and variation in local supply elasticities for private sector housebuilding. In this section the results of the supply modelling work are put together with two other elements to give an overall assessment of supply elasticities. The two other elements are the second order "induced supply" response via the planning system and the place of new-build in the overall supply of units for sale in the market. The modelling of planning permissions (Ch. 7) provides a basis for the induced supply estimates, while the overall supply issue requires us to take account of turnover, as discussed above.

Given a choice of output model the computation of supply elasticity is a mechanical operation. The preferred output equation is that in column 3 of Table 6.3. This gives a basic elasticity of new-build with respect to price which varies locally according to the availability of land with planning permission and actual price and output levels. The average value is 0.99 and the range of variation is from 0.29 (Birmingham) to 2.11 (Worcester). The low values are unsurprising, but some of the high ones are affected by extreme values, for example a low existing level of completions.

The average new-build elasticity is very similar to that obtained from time-series analysis for the Bristol subregion in Bramley et al. (1990: 65–7). It may also be compared with results from other time-series studies of 0.75–1.62 (Whitehead 1974) and 0.27–0.55 on profitability (Mayes 1979: 93). Ermisch (1984: 56) suggests from a review of other literature a figure of 0.6 for Britain.

The allowance for a secondary induced supply effect adds some complication to the computation but it remains essentially mechanical. The preferred equation for planning permissions flow is that shown in Table 7.1 in Chapter 7. This equation has the virtue of having plausible or "correct" signs on the relevant variables although the fit is poor and the statistical significance of the coefficients is low. It serves to illustrate the kind of order of magnitude of a possible induced supply effect, within the same two-year period, rather than an accurate final estimate.

The average supply elasticity rises from 0.99 to 1.15 after allowing for the induced land supply effect. This is not a very large increase, because the relevant coefficients in the planning permissions equation are, as we have seen, small in magnitude. The range of variation is now wider, from 0.26 (Birmingham again) to 3.94 (Oxford). The very high values look to be rather freakish, as they are areas with very tight constraints (very low existing output is the explanation in the case of Oxford).

The final stage in the calculation is to re-estimate the elasticity in terms of proportional change in net supply, using the information on the other components of net supply developed above. The result is to divide the elasticity of supply by rather more than three, to give an average figure of 0.31. This may be closer to the correct figure to compare with estimates such as Ermisch's (1984) referred to above, where the concern is with subsidy impact in the short to medium term. The range of variation now is from 0.04 (Birmingham) to 0.86 (The Wrekin, which includes Telford new town); other high values include Northavon (0.80) Worcester (0.71) and Bracknell (0.61), the common factor being that these are growth areas with high existing stocks of land with planning permission.

The finding that elasticities are low in the most urbanized areas in the sample (e.g. West Midlands metropolitan area) is precisely in line with our *a priori* and theoretical expectations. The identity of some of the districts with high elasticities is surprising, but may be affected by the output or net flow elements of the denominator. Overall, as Table 6.5 shows, elasticities are higher in the South East.This result may still be affected by the arbitrary restrictions of the functional form used.

Table 6.5 Price elasticities of supply by county, 1988.

Region/county	New-build direct	With induced land	Market net flow supply
South East			
Berkshire	1.23	1.73	0.36
Hampshire	0.91	1.12	0.28
Oxfordshire	1.31	1.82	0.36
South West			
Avon	0.98	1.15	0.31
Dorset	1.19	1.41	0.35
Gloucestershire	1.08	1.19	0.35
Somerset	0.80	0.88	0.30
Wiltshire	0.98	1.12	0.36
West Midlands			
Hereford & Worcester	1.11	1.14	0.38
Shropshire	0.89	0.86	0.31
Staffordshire	0.73	0.69	0.21
Warwickshire	0.82	0.84	0.22
West Midlands Met Area	0.77	0.72	0.15
Whole sample	0.99	1.15	0.30

Figure 6.4 summarizes the essential features of the demand and supply model in conventional economic form. Districts vary widely in their demand characteristics and consequently in the level of the their house prices, represented by differing demand schedules D1 and D2. These are shown with a shallow downward slope to reflect the small local price response to supply, equivalent to a

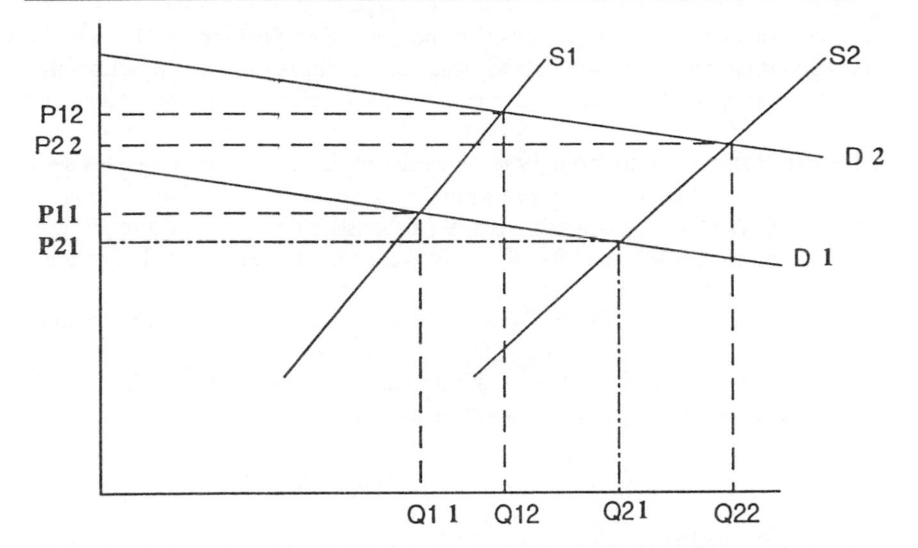

Figure 6.4 Local supply & demand model, with elastic demand and supply varying with land availability.

large negative local price elasticity of demand. Districts also vary in the amount of land they have available for housing, and hence the supply schedules (S1, S2) differ in both position and slope. Price and output levels are determined by the interaction of these differing demand- and supply-side characteristics, with demand-side factors dominating the explanation of prices while land availability dominates the supply side.

Simulations

The estimates of supply elasticity just presented provide a useful shorthand indication of the responsiveness (or lack thereof) characteristic of the private housebuilding industry operating in the British land-use planning context. However, to gain a fuller picture of the impact of particular types of change, it is preferable to see how the whole system might change over several years, allowing for various feedback effects. This is the role of simulations, which use the whole model depicted in Figure 6.1, including estimated forecasting equations for prices, output and planning permissions, together with certain definitional identities and assumptions, to construct alternative scenarios for the development of the housing market in our quasi-national system of 90 districts over several years.

How a typical set of simulations operates for one annual cycle, and how the results in that year form the inputs into the next annual cycle, may be judged from Figure 6.1. The sequence is roughly to forecast first the flow of new planning permissions, then update the stock of permissions, then forecast output, then estimate prices. Price levels and changes and other variables, including output, then feed into the projections for the following year. At this point the national output-price feedback mechanism (Eq. 2) applies. First a baseline projection is made, and this is checked to ensure that its results look reasonable. The work done so far is for a 6-year period from 1987 to 1993. The baseline assumes stable national conditions from 1988 onwards, in respect of key variables such as interest rates; it also assumes zero inflation for convenience. Thus, it is nothing like a forecast of the emerging reality, because it does not build in the dramatic downturn in 1989 and 1990 that was caused by the record level of interest rates, nor the subsequent general recession.

Broadly speaking we are interested in two types of simulation, one dealing with changes on the demand side and the other dealing with changes on the supply side associated with planning policy. These are illustrated in Chapters 9 and 7 respectively, where the results are discussed in terms of relevant policy issues.

6.5 Conclusions

This chapter has demonstrated the feasibility and usefulness of an approach to the analysis of housing markets based on the cross-sectional models at the inter-urban level. By incorporating explicit local data on land-use planning policies and outcomes, the importance of this particular British form of intervention for housing market response is confirmed. At the same time, the practical difficulty of compiling systematic land and planning data should not be underestimated, although the situation is gradually improving.

The analysis provides support for several of the theoretical ideas put forward in earlier chapters, based on the work of others as well as ourselves. Evans' (1983) view of land supply as an upward-sloping function within a given time period is very consistent with our model results. New housebuilding responds to the market with certain crucial time-lags. Supply of land with outstanding planning permission at local level is, in conjunction with profitability, a crucial determinant of output. Developers' expectations of future local land supply, based on planning policies and constraints, shape current housebuilding decisions.

The study shows that the elasticity of supply of new private housing in Britain is quite low, although far from negligible. The elasticity of new-build with respect to price change is on average around unity after two years, or 1.15 including induced land supply. Assuming other components of stock supply are essentially demographic and unresponsive to price, the net flow supply of housing units for sale in the market has a price elasticity averaging 0.3, with local values ranging widely, from 0.04 to 0.86

Low supply elasticity has policy implications. Subsidies and tax reliefs to house buyers will tend to push up house prices rather than housing output. This issue is discussed further in Chapter 9. Another major implication of low short-run supply elasticity is that macroeconomic fluctuations in demand are likely to impact sharply on prices and risk destabilizing the economy (Muellbauer 1988,

Wilcox 1993). Sharp changes in interest rates and other factors caused housing demand to swing wildly in Britain in the late 1980s and early 1990s, and very large changes in house prices resulted, as shown in Chapter 5.

Although the supply elasticity is low, it is not zero and it builds up over time. This means that large demand-induced price fluctuations are not just a monetary and price phenomenon; they also have large effects on output and employment in the construction and allied industries. The debilitating effects of chronic instability in this industry, which we discussed in Chapter 5, is arguably a serious policy issue in its own right.

We examined carefully the evidence on how much new housebuilding supply feeds back into reducing house prices in local markets. Our conclusion is that the local feedback effect is very weak as far as the general price level is concerned, although there may be somewhat more effect on the price of new homes. The main reason for this is the openness of local housing markets in Britain, at least in the regions we examined. Many housing consumers shop around, and local migration rates are strongly related to local owner-occupation supply, especially new private building. This also has policy implications for planning and for social housing, which we take up in the next chapter.

CHAPTER 7
Modelling planning

In this chapter we continue to develop and use the modelling approach set out in the previous chapter, with particular reference to some key issues in planning policy. Although still using the same modelling approach to analyze policy, this chapter is less technical and involves a broader discussion of policy issues. First, we discuss some of the practical issues that arise when we try to measure planning policies in a systematic way. Secondly, we address one of the questions posed in Chapter 3, as to whether planning is autonomous or responsive to market forces, in the case of housing. Thirdly, we examine the policy issue of the amount and location of land released for housing through the planning system, by using model simulations to assess market impacts. Finally, we examine the topical issue of planning policies and agreements for social housing in the same way.

7.1 Measuring planning policies

It is not easy to incorporate planning in economic models, because planning is not a simple phenomenon. As explained in Chapter 3, planning has operational objectives, which may to some extent conflict or qualify each other, and its overall function in society is not necessarily clear. Plans may be expressed in terms of goals (e.g. containment) or in terms of instruments (e.g. zones). Thus, planning policy is not easily reduced to a one-dimensional phenomenon that can be readily measured. This is true even within the one sector of housing, but even more so when housing is recognized as being but one of several sectors competing for land and the attention of the planners. We see the British planning system, in comparison with that found in many other countries, as being characterized by high levels of both comprehensiveness and discretion. These are both features that add to the difficulties of measurement.

We can draw distinctions between different kinds of measures of planning policy for housing. First, there is the distinction between qualitative and quantitative measures. The former cannot be meaningfully expressed in numbers of units, although it may be possible to classify different observations (e.g.

districts, local plan areas) into different categories and from this to make some judgements about whether category A is likely to have more of a certain type of effect than category B. Secondly, there is a distinction between quantitative measures that express objectives (e.g. structure plan housing targets), measures that represent legal instruments (e.g. zoning allocations of land), and measures that represent effective constraints on development decisions (e.g. built-up areas). Thirdly, we can distinguish measures of stocks of land or housing units (e.g. outstanding planning permissions) from measures of flows through stages in the development process in a period of time (e.g. new permissions granted in a year). The measures used in this study, which were introduced in the previous chapter, are a mixture of all of these types.

In building up the empirical database for this study, some measures were easier to obtain in practice than others. The two aspects that were most difficult to measure were stocks of land subject to various kinds of constraints, and the qualitative categorization of local planning policy stances towards housing development.

Land stock constraints

We found in the course of our research that it would be difficult to obtain an adequate set of data to describe fully the potentially available land and specifically constrained land. Land-use data remains one of the most important gaps in official data series available in Britain, although steps are being taken to improve this situation. It was originally hoped that county planning departments would be able to produce estimates of the relevant areas; rather surprisingly, most could not.

Estimates for each district were required of the amount or proportion of the total land area that fell into the following categories:

(a) urban, or built-up
(b) non-urban but subject to overriding planning constraint in form of green belt designation
(c) non-urban but subject to strong planning constraint by virtue of being Areas of Outstanding Natural Beauty (AONB) or national parks
(d) non-urban but subject to other strong planning constraint
(e) non-urban not subject to specific constraint.

In the event, it became clear that no standard definition could be found for category (d) on which systematic data could be obtained. This is unfortunate as it appears that planning policies incorporate a growing array of devices of this kind, often in areas close to urban settlements that might otherwise be attractive to housebuilders. The terminology used varies, including such concepts as green wedges or buffers, areas of restraint, and so forth (Evans 1991). However, it can be argued that, because green belts and AONBs are both long-standing and given official/statutory backing, they carry more force in relation to the approval of plans and the outcome of planning appeals.

For the remaining categories, two methods were initially used to generate estimates. The first involved using satellite (LANDSAT) photography data for counties and statistical analysis to predict urban areas for districts, together with visual map inspection to estimate rough proportions of green belt and AONBs. Although the totals could be adjusted to conform with known county or regional totals, this method remained very rough. This was then superseded by the second method, which involved the South East Regional Research Laboratory (SERRL) in calculating the areas from digitized boundary data held under licence from the DoE. These included boundary data for the districts, for OPCS 1981 Urban Areas, for approved green belts and for AONBs. As explained in Chapter 6, having two methods provided a cross-check on the second, enabling certain discrepancies to be ironed out.

It is hypothesized that green belt is a more potent constraint than AONB, because by definition green belt tends to be located on the land at the urban fringe that would otherwise be of greatest interest to developers. One of the striking characteristics of the 1980s has been the high proportion of housing development taking place on "recycled urban land", something like 40% according to recent studies and statistics (DoE 1991a). This has been partly a matter of policy, but in general such land would be the second choice of housebuilders, because it is likely to involve higher costs (e.g. site preparation, demolition, compensation, etc.). This is allowed for in our supply equations by the inclusion of density or measures of urban land share. The main indicator of density used (D_w) is the population-weighted average of ward densities in 1981, trended forward to 1986. Density may affect the attractiveness of areas and may therefore feature on the demand side, as well as the supply and planning equations.

In the future, it may be possible to obtain measures of the quantity of land transferring between different uses or redeveloped within the same use class. The Ordnance Survey is building up such a database for the DoE and some early results were used in the study of rates of urbanization (DoE 1991a). At present the data are not considered reliable enough to release below the county level, but, for modelling of the kind we are pursuing, data would be needed at district level. In principle, measures of the proportion of housing development taking place on various categories of former urban land would be superior to the crude proxy indicators, such as density, mentioned above.

Planning policies

The other problematic measure of planning policy is the qualitative assessment of the general stance of the local authority. We tried to use our inquiry with county authorities to generate a systematic qualitative characterization of the basis for structure-plan policy targets for each district. Research by Coopers & Lybrand (1985) into structure planning for housing in the South East suggested a framework of categories for this purpose. This study suggested that the derivation of housing targets could be categorized in the following way:

(a) land supply constraint overriding
(b) zero net migration
(c) consistency with employment targets
(d) extrapolation of past migration rates
(e) other (specify).

Chapter 3 suggested that there was a standard demographic approach to this task followed by British planning authorities, and drew attention to the fundamental difficulty that the analysis tends to be circular. The Coopers study, and other case studies mentioned in Chapter 4, indicate that within this general demographic framework there may several different ways of resolving the matter. The key variable is clearly net migration, and we have ourselves demonstrated in Chapter 6 how sensitive migration is to the supply and price of housing at the local level. The above typology suggests that planners may adopt different strategies with regard to migration, ranging from at one extreme ignoring potential migrant demand (category (a)) through an emphasis on local needs (b) or the labour market (c) to the "trend planning" implicit in (d).

Although this kind of typology seems to be conceptually helpful, and should certainly help in making sense of some structure plans, it was a tool that we could not operationalize in our research. Reviewing the responses from the county planners, it was clear that the majority could not or would not respond in these terms. This may or may not be some comment on the Coopers typology.

As a substitute, one of the authors read through all of the relevant planning documents (structure plan policy and technical reports, review documents, etc.) and attempted crudely to classify the overall policy stance for each district. This classification was inevitably influenced in part by the quantitative targets; for example, where the target was below past targets and recent performance, there would be a presumption of a restrictive stance. The resulting planning policy dummy variables (PPD1 – very restrictive; PPD2 – restrictive) can only be described as crude, but they do have the expected effects in the statistical modelling work. Overall, this aspect of the study has been disappointing but perhaps instructive.

There are other, quantitative, measures of policy stance. The most important is the operative structure plan policy target for housebuilding (LP, in housing units per annum, on the same definitional basis as land supply and completions, per 1000 owner-occupiers). This ought to be the best single quantitative indicator of relevant planning policy.

The ratio of successful to total planning applications (PPRAT) is another measure used. This is subject to limitations of both measurement and interpretation. Based on numbers of planning applications for housing, classified simply into major and minor, it does not take account of variations in the number of plots per application. Neither does it distinguish applications that are clearly in conformity with current plans or allocations from those that clearly are not, or applications subject to appeal. It is also clearly subject to local and cyclical fluctuations in the state of demand. When and where demand is high and expectations buoyant, there are likely to be more applications in total and more speculative or non-conforming applications, so the success rate is likely to fall, even though the policy stance has not changed. At local level this indicator may be affected by the strategies of important local developers, of the kind identified by Short et al. (1986) and discussed in Chapter 5.

7.2 Planning policy and market forces

Autonomy versus responsiveness

It would be surprising if planning were not to be in some degree independent and autonomous of market forces. As a process rooted in law, public administration and local politics, it can be expected to follow imperatives different from the housing market. Chapter 3 discussed at some length the goals and procedures of planning and their implications for housing supply. Of the broader views of the functions of planning in society (what might be termed the "political economy" of planning), most seemed to predict that planning would be relatively autonomous and unresponsive. The main exception was one strand of thinking in Marxian political economy that gives priority to corporate business interests, rather than landowning interests. Clearly, there are also features in the norms of planning practice that give rise to policies independent of and in some ways in conflict with market forces, for example the maintenance of green belts. The provision of forward targets for the allocation of housing land are based on medium-term projections of demographic need, as opposed to economic demand, on the basis of assumptions and priorities that are likely to vary between areas (Coopers & Lybrand 1985). These targets are then implemented, with varying commitment and success in different cases (Healey et al. 1985), by the district councils through their local planning and development control procedures.

Autonomy is then the baseline assumption. The more interesting question is whether planning is, as sometimes portrayed in the economic literature, a rigid and unyielding constraint on supply, or whether it in practice has a degree of responsiveness to market demands. Several possible mechanisms may be posited. The most obvious is the development control bombardment factor. Planning authorities operate in responsive mode in granting planning permission, so that the number of permissions given is bound in some measure to reflect the "demand" expressed through the medium of developers applying for planning permission. A second factor, increasingly important in the 1980s, is the "adequacy of land availability" requirements enshrined in DoE Circulars (especially 9/80). If land with outstanding permission falls short of a five-year supply, there is strong pressure to release more. A third factor is the alleged tendency to determine both planning targets and land availability assessments on recent past housebuilding performance. If the relative demand conditions in different areas show some stability over time, then new permissions may appear to be positively related to demand. Expressing this in a different way, Bate (1991) argues that the planning system tends to allocate permissions to replace those used up in actual development. In recent years, more particularly, concern about house price escalation, and its implications for housing access and affordability, may have had a further effect in terms of making planners more sensitive to market conditions, as indeed some semi-official advice (Coopers & Lybrand 1987) encouraged them to be.

Some of the literature on planning in the 1980s argued that the system, under government pressure, became more responsive to the market. This issue is discussed in relation to housebuilding land requirements by Coopers & Lybrand (1985), Rydin (1986), Elson (1986), and Monk et al. (1991), and official policy was spelt out in DoE Circulars 9/80 and 15/84. Other aspects of planning policy, relating to commercial and industrial development and urban regeneration were also seen in this period as seeing a shift in favour of less regulation and the promotion of market-led development.

We would expect the effect of demand to be clearest in the determination of the flow of new planning permissions. This is most likely to operate through the flow of new applications; whether it also affects the probability of success of applications is an interesting question that may be more difficult to test. Moving back a stage, it would be even more interesting if market forces could be shown to influence the planning targets set in structure and local plans.

We now go on to examine this question empirically, using the standard statistical technique of regression analysis introduced in Chapters 1 and 6. Here, the models are essentially exploratory in character. We have a much less clear view of the true structure of the system we are modelling than in the case of the supply of and demand for housing. The order in which we examine relationships is the reverse of that in the previous paragraph and it corresponds to the conventional procedural model of planning, starting with strategic policy targets in structure plans, and moving through applications and their success rate in development control to arrive at the "output" of the planning system in the form of the flow of planning permissions. Figure 7.1 illustrates this procedural model of planning. We do not model the local plan stage identified in this figure, because our data refer to the period of the 1980s where most areas did not have comprehensive local plan coverage.

Structure plan targets

A statistical model predicting structure plan policy targets (also known as "provision") is shown in the first column of Table 7.1. This model is reasonably plausible and explains nearly half of the variance in target numbers of units per year per 1000 owner-occupiers.

The results suggest that planning policy is relatively autonomous viz-à-viz the market. Our primary market demand indicator, price/profit (PCS6), has an insig-

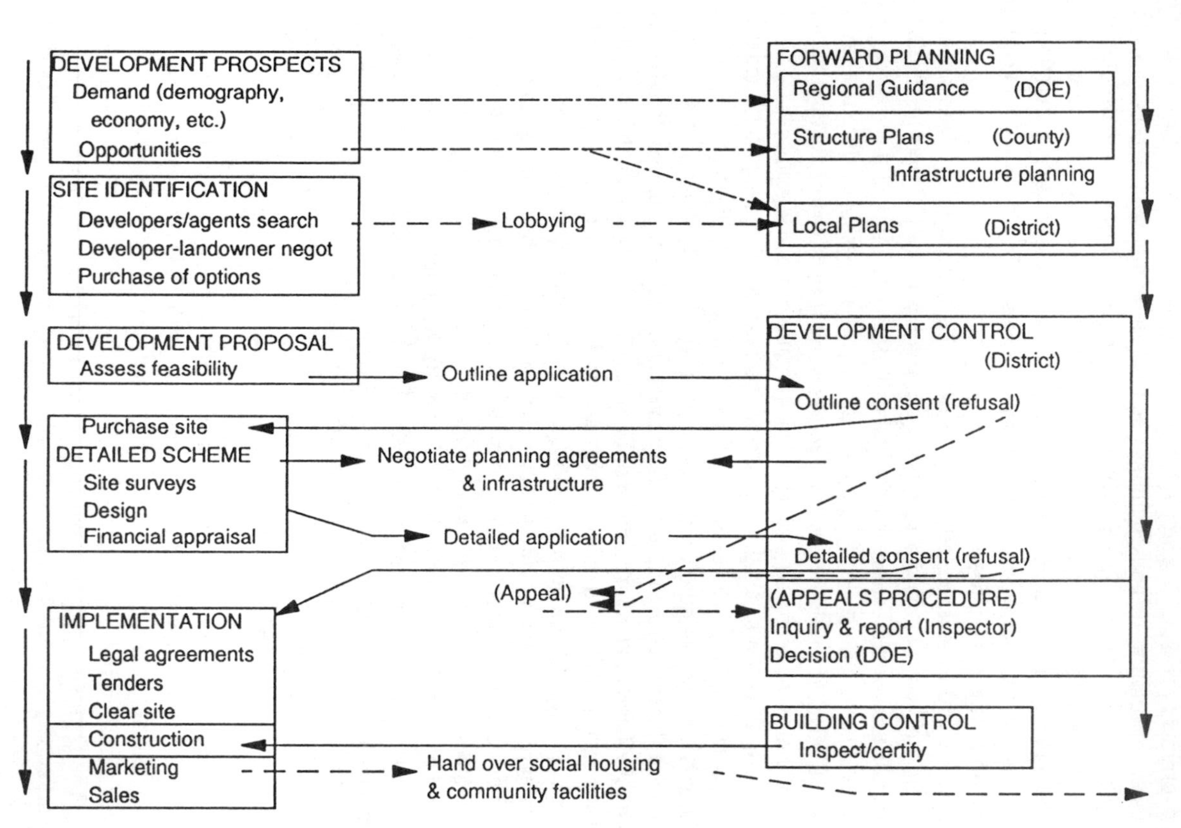

Figure 7.1 Model of development and the planning process.

Table 7.1 Alternative regression models for planning policy provision, planning applications, and their success rate (1986-8).

Explanatory variables	(1) LP Structure plan target	(2) LAP78 Applications	(3) PPRAT Success rate
Constant	13.42	27.0	159.8
	(0.79)	(3.79)	(7.59)
Demand			
PCS6 Price/profit '86		0.102	−0.26
		(0.42)	(−1.16)
PAV26 Price change 82–6		0.0824	
		(0.70)	
DEMANDS1 structural demand	0.013		−19.58
	(0.0)		(−3.97)
DEMANDL1 local demand	1.21		
	(0.44)		
Constraints & location			
G18 Green Belt	0.0014		−0.0496
	(0.05)		(−1.37)
LTR2LN Unconstrained land	0.842		−1.32
	(2.13)		(−2.71)
CONST1 composite		18.76	
		(7.37)	
G7LN Distance London	−1.53		−15.27
	(−0.45)		(−3.63)
Planning policy			
PPD1 Very restrictive	−6.71		−6.09
	(−2.61)		(−1.77)
PPD2 Restrictive	−1.17		−0.661
	(−0.68)		(0.31)
LP Structure Plan provision			−0.0449
			(−0.33)
PPS1 composite		−3.44	
		(−0.84)	
POL3 Labour control	2.00		−4.49
	(0.95)		(−1.34)
POL1 Conservative control			0.311
			(0.11)
Stock adjustment			
LS6 Land o/s PLG perm		0.077	
		(1.49)	
QD802 Output 1980–2	0.227		0.117
	(5.2)		(1.91)
QD6 Output 1986		−0.306	
		(−1.33)	
Interactions			
PCS6*PPS1		−0.164	
		(−0.50)	
Adjusted *r*-squared	0.476	0.546	0.550
F	10.0	13.2	9.76
N	79	71	80

Note: LP and LAP78 are expressed as housing units per year per 1000 owner occupiers; PPRAT3 is the percentage of successful private housing applications (weighted for major/minor). LAP78 and PPRAT3 refer to 1987 and 1988 averaged; LP refers to operative policy in 1987. Regressions for LP and PPRAT are weighted by size of market (number of owner occupiers) nificant effect and is excluded from the model shown. Local variable demand factors (DEMANDL1) have the expected positive effects, although this relationship is not statistically significant (shown by the small *t* statistic in brackets). The factors included in this composite variable are the employment and demographic variables that would generally form part of the legitimate factors taken account of in setting planning targets. It would be possible to explore whether particular variables in this set relate more strongly to policy variance. There is no apparent relationship with the structural component of demand (DEMANDS1) after allowing for other factors in the model. Demand also enters, indirectly, through the strong element of momentum or incrementalism represented by the variable for past completion rates (QD802, which is the average for 1980–2). Some commentators have observed the importance of this phenomenon (Grigson 1986, Bate 1991).

The constraints variables have plausible effects but these are neither very strong nor statistically significant. Green belt (G18) does not have the expected negative effect in the model reported, although this does appear in some other formulations. The total supply of unconstrained land (LTR2LN) does have the expected positive effect in the model shown, although this result is rather unstable. In the 1980s this effect might have been weakened by the overall policy emphasis on using former urban land. In addition, most unconstrained land is rural land away from towns and cities, and is often subject to less overall housing demand.

The two subjectively coded planning policy dummies work in the expected way, with PPD1 ("very restrictive") having a much stronger and more significant effect. Labour-controlled councils appear to set higher targets, although the statistical significance of this relationship is not strong.

These results for structure-plan housing policy targets are quite reasonable and informative given the limitations on the exercise. Nearly half of the variance is explained. To take this work further it would probably be necessary to have a closer look at the planning documentation and to try and come up with some more discriminating classifications. The differential role of certain employment and demographic variables in affecting local policies could be another area of exploration. Interaction terms or partitioning of the sample could be used to test propositions about different patterns of policy determination in different types of area.

Planning applications

The model for planning applications gives a reasonable fit, with over half of the variance in the rate of applications being explained. The dependent variable is somewhat crude, with a good many missing cases. We would expect this indicator to be more strongly related to market demand-side factors and less to constraints and policies. It should have some similarity with output, insofar as both sets of decisions are initiated by developers and represent different stages in the same production pipeline. In fact, the model does not match these expectations very well, and indeed most of the coefficients are not statistically significant. Some also have the wrong sign; in other words, the effects run in the direction opposite to what we expect. One reason for the weakness of this model is that the mix of types and sizes of applications may vary in ways which confound things. For example, areas with positive policies and demands may have fewer, larger applications and fewer small and medium-size speculative applications.

Price/profit seems to have a weak positive effect, and when interacted with planning policy the effect is negative. The effect of lagged rate of price increase is also weaker than we would have expected. The signs on outstanding permissions (LS6) and completions output (QD6) are the opposite of what we would expect from a "stock adjustment" perspective. This means that developers would be expected to have a desired level of land with permission that they wish to hold, so that if the stock falls below this level they make more applications to replenish it. In fact, applications are higher when existing stocks of permissions are higher, and lower when recent output is higher, so the stock adjustment mechanism does not seem to work.

Land constraints completely dominate this equation. One standard deviation in this composite index would increase the rate of applications by 48% or 0.7 standard deviations. So the rate of applications is clearly more strongly conditioned by supply than by demand. Applications are unlikely to be made where there is not suitable land on which to make them.

Constraints should be clearly distinguished from policy (assuming, as we do, that green belts are relatively immutable). Planning policies have a weak (statistically not significant) negative relationship with applications, other things being equal. It should be noted that this applies both to the policy composite variable itself and to the interaction term with price. Although we saw in Chapter 6 that developers' output decisions seemed to be influenced by planning policy, their planning applications do not appear to be influenced in the same way. It is difficult to know why this should be so. We have seen that policies do not correlate with market demand, but the effects of these discrepancies ought to work through the price/profit variable. If nothing else, this result illustrates the difficulties planners have implementing their decisions when they must operate in a responsive mode.

Success rate

The final link in the chain of a multi-stage model of planning would be a model for the success rate of planning applications, that is permissions as a percentage of applications (PPRAT3). Similar comments on the limitations of this model apply as to the previous ones, although on the whole it is easier to interpret.

Both price and the structural demand composite indicator are negatively associated with the chances of success. However, allowing for this success also falls with greater distance from London(G7LN). High demand/price districts are apparently more restrictive. It is tempting to suggest that such districts are more bombarded with dubious or nonconforming applications, but the model just described for applications did not directly support this hypothesis.

Green belt (G18) has the expected negative effect. Rather surprising is the negative association with the overall supply of unconstrained land (LTR2LN). This may be acting as a rural proxy and telling us that rural areas have a more restrictive stance, or that our measures of constraint are seriously inadequate.

The planning policy dummies are not very significant, although the very restrictive one (PPD1) has the expected greater negative effect. Another very surprising finding is that structure plan policy targets have no significant effect on the success rate of planning applications (LP). This provides further evidence for the ineffectiveness in implementation terms of this style of planning.

Labour councils (POL3) appear to be less likely to approve applications. This is the opposite of the pattern observed with planning targets, but again the statistical significance is marginal. Labour councillors may be less sympathetic to private developers.

Planning permissions

The final stage in the planning process is the granting of planning permission. As we showed in Chapter 6, this stage is an important one in modelling the interaction between planning and the housing market. The theoretical presumption behind the model sketched in Figure 6.1 is that the flow of planning permissions will reflect policies, constraints, existing stocks and flows, and to some uncertain degree the pressure of demand reflected in development profit. If planning policies are systematically implemented, then there should be a relationship between policy (and constraint) variables and the flow of planning permissions. The planning system may be responsive, though, and permissions follow from developers having taken the initiative with applications. Developers may be expected to be strongly influenced by market conditions. In addition, the planners themselves may be subject to market demand pressures, for reasons discussed above. A model for the planning permissions stage of the process in a sense combines the previous stages in the planning process just described.

Table 7.2 gives results from three variant regression models for the average flow of permissions in 1986–7, using a model structure similar to the supply model. The first two models differ in how far constraints and policies are disaggregated, whereas the third model is weighted by size of market. This improves the fit of the model noticeably, from what would otherwise be a very poor performance.

Lagged stock of permissions (LS6) is included to reflect a stock adjustment perspective, and lagged output (QD6) is included to reflect a possible momentum of development effect. The first of these does not work in the expected way, as we found with applications. Demand is reflected through profit and lagged price change, and an interaction term with policy; direct demand indicators were also tested and rejected. Model 2 is used as part of the overall set of equations for simulation purposes and for the estimation of supply elasticities.

The performance of these models is much more disappointing than the supply

Table 7.2 Regression models for the annual flow of new planning permissions (LF67, housing units per 1000 owner occupiers, 1986–7).

Explanatory variables	(1)	(2)	(3)
Constant	17.2	-6.95	7.38
	(1.2)	(0.97)	(1.46)
Demand			
PCS6 Price/profit '86	0.052	0.0496	
	(0.2)	(0.19)	
PAV26 Price change 82–6	0.276	0.222	0.171
	(2.1)	(1.72)	(1.83)
Constraints			
DW Ward density	−0.408		
	(−2.3)		
G18 Green Belt	−0.048		
	(−0.8)		
LTR2LN Unconstrained land	−0.38		
	(−0.4)		
CONST1 composite		7.64	5.96
		(2.90)	(2.73)
Planning policy			
PPD1 Very restrictive dummy	−0.81		
	(−0.1)		
PPD2 Restrictive dummy	−4.58		
	(−1.3)		
LP Structure Plan provision	0.15		
	(0.8)		
PPS1 composite		3.85	3.07
		0.87)	(1.07)
POL3 Labour control			−1.96
			(−0.58)
Stock adjustment/momentum			
LS6 Land o/s PLG perm		−0.0064	
		(−0.17)	
QD6 Output		0.142	0.226
		(0.68)	(1.44)
Interactions			
PCS6*PPS1	0.381	0.117	
	(1.0)	(0.33)	
Adjusted *r*-squared	0.188	0.181	0.295
F	3.0	3.4	8.3
N	75	77	87

Note: LF67 is indirectly calculated from outstanding permissions and completions, averaged for 1986–7. Equation (3) is weighted by size of market (number of owners)

models, with most of the variance remaining unexplained. Individual coefficients are often of marginal statistical significance and there is some instability between alternative models. Part of this may be attributable to random year-to-year fluctuations in permissions, associated for example with large sites, and also with some data-recording weaknesses in relation to the timing of records. Part also may reflect the difficulties mentioned previously in classifying or measuring planning policies. Beyond this, it suggests that the determination of planning permission flows is not very systematic. This may be because of the inherent variability in the qualitative characteristics of key sites or applications; or because of the influence of particular officers or elected members.

Subject to these important qualifications, the results in Table 7.2 do suggest that market prices affect the flow of planning permissions slightly. Whereas the effect of profit itself is weak and inconsistent, the lagged rate of price change (PAV26) seems generally to have a significant positive effect. The interaction of profit and policy has the right sign but is not statistically significant and does not improve the model overall. So the hypothesis of planning responding to the market is supported, but not very strongly. The responsiveness is rather less than was expected on the basis of prior reasoning and recent literature about planning and housing in the 1980s.

The constraints on land supply seem to be important in determining planning permissions, especially when combined in the composite indicator (CONST1). Density has the strongest individual effect and unconstrained land the weakest; the earlier comments on possible reasons apply here also.

What is really surprising in these results is the weak effect of planning policy variables, individually or when combined in the composite (PPS1); none are statistically significant. The structure plan provision variable (LP) is a consistent, continuous quantified measure, and ought to be the main expression of planning policy; yet its effects are weak and insignificant. In other words, there is very little correlation of planning permissions with target numbers, allowing for other factors. This is surely evidence of a considerable "implementation gap" (Barrett & Fudge 1980) in the planning system as it was in the 1980s, something that practising planners were themselves aware of to some extent. This observation is slightly mitigated by the results of the supply model described in Chapter 6, which showed planning policy having a significant effect on output, interpreted as an expectations effect. Thus, the policy is implemented to some extent by developers in spite, as it were, of development control.

Local plans and allocated sites

The policy-implementation process in British planning is also undergoing a significant change. Whereas structure plans will remain in some form, if only as regional guidance, at local level statutory district-wide local plans are required in all areas in the near future. Planning decisions will be much less discretionary and much more plan-led. Practitioners generally believe that this will strengthen the implementation link, although additional measures such as phasing agreements may be required as well.

We can give a pointer to this change by referring to data on "allocated" land in our dataset. This is land in specific sites which has been allocated for housing development within the next ten years, either in an approved local plan or by virtue of a local council committee resolution, but which has not yet received planning permission. In the mid-1980s many areas did not have operative local plans and consequently had no land in this category, whereas others did. In our sample of districts, land in this category was equivalent on average to about two years' building or 43% of the amount of land with planning permission. But, it should be stressed, its incidence varied, from zero or negligible in a third of districts to quite large volumes in other districts (7 out of 90 had allocated land equivalent to 10% of the present owner-occupier stock, while another 9 had allocated between 5% and 10%). Comparing the performance of the system in delivering planning permissions in these differing cases provides an interesting test of propositions about the properties of the new "plan-led" system, analogous to the trial of a new drug in medicine where a "control group" of patients is used for comparison.

The inclusion of allocated land in the predictive model for planning permissions (see Table 7.3) slightly improves its predictive power. The coefficient for the allocated land variable is positive and significant at the 10% level, whereas the structure-plan policy target variable is not significant. The effective size of the allocated land coefficient (6 permissions per year per 100 allocated sites) is effectively much larger (four times) than the coefficient for the structure-plan target variable, when both are adjusted to be on a comparable basis. Thirdly, if we split the sample into two groups, according to whether they had significant allocated land in 1987, we find quite a different predictive performance in the planning permissions model. For the sample with significant allocated land (column 2 in Table 7.3), the model is four times more effective in predicting the number of planning permissions. Where land is formally allocated, both structure plan policies (LP) and market forces (price change PAV26) have more effect on the supply of planning permissions.

These results are encouraging both analytically – we are making more sense of the data – and in terms of policy implementation. They suggest that the plan-led system of the 1990s may be more effective at implementing policy, and possibly even more capable of responding to demand, than the 1980s system. However, it is intended to research this issue further.

Table 7.3 Regression models for the annual flow of new planning permissions allowing for allocated land (LF67, housing units per 1000 owner occupiers, 1986–7).

Explanatory variables	(1)	(2)	(3)
Constant	20.33	−13.8	17.05
	(1.7)	(−1.7)	(1.1)
PCS6 Price/profit '86		.047	−.79
		(0.2)	(−1.1)
PAV26 Price change 82–6	0.193	.384	−.050
	(2.0)	(2.7)	(−0.2)
Constraints			
DW Ward density	−0.364		
	(−2.3)		
G18 Green Belt	−0.068		
	(−1.2)		
LTR2LN Unconstrained land	−0.73		
	(−0.8)		
CONST1 composite		11.7	2.11
		(3.6)	(0.4)
Planning policy			
PPD1 Very restrictive dummy	−2.72	2.82	8.54
	(−0.6)	(0.6)	(0.7)
PPD2 Restrictive dummy	−1.64	−1.11	−1.76
	(−0.5)	(−0.4)	(−0.2)
LP Structure Plan provision	0.175	0.30	−0.24
	(1.0)	(1.6)	(−0.5)
POL3 Labour control	−1.49	5.88	−10.8
	(−0.4)	(1.5)	(−1.6)
LA7 Allocated land	0.0625	0.030	1.11
	(1.7)	(0.8)	(1.4)
Momentum			
QD6 Output		0.38	0.41
		(1.7)	(1.3)
Adjusted r–squared	0.296	0.492	0.127
F	5.1	6.2	1.5
N	87	48	28

Note: LF67 is indirectly calculated from outstanding permissions and completions, averaged for 1986–7. All equations weighted by size of market (number of owners). Equation (2) fitted to districts where allocated land at least 20% of land with outstanding permission, Equation (3) the remainder. F test on equation (3) as a whole is not significant at 20% level.

Overall patterns

Overall, the results of this rather exploratory exercise are mixed. They do provide some interesting and suggestive material for discussion. The main provisional conclusions are:

- severe land supply constraints are the most important influence on most stages in the process of bringing land forward for housing development;

- demand and price factors do not have either as great an influence or the kind of influence expected; on the whole, planning targets are uninfluenced, whereas the success rate of applications is negatively associated with price/ demand pressures;
- the interpretation of the effects of constraints is complicated by urban–rural differences and the incomplete measurement of softer constraints;
- the effects of structure-plan policy targets on applications or permissions is very weak, suggesting that this style of policy is difficult to implement; allocated land seems to have more effect and areas with more allocated land seem to generate outcomes more responsive to both policies and the market;
- the planning application and permission process certainly does not act like a stock adjustment process in the short term, but the whole process of target setting for the longer term is clearly incremental, and this is the main (indirect) way in which demand is influential.

The overriding question posed at the beginning of this section was whether planning is autonomous or responsive to market forces. The conclusion we have to draw from the statistical evidence is that planning for new housing is relatively autonomous and is not strongly influenced by market forces. The way we have approached this (using statistical models) is rather novel, and contrasts with the bulk of recent literature on planning where the main empirical device is the case study. As such it provides at least some additional insight into the complex nature of the planning beast. In terms of the broad views on the nature of planning set out in Chapter 3, our findings are more consistent with the views that emphasize pluralist politics or bureaucratic process, than with some structural political economy accounts.

7.3 Land release policies

The unresolved debate

Many planning practitioners do not accept that planning pushes up house prices, despite the general theoretical presumption that it does. The debate between Evans (1987, 1988b) and Grigson (1986), rehearsed in Monk et al. (1991), illustrates this. Grigson argues that prices are determined by demand, not supply, because new-build supply is only a tiny part of the total supply and cannot adapt quickly to the major demand fluctuations induced by financial and other factors. He also expresses the view that "enough" land is made available through the planning system to meet the effective demand. Evans, by contrast, argues that restricting the total supply of land is bound in the longer term to raise prices, and also to raise densities (thereby reducing welfare). A variety of indirect evidence is adduced for these tendencies, particularly in South East England, including land prices and transactions, densities and house type mix (Evans 1988b). However, direct and systematic evidence of the extent of the impact of planning on prices is very limited.

Cheshire & Sheppard (1989) and DoE (1992b) are the main recent attempts to measure the impact of planning on the housing market empirically. The former study applies statistical intra-urban house price and land rent functions to two "similar" cities, Reading and Darlington, which differ in their degree of planning restrictiveness, and estimates the amount of difference in prices attributable to this factor. It finds surprisingly modest price impacts, on average (6–8%), but goes on to show that removing constraints on total land area allocated to housing would lead in the long run to a dramatic fall in densities and increase in "built-up" areas. The DoE study also used matched pairs of local case studies, and tracked prices of particular house and land types over long periods. The results are interesting but somewhat inconclusive. Local markets seemed to be very open, or "substitutable", so that the apparent high house and land prices resulting from planning constraint in the South East leak out of the particular localities of constraint and affect other districts in the region, even where there is less constraint. This finding is consistent with our own, reported in Chapter 6.

The housebuilding industry has long argued that planning restricts output and forces up prices. Chapter 4 described how studies of land availability and debate about this issue led to the institution of procedures for ensuring short-term land availability consistent with plan targets. However, the wider issues of whether the plan targets are themselves adequate, and about implementation, remain.

The crucial question arising out of this debate is: what difference would it make to house prices if significantly more land were released by the planning system? It is important also to consider what would happen to output, since this is the main transmission mechanism, and since output is of policy interest in its own right. One advantage of the simulation model is that it is possible to examine fairly extreme scenarios, which might be rather difficult to operate politically or on an experimental basis in reality. As a suitable starting point, we ask what would happen if the government required local planning authorities to *double* the amount of land to be released over the ten-year plan period 1986–96.

Land release options and constraints

This leads into more detailed issues of policy implementation. First, it is assumed that the primary expression of planning policy is the structure plan provision target (LP). This is adjusted where feasible, and consequential adjustments are made to values for other policy variables (PPD2, PPRAT, and PPS1). But the "where feasible" phrase is crucial. The supply and permissions modelling results showed the importance of land supply constraints, as does any practical familiarity with local planning situations.

Three alternative scenarios are constructed. The first assumes that all additional land for housing comes from the "unconstrained" pool (i.e. not urban, not green belt, not AONB), and that local authorities are not expected to exhaust their unconstrained land in less than 100 years (i.e. at a rate above 1% pa). The result of this interpretation of constraints is that more than half of the districts (49 out of 90) have unchanged levels of provision, while another nine have increases below double. Despite this, total planned provision jumps by 65%, because certain districts provide a disproportionate share of both existing and, more especially, extra provision. This point is brought out by the map in Figure 7.2.

A hundred years might be considered a long time, and too great a constraint on the land release policy. The housebuilding industry might argue that this is treating the rural/NIMBY lobby with kid gloves. To go to more drastic lengths to release land, we could set the maximum exhaustion period at ten years. In other words, within a very foreseeable future (the plan period) all unconstrained land might be allowed to be allocated in many districts, using a conservative definition of constraints. Under this scenario, most authorities (all bar 14) can double their planned provision, and the total provision increases by 90%; the growth is slightly less concentrated. A third scenario, involving green belt land, is considered further below.

Impact on output and prices

The results of the simulation for overall housebuilding output and house prices are shown graphically in Figures 7.3 and 7.4, and Figure 7.5 shows the impact in different counties and types of district. In interpreting the pattern of the simulations over time, a point to be borne in mind is that the time-lag mechanisms assumed are rather crude and hence the dynamics of the system may not be quite realistic, although the system as whole is fairly stable. In addition, a key parameter in determining prices is the national price feedback, based on an assumed price elasticity (-0.7) applied to a net flow supply calculation. Alternative assumptions and approaches have been examined. Different assumptions about the elasticity would alter the dynamic profile but would have less impact on the general pattern of results, except perhaps in giving more or less persistent price effects. Alternative adjustment mechanisms can be modelled at local level, involving migration and affordability together with various lags and damping mechanisms, and are described in more detail in Chapter 9. These suggest that the effects on price might be less initially than shown here, but persist over a longer period. It should also be emphasized that the results here depend on the style of planning policy and its implementation characteristic of the 1980s. There are indications that the more plan-led system intended for the 1990s could increase the responsiveness of the system.

Under the first scenario (100-year exhaustion) new-build output climbs quite steeply to a peak rate about 23% above the baseline, then falls to about 11% above at the end of the period (Fig. 7.3); the average increase is 16%. Under the alternative local price feedback model mentioned above, the average effect is similar but persists more at the end of the period. The second scenario (10-year exhaustion) increases these figures to 28%, 13% and 19% respectively. What is really striking in these results is the finding that at no point, even before the price feedback causes a fading of the initial output boost, does the increase come anywhere near the 65% or 90% increase in the structure plan targets. This dramat-

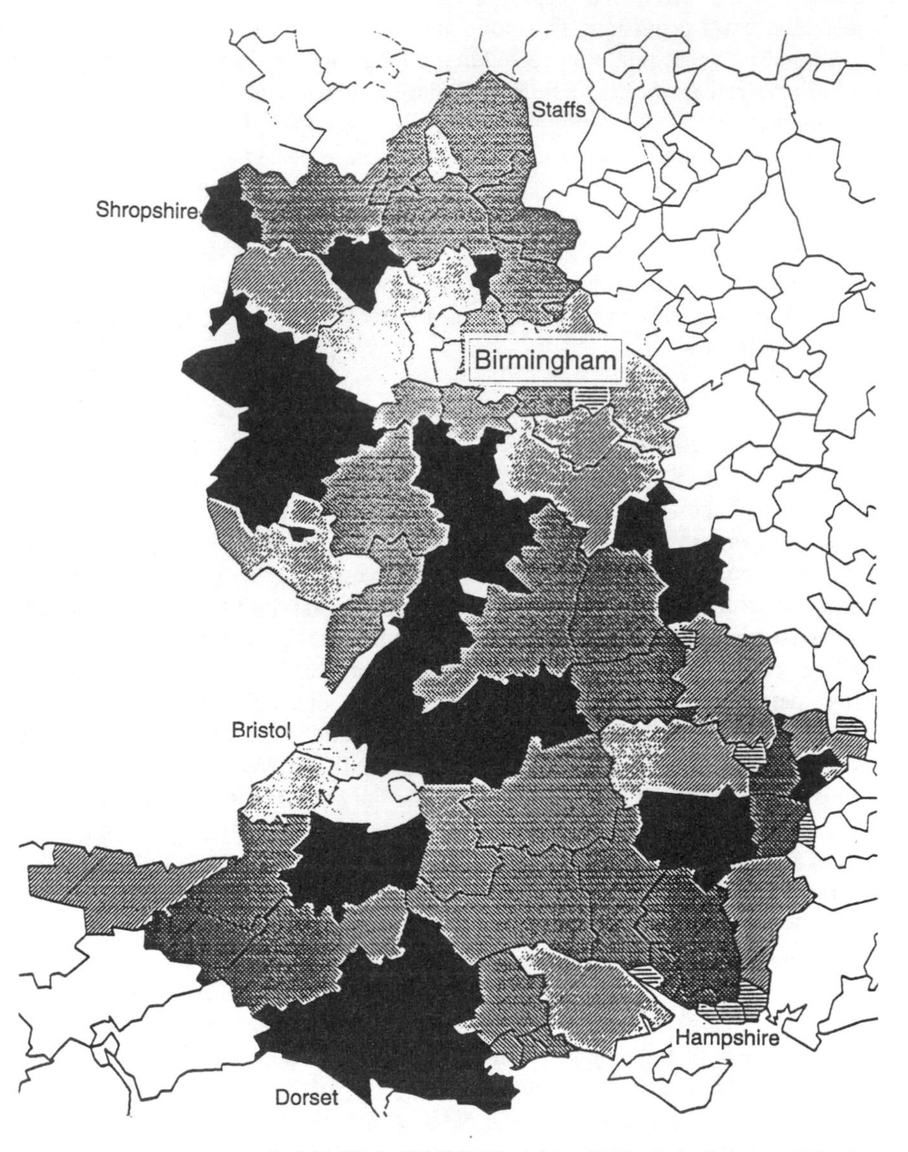

Figure 7.2 Outstanding planning permissions for private housing in 1987 (per thousand owner-occupiers).

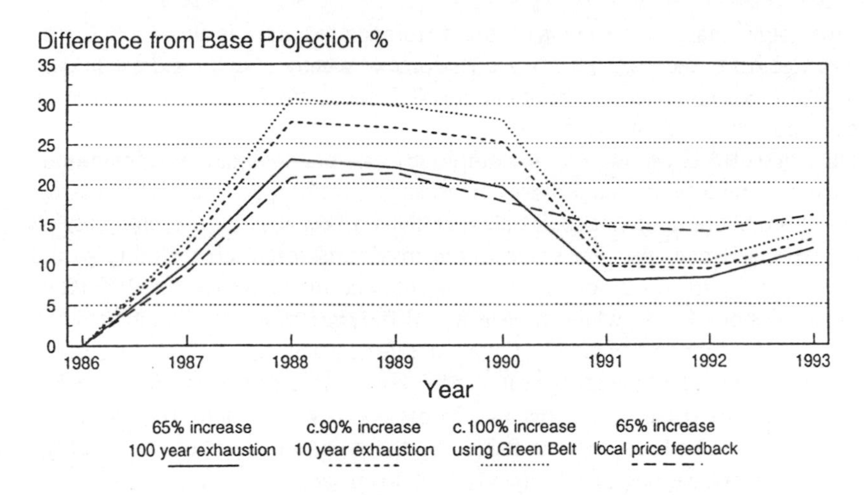

Figure 7.3 Impact of additional planned land release on new-build output.

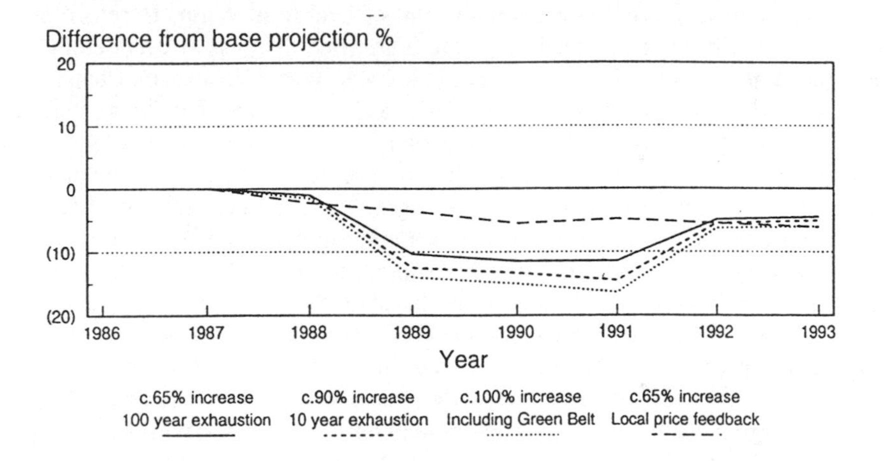

Figure 7.4 Impact of extra land release on house prices, with differential constraints on release strategy and different price feedback.

ically illustrates the point about there being an implementation gap. It is private developers, not the planners, who normally initiate developments (or not as the case may be). The flow of new planning permissions increases by even less than the figures for output quoted here, following the model described in the previous section, and this is one reason for the muted output response. A second reason is that, as greater supply reduces prices, the profitability of housebuilding falls and this reduces supply again.

It is also apparent that the output gain from adopting a drastic version of the land release policy, by allowing unconstrained land to be exhausted in 10 years, is really rather marginal. The maximum difference in output is about 5.5%, and the average difference is 2.7%. It is questionable whether such a gain would be worth the environmental and political costs. Indeed, such a question would be posed about even the first scenario.

The price effects follow from the output effects, but are smaller in magnitude because new-build is only a minority of total market supply. Most of the effect comes through the national feedback mechanism, because of the openness of local markets. Under the first scenario the maximum price fall resulting would be 11.5%, and this too is not sustained; by the end of the period the difference is down to about 4.5%, while the average difference is 7.3%. The alternative local price feedback model gives a flatter profile of price impact over the period, with a lower peak and average (only 4.5%) but a more persistent effect (6.1% at the end of the period). The second scenario (10-year exhaustion) increases these figures to 14.5%, 5.1% and 8.7%. So the point about the drastic strategy giving only marginal pay-offs is equally true for prices.

Figure 7.5 gives a geographical picture of the output effect of these land-release policy scenarios, looking at the effect at the end of the simulation period. Initially, output is boosted in areas with a lot of land (e.g. Avon, Hereford & Worcester, Staffs), but eventually it is the high-price South East counties that show the most persistent increase. Output falls in the West Midland conurbation, because of falling prices and constrained land, and barely rises in the more rural western counties. The types of district to experience the largest increase are the growth areas (e.g. former new towns). This reinforces the tendency of the planning system to concentrate growth (see also Fig. 7.2), an interesting parallel to the similar tendency within districts to concentrate growth on a few major sites which we identified in Chapters 4 and 5. Affluent suburbs and resort and coastal areas also show relatively high growth, perhaps a reflection of a British version of the "sunbelt". Declining industrial and rural areas see the smallest increase. Very similar patterns are observed for output in the alternative local price feedback models. This version of the model generates more local variation in price impacts, ranging from a 9% fall in Berkshire to only 1.5% in the West Midlands county, or from 8.9% in growth districts to 2.2% in declining industrial areas.

Impact on affordability

One of the main reasons used by the pro-development lobby in arguing for more land release is the proposition that this will lower prices and increase access to owner-occupation and housing affordability in general. It is clear from these results that this argument is weak. First, the simulations reported here represent what must be close to an extreme form of the proposed policy. Despite this, the impact on average prices is rather modest. Secondly, we can translate this into access to owner-occupation terms, using the kind of estimates reported in Bramley (1991a). These suggest that a 10% price fall would increase the number of

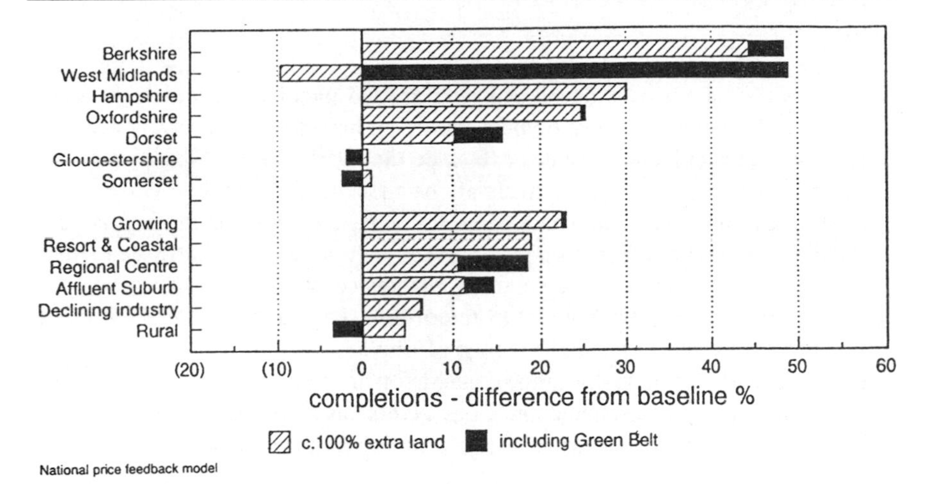

Figure 7.5 Impact of extra land release on housebuilding output (by selected county and type of district).

new households able to afford to buy by about 4–5%. This is equivalent to an elasticity of between about -0.6 and -1.0, depending on the initial level of affordability, comparable with the elasticity estimates from earlier literature referred to before. These results mean that large-scale land release could increase the proportion of new households able to buy by about 3–6% points. When typically between 30% and 50% cannot buy, this is a rather small gain. It will not be sufficient to solve the social housing need problem. The alternative local price feedback model contains an estimate of the waiting list for social housing; this suggests a reduction of only 11% in the average list as a result of the 65% extra land release scenario. Recent estimates suggest a need for around 100000 units of social housing per year in England, whereas the improvements in access mentioned above could at most help between 12000 and 24000 households.

Thirdly, it is manifestly not worth an individual local authority following this strategy, because of the openness of local markets. Doubling one district's plan provision will raise output by an average of 19%, which will lower that district's prices by £400 or 0.75% (using the price model in Ch. 6). Insofar as local officials and elected members perceive this, which some appear to, judging by their comments about prices not being under their control, then this helps to explain some of the reluctance of individual local authorities to release more land for housing. This also helps to explain the interest in more direct mechanisms for securing affordable housing, discussed further below.

Green belt

Green belts are areas of undeveloped land around major cities which are given statutory protection from development, and they have been a generally accepted part of the British planning framework since the 1950s. In the 1980s, green belt policies became somewhat controversial. At first the Conservative Government sought to lessen the restrictiveness of green belts, but, after political grassroots opposition from within their own party, green belt policy was reaffirmed (Elson 1986). At the same time, some counties introduced or extended green belt designations. Green belts are thus quite important. They account for 27% of the non-urban land area in our sample wedge of England, and very often this is urban fringe land with a potentially high demand for housing. Figure 7.6 shows that this proportion is quite high in counties as diverse as Avon, Berkshire, Staffordshire and Dorset, reaching virtually 100% in the West Midlands.

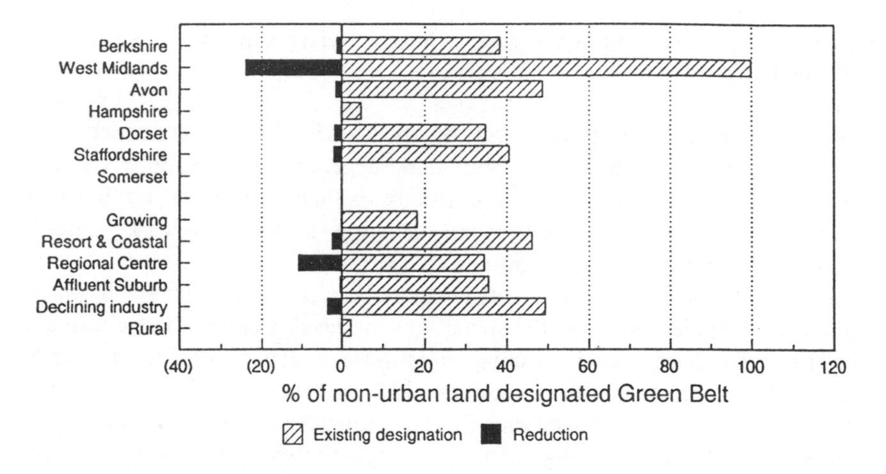

Figure 7.6 Reduction in green belt required to double planned provision for housing over ten years (by selected county and type of district).

Suppose the generally firm policy line of protecting the green belt were to waver. What effect would a land release strategy such as that just discussed have, if green belt land could be used as well as unconstrained land? Intuitively, one would expect a significant effect, since green belt land is land which is most attractive to developers, i.e. greenfield sites in an attractive environment close to major urban centres. This might be somewhat offset by reduced development within the urban area, especially in regions of lower demand.

This can be tested using a variant of the second land release scenario described above, where green belt land is used (at the same rate as unconstrained land) if necessary to achieve a doubling of plan provision. This has the effect of increasing provision in most of the remaining districts, which were constrained under the previous version of this scenario, typically large urban authorities including those in the West Midlands conurbation. The shaded bars on the left of Figure 7.6 show the amount of reduction resulting from this policy scenario, with the existing designation (as a percentage of non-urban land) shown by the pale bars on the right. Strictly, this is a potential reduction, as this is plan provision rather than actual output. This shows that the reduction is chiefly significant in the West Midlands and in the large city (i.e. Regional centre) type of district.

The dotted line in Figure 7.3 shows that this strategy would result in a higher level of extra housebuilding output, although the marginal gain from the specifically green belt release is a modest 3% at the peak, falling to 1.2% at the end of the period, an average of 2% over the period. Figure 7.5 shows that there would be a massive boost to housebuilding in the West Midlands, more modest boosts in Dorset and Berkshire, but offsetting reductions (attributable to price feedback) in rural western counties. Figure 7.4 shows that the marginal price reductions are small in magnitude and fade after about four years; the maximum is 1.9% and the average 1.2%.

These results should be qualified slightly, in relation to the limitations of the model. First, the version of the price model used in the simulations does not contain the green belt variable. Other versions (see below) suggest that green belts may increase house prices somewhat. If so, then reductions in green belt designation would reduce prices directly as well as through the supply effect. Secondly, the former green belt land might be disproportionately attractive to developers, who would bring it forward for development much faster than normal sites. It is not clear that the supply model used here, although it gives a considerable weight to constraints, would fully reflect this point. Even if the reality were to be a stronger effect on prices than that quoted above, it seems hard to believe that its overall magnitude would be very large. One reason for this is the point that it is only in certain areas that much extra land would be released under this strategy, and price effects are diffused through the whole system.

Again, these results point strongly to the conclusion that the benefits of extending a land release strategy into the green belt are very marginal, and would surely be outweighed by the political and environmental costs. The policy would represent a further movement away from an unambiguous planning framework, reducing certainty and the credibility of the planning system and provoking many nonconforming (rent-seeking) applications and appeals. Although occasional incursions into the green belt do occur, these are usually industrial/commercial developments that are sold on the idea of economic development and job creation.

Long-term effects of planning

It has been suggested that the effects of planning are felt much more in the longer term than in the short term (Evans 1988b, Monk et al. 1991, DoE 1992b). The model used here is not a long-run model. It is quite defensible to focus on the medium term, as in this part of our research, particularly when informing a practical policy debate. But can the dataset assembled for this study give any clues about the longer-term effects of planning?

One alternative approach to modelling the system, instead of the lagged response structure described in Chapter 6, is to treat it explicitly as a simultaneous system. The normal technique then would be first to estimate "reduced form" regression equations in which endogenous variables (prices, planning permissions, and output) would be regressed on all exogenous variables. Thus, planning policy and constraint variables would appear in a price equation. Assuming planning policies and constraints were relatively stable over time, then one could interpret any relationships revealed as being longer-term ones.

Without going into further detail, tests of this approach indicate that the planning and constraints variables have effects of broadly the expected direction but small in magnitude and often not statistically significant. Using the composite variables, one standard deviation change in policies would lower prices by 1.6%, whereas for constraints the effect would be 2.5%. Using individual variables, structure plan provision would affect prices by only 0.7% for one standard deviation (nearly doubling provision produces a 3.1% fall), whereas for green belt the effect is slightly stronger at 2.8%. The most restrictive districts (PPD1) have prices 3.4% higher, other things being equal.

These results are consistent with the conclusions presented earlier on both planning and supply, that harder constraints have more effect than discretionary policies. They are also consistent with the simulation results that the effects fade over time (more in some versions than others). But it should be remembered that, unlike the simulation figures for price reductions, these are differential price effects at the local level. This in turn reinforces the point that local markets are very open and that price effects diffuse through the national system.

There is another important point to be made about longer-term effects, however, which is that the important effects may be not so much on the numbers of housing units and the price per unit, but more on the type and size of units and the density at which they are developed. This is the focus of much of the theoretical literature on supply reviewed in Chapters 2 and 3. The work of Evans (1991) and Cheshire & Sheppard (1989) points to density effects being predominant. We take up this theme in the next chapter. At this point it is enough just to hint at what may be going on in the longer term. Tight planning controls in areas of high potential demand, such as the South East, may have the effect of shifting the type mix of output (more flats, fewer bungalows) and increasing the density (smaller gardens). The price of a housing unit, even of a given type such as modern semi-detached, may not be much higher as a result, but people have a lot less space for their money.

7.4 Planning agreements

Social housing targets

Chapter 4 explained the evolution of a new approach to the provision and subsidy of "affordable" social housing, based on the use of planning agreements and backed by local planning policies. Chapter 5 suggested that housebuilders were not necessarily opposed to these arrangements and were learning to work with them. The more important part of the new policy described in *Planning policy guidance note 3* (PPG3 for short, DoE 1992a) refers to medium and larger private housing sites and enables the local planning authority to negotiate with the developer for a proportion of affordable social housing units to be included within the development. In the evolution of this policy, such proportions as laid down in local planning policies were referred to as "quotas" (Bishop & Hooper 1991), but DoE (1991a, 1992a) guidance disallows rigid quotas. Thus, the general approach may be to set broader "targets", based on evidence of needs, but to negotiate around these in the light of individual circumstances.

Under optimal conditions the land value on the social housing units, together with a cross-subsidy from part of the land value on the private units, can enable such schemes to produce "affordable" social housing without direct public subsidy. A worked example is given in Box 7.1. Very often in practice, schemes involve a mixture of land value and public subsidy. Clearly, the potential for schemes or targets aimed at minimizing public subsidy varies roughly in proportion to residual land values. Social housing produced in this way is an example of a broader class of social benefits from planning decisions known as "planning gain".

The approach is relatively new and has not been thoroughly tested. Initial survey evidence suggested a rather modest impact (Barlow & Chambers 1992), but more recent updates suggest that by 1993 the impact of the new arrangements appeared to be quite substantial (Barlow 1993b). Many local authorities are interested, but not all push the approach to its limits, and market conditions in the early 1990s are relatively unfavourable. In general, negotiated targets for affordable social housing are typically of the order of 20–25% of units.

Barlow & Chambers (1992) and Chapter 4 both suggested that there are uncertainties involved in the implementation of this approach. But two major questions have not been strongly emphasized or systematically examined so far. These are (a) the likely maximum scope of the approach, given the basic economics of the housing market, and (b) the second-order effects, or costs, of the policy, consequent upon behavioural reactions of the housebuilding industry. Our simulation model can be used to tackle these questions. The first relates mainly to the pattern of residual land values, but also to the level of subsidy needed to achieve "affordability". There is also an issue about the geographical coincidence of potentially viable schemes and existing social housing needs. The second question is applicable to any example of planning gain that acts like a tax

Box 7.1

Alternative subsidy arrangements under planning agreements for social housing

The following table sets out a worked example of a typical mixed tenure housing scheme negotiated with a private developer under the provisions of PPG3. The site accommodates 100 new homes, of which 25 are to be affordable social rented units managed by a housing association, and the remaining 75 are to be for sale on the open market (i.e. the "target" or "quota" here is 25% of units). The three columns refer to three different ways of financing the subsidy which the social rented housing requires to make the rents affordable.

Subsidies:	(1) Public	(2) Land	(3) Cross
Number of units – total	100	100	100
– market sale	75	75	75
– social rent	25	25	25
Construction & development costs @ £42000 /unit	£4.4m	£4.4m	£4.4m
Market value @ £55000 /unit			
– whole scheme	£5.5m	£5.5m	£5.5m
– private sale units	£4.125m	£4.125m	£4.125m
Cost to HA for rented units			
– land	£0.275m	0.0	0.0
– houses	£1.1m	£1.1m	£0.55m
Housing Association Grant	£0.825m	£0.55m	0.0
– as % value	60%	40%	0%
Net capital cost to HA	£0.55m	£0.55m	£0.55m
– per unit	£22k	£22k	£22k
Annual loan charge (8.5% annuity, 25yr)	£2150	£2150	£2150
Annual provision for maintenance, mgt, major repairs, voids	£935	£935	£935
Annual cost rent	£3085	£3085	£3085
Weekly cost rent	£59.32	£59.32	£59.32
Land value subsidy	0.0	£0.275m	£0.275m
Cross subsidy	0.0	0.0	£0.55m
Residual land value or gross development profit	£1.1m	£0.825m	£0.275m

Col (1) shows the way the scheme would be financed when the HA pays full market value and receives full HAG (i.e. public subsidy). The 60% grant reduces costs sufficiently for the HA to charge an "affordable" rent of £59.32 per week. The landowner receives the full market value of the site, £1.1m. Col (2) shows the effect of the land for the social rented units being passed to the HA at zero cost while the dwellings are procured at the full construction and development cost of £42,000 per unit. HAG is reduced to reflect the land subsidy, from the normal 60% to 40%. HA rents are unchanged, but the HAG is "stretched" so that a given budget buys more units (50% more in this example). The landowner receives three-quarters of the full market value of the site. Col (3) shows the effect of introducing a cross-subsidy element as well, to support the cost of the social rented units from the development profit or land value associated with the market sale units. In this case the cross-subsidy of £0.55m completely replaces the HAG, and shows how it is possible in theory to provide social housing in this way without public subsidy. The landowner still receives a small residual value of £0.275m.

The theoretical maximum social housing target which can be financed from land value and cross-subsidy may be derived as follows. Let q be the quota or target of affordable social units, P be the market price per house, N be the total number of units, v be the share of land value in full market value, and s be the standard rate of HAG subsidy designed to bring cost rents down to an affordable level. The developer will receive $(1-q).P.N$ from the market sale units and $q.(1-s).P.N$ from the social units, and will incur costs of $(1-v).P.N$ in developing the houses (assuming in the extreme case the residual land value is driven down to zero). Thus, equating revenues and costs for the developer,

$$(1-q).P.N + q.(1-s).P.N = (1-v).P.N$$

Cancelling out the P.N terms and expanding, we have

$$1 - q + q - q.s = 1 - v$$

which simplifies to

$$q = v/s$$

This indicates the maximum theoretically feasible social housing quota or target achievable without public subsidy. If it is thought that only a proportion of residual land value can be tapped, then v should be adjusted accordingly. In the example in the table, $v = 0.2$ and $s = 0.6$, so q is 0.33; this means that a social housing proportion of 33% of units would have exhausted the residual land value.

or charge on development, and this is a broader issue taken up in Chapter 9.

The analysis in Box 7.1 indicates that the theoretical maximum proportion of social housing that can be provided without public subsidy is equal to the ratio v/g, where v is the residual land value as a share of house value and g is the subsidy (HAG) rate required to produce affordable housing. This assumes land subsidy from the value of the land on which the social housing units are built, plus cross-subsidy from the land on which the private sector units are built, but zero public subsidy. New homes would be delivered to housing associations at a net cost equivalent to the cost of normal social provision after receipt of Housing Association Grant. Developers have to bridge the gap between construction cost and this figure with cross-subsidy, so reducing their overall profit. Typical average values of 0.2 for v and 0.6 for g imply that social housing targets of 33% would be theoretically viable without public subsidy. In practice, lower figures than this are the most that is likely to be achieved, because landowners will require some positive incentive to bring land forward under these terms.

The case we test on our model is of all the districts in the sample attempting to apply social housing target to all new private development, but with the size of the target varying around an average of 20% in proportion to residual land value. Where land value based on second-hand prices is negative, quotas are set at zero (this applies to 18 out of 90 districts, mainly in the West Midlands). The 20% figure is pretty typical of the actual targets being negotiated in those areas where authorities are actively pursuing this policy. It is less than the theoretical maximum (we take two-thirds of residual value after allowing for infrastructure costs), but in other ways it might be considered unrealistically generous. The PPG3 approach is not so easy to apply on small sites or former urban sites, both of which are important in practice. Developers have to be willing to negotiate around these norms, which depends partly on their expectations of the regime persisting.

The policy targets have to be supported by demonstrable need. We attempted to test this for the 90 districts by comparing viable targets with social housing needs estimated in two alternative ways, the first based on Bramley's (1991a) affordability method, and the second based on statutory homelessness and a small proportion of general council waiting lists. The needs estimates are essentially conservative. The 90 districts divided as follows

(a) positive target less than needs 29
(b) positive target less than one needs estimate 10
(c) positive target constrained to level of needs estimate 28
(d) zero target and positive needs 13
(e) zero target and zero net needs 10.

In other words, districts vary considerably in how the potential of this approach to contribute to social housing supply matches up against needs, although in general there is some positive correlation between net needs and land values. A third of districts could justify the maximum feasible targets. A quarter would face a situation where either targets were unviable or they were not justified, or both.

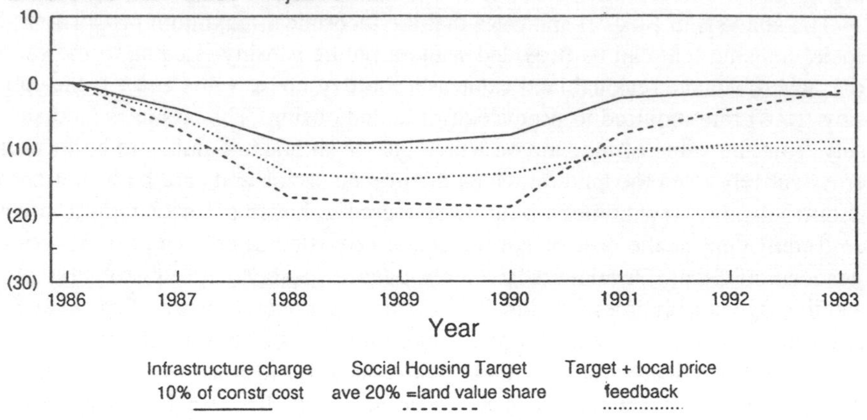

Figure 7.7 Impact of infrastructure charges or social housing targets on new-build output.

Nearly a third of districts might have difficulty in justifying in need terms the targets that appeared to be economically viable. Across the whole system, the amount of social housing that a targets system could produce is reduced by 23% by constraining targets to needs in the way just described.

The results of this simulation are shown in Figures 7.7, 7.8 and 7.9. Figure 7.7 shows that this version of the targets policy would, if applied from 1987, have led to quite a large initial drop in total housing output, even including the social units. The maximum reduction relative to baseline would be 17.5% in 1989, but this drops away to quite a low level (1%) by 1993, giving an overall average lost output of 11.3%. The alternative local price feedback model gives a similar average loss (11.9%) with a lower peak but a more persistent effect (8.9% lower in 1993). This is quite a worrying consequence of a policy concerned with meeting housing needs, although the fact that the loss seems to fade to smaller proportions later on is more reassuring.

Figure 7.8 shows the geographical impact of the policy. First, social housing targets would be quantitatively important in South East counties such as Berkshire, and fringe counties in the South West, but would barely feature in the less prosperous parts of the West Midlands (nor, by implication, in most of the North of England). This result is exactly parallel with the findings of Barlow & Chambers (1992). Targets would be important in growth, rural, resort/coastal and affluent suburban areas, but much less so in declining industrial areas. An arguably beneficial consequence of this pattern is that the social housing stock would tend to be boosted most in areas that currently have least, and vice versa. Secondly, the lost output would tend to be concentrated in the same areas where the social targets were most significant, particularly in the South East fringe counties such as Wiltshire and Dorset, and in the resort/coastal areas. Thirdly, lower-priced areas such as Staffordshire would actually experience a growth in private

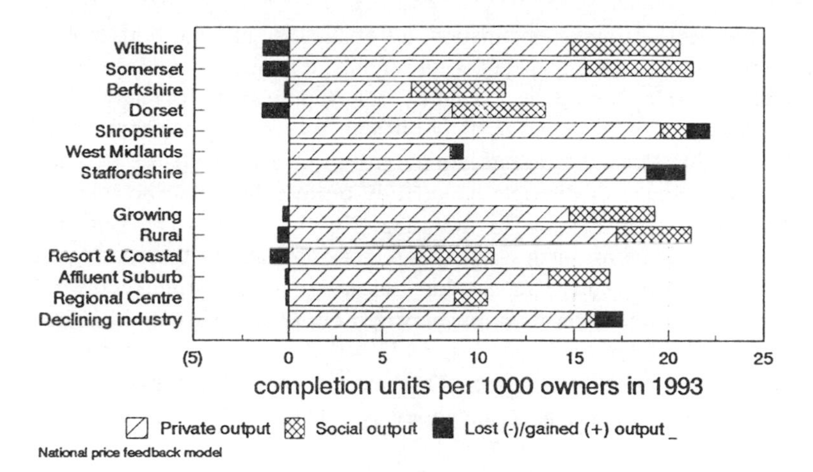

Figure 7.8 Impact of housebuilding output of social housing targets.

and total output, as a consequence of the higher prices. This also might be regarded as not unhelpful.

Figure 7.9 shows the impact on house prices. The model suggests that the targets policy would raise prices by an average of 5.6%, ranging from a peak of 10.5% to a level of only 1.9% at the end of the period. The alternative local price feedback model suggests a much smaller effect on prices overall, averaging only about 1.5% (this model takes account of the way the additional social housing meets demand).

How counterproductive would these price effects be, in terms of a policy to meet the needs of households who cannot afford to house themselves in the owner-occupier sector? Bramley (1991a) suggests that a price change of 5.6%

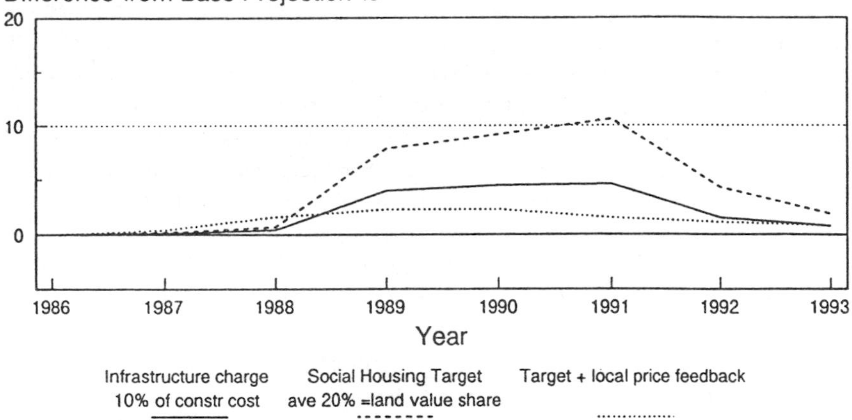

Figure 7.9 Impact on house prices of social housing targets.

would reduce access to owner-occupation by about 2% of new households. Nationally this could be as many as 8000 households, but detailed analysis using the local model and allowing for needs and existing supply suggests many fewer households priced out of the market. It is difficult to gross up the number of social units resulting from the targets policy from our sample to the national level, because the sample of districts is not fully representative in the relevant respects, but rough estimates lie in the range 16000–22000. The outcome depends on many unknowns, such as the degree of applicability to urban areas including London. The results suggest that the policy would produce several extra social units for every marginal buyer priced out of the market. In aggregate, the extra social units could represent a 30–45% increase on the current social housing programme in England. On balance, taken together with the generally favourable spatial impacts, the policy would seem to be one worth pursuing.

The finding that the theoretical potential of the policy is as large as this is encouraging, but not the same as saying that this is what the policy will actually deliver. This remains to be seen. In practice, it will take at least five years or more for the full potential to be established, because it chiefly applies to sites that have not yet been allocated or granted permission for housing, and most areas have at least a five-year supply (the average for our sample in 1987 was 6.5 years, or 4.5 years excluding allocations not yet granted permission).

Barlow & Chambers (1992) were much more cautious in their assessment, suggesting that the total number of affordable units resulting would not exceed 2000 per year in the immediate 5-year period. More recent research by Barlow (1993b) gives a more positive picture in some respects, with far more local authorities with policies and more schemes being negotiated, albeit smaller on average in size. In early 1993 there were 11125 affordable units identified in schemes in England, of which 60% followed the clarification of policy in May 1991 and 34% were under construction. This suggests an annual rate of output of about 3750 per year. This research also shows that the policies in practice fall considerably short of the pure form represented in our model. For example, in the recent sample only a third of authorities felt able to specify a target percentage, although more would doubtless do so if it were seen as more legitimate in the eyes of DoE. The most common arrangements involve land for social units at nil or agricultural value, but still involve some public subsidy. The use of cross-subsidy to provide schemes without any public subsidy seems to be less common.

One way of making the policy seem more positive overall would be simultaneously to release more land for housebuilding overall, as in the earlier scenarios. This in fact is the view that the House Builders Federation have put forward: that social housing requirements should have a corresponding additional land release. The earlier results in this article sound a caution here, in that the amount of extra land release, under the existing style of planning, would have to be considerably greater numerically than the number of social units.

7.5 Conclusions

In this chapter we have tackled some of the large policy issues in planning for housing. We have used our models of the housing market to conduct the sort of experiments that can rarely be carried out in practice, pushing policy as far as it can logically be pushed in particular directions to see what happens. Modelling techniques have also been used in a more exploratory way, to see what general patterns can be observed in the way local authorities set and implement planning policies for new housebuilding. At the same time we have referred, where appropriate, to the findings of other research using different approaches to the same issues.

Is it possible to measure planning policies in a meaningful way, and subject them to a process of quantitative modelling? Our answer to this question, in the British case, is "yes, up to a point". The British planning system is well established, comprehensive, professionalized and relatively well documented. Measures of aspects of policy, constraints and throughputs can be constructed and compared across localities for recent points in time, and some relationships established. Nevertheless, certain important aspects are more difficult to measure. Land use stocks and (at local level) changes can be costly to measure accurately, and on certain more discretionary policy zonings it is difficult to collect general data. The qualitative aspect of the general policy stance towards housing is also difficult to assess, and certain measures that are available are difficult to interpret (for example success rates of planning applications).

How responsive is planning to the market, or is it relatively autonomous? Planning policy targets are mainly autonomous, whereas the output of planning permissions shows some slight responsiveness to market demands. Neither is the supply of planning permissions strongly explained by planning policy, which reinforces the message that the 1980s-style British planning system suffered from an implementation gap. Firm constraints (e.g. green belts) have much clearer influence than discretionary policies. Overall, the patterns are more consistent with broader theoretical views about the nature of planning that predict autonomy, pluralist politics or bureaucratic process.

The greatest practical policy question is probably: what would happen if the planning system released much more land for housing? This study shows that the effect of large-scale land release would not be as great as expected, because of the implementation gap mentioned above. Output effects would be larger than price effects, but still on average only a quarter of the nominal release of land capacity. The benefits of this policy in terms of access to owner-occupation can only be described as modest. The price effects would be fairly uniform geographically, because local markets are very open, and for this reason the large land release strategy is unrewarding to individual local authorities. But the physical concentration of growth in certain districts would be heightened by this strategy, possibly increasing the pressure for new settlements and local controversies about large-scale developments.

The model suggests, overall, that it would make only a slight difference if the land released were green belt land where appropriate. The housing benefits of breaking into the green belt are marginal (2% more output, 1.2% lower prices). The greatest impact would be on the conurbation fringe in cases such as the West Midlands.

Are the effects of planning on prices more apparent in the long term? On the data collected for this study, it appears as though the long-run effects of planning on local prices are small. Simulations show fading effects of planning changes, whereas reduced-form equations for prices also show small effects of planning. Hard constraints such as green belt seem to have slightly more effect. These results are consistent with some other studies, although at variance with some interpretations of theory. Part of the reason for the small effect is the openness of local markets, which cause price effects to diffuse more widely, and part may be attributable to offsetting changes in density and other housing quality attributes.

This issue illustrates a general theme in policy analysis. Different policy goals often conflict and policy-makers have to choose between options that give more of one goal at the expense of less of another. In this instance the major goals in apparent conflict are the planning goals of containment and environmental conservation on the one hand, and housing policy goals of more output and lower prices on the other. Research and information cannot make the decisions for politicians, but they can highlight and even quantify the policy trade-offs. How much extra housing need can be met by sacrificing a given amount of containment? Our results suggest that the trade-off involved in releasing more land for general housing, through structure plans, is not very favourable and hence not very attractive politically.

This leads on to consideration of alternative policy options that target particular policy goals in a more direct or discriminating way than the blunt instrument of general land release. A highly topical example is the use of planning policies and agreements to secure affordable social housing on private housing sites. Our model can explore what might happen if planners attempted to make full use of their new ability to negotiate for target proportions of affordable social housing. These policies would lower output and raise prices slightly, diverting private into social output and reducing total output in high-price areas. But they would be inoperative in low-price (and low need) areas, where output would rise slightly with prices. These policies are worthwhile in terms of the net gain in social housing opportunities, and could be combined with greater land release scenarios.

These conclusions refer to the British planning system as it was operating in the 1980s. Its lack of implementation power can be linked to three key features: the generalized nature of structure plan targets, the growing importance of urban and windfall sites, and the fundamental fact that it is developers or landowners who initiate developments, whereas the local planning authority can only respond. The first of these features may be significantly different in the 1990s, because a system of universal, statutory, site-specific local plans is coming into being. Some practitioners have claimed that this will strengthen implementation, and our preliminary look at the effect of allocated land gave some support to this.

A relatively restrictive overall climate surrounding urban development is likely to remain, in this environmentally conscious era, although in a deep recession economic development arguments may at times override environmental considerations.

In the short term, lack of demand is manifestly the chief problem facing the housebuilding industry. In the longer term, the kind of problems highlighted by this study are likely to reassert themselves to some extent, although the social housing targets approach provides one new way forward. If it were felt important to go beyond the responsive mode, so that housing investment might operate more counter-cyclically and/or with a greater elasticity of supply during demand surges, then the long-standing issue of the role of the state in the ownership or bringing forward of development land might once again have to be considered. The taxation of development or development land might also be seen as an attractive option. Chapter 9 examines taxation, while the final chapter pulls together the broader threads of planning policy for the 1990s and beyond.

CHAPTER 8
Housing density and quality

8.1 Policy issues

In this chapter we relax the restrictive assumption of Chapters 6 and 7 that "a house is a house is a house". We recognize again that houses differ a great deal one from another, in a whole host of ways. Some houses are larger than others, some are more tightly packed together, some are better built and some are better equipped. Some dwellings of course are apartments in large blocks rather than single-family units. Most of us would say that some houses are a good deal more pleasant to look at than others, although we might well not all agree which are the most attractive aesthetically.

In the first part of the chapter, we review a wide variety of policy issues that relate in some way or other to the quality, as opposed to the number, of houses produced. The main emphasis is upon new housing and on policies that operate in some way through the planning system, or the related regulatory systems such as building control. However, some of these policies do have implications or effects in the existing stock.

We then home in on density as a particular but important aspect of quality, and analyze this more closely. This provides a direct link back to Chapter 2, where we outlined the economic theory of housing supply and showed how density was central to one strand of this theory. We report on the application of this approach to a representative British city, Bristol, in order to see how this aspect of the elasticity of supply measures up in comparison with the US literature. The approach can also be applied across cities, using the dataset underlying the model reported in Chapters 6 and 7. The last part of the chapter discusses the results of doing this, and relates these more generally to the influence of planning policies and to related issues such as housing mix.

Density and welfare

The urban economics literature reviewed earlier in this book emphasizes the fact that both market forces and planning intervention may have powerful effects on residential densities. How much does this matter? Does higher density significantly affect the quality of life of urban residents, individually or collectively? Economists such as Evans (1988, 1991) argue that, when planning restricts the supply of land for housing, it inevitably tends to raise densities and that this obliges households to consume less space (e.g. have smaller gardens) than they would prefer, which reduces their private welfare. Cheshire & Sheppard (1989) estimate that the magnitude of this reduction in space consumption in a tightly constrained city such as Reading would be very substantial, of the order of 60%.

Nevertheless, planning intervention may not always operate in this direction. In some circumstances the planning system may be used to place upper limits on density, as in much of the zoning characteristic of American suburbs (Monk et al. 1991: 17–19). Here, the economic criticism is that of inflexibility and the limiting of choice about space consumption (Harrison 1977). The social criticism is of the potential exclusion of certain lower income, demographic or ethnic groups from better quality housing and living environments within metropolitan areas (Downs 1973, Bogart 1993).

High density may have second-order effects on welfare through the external or public good aspects of having whole communities living at high densities. For example, there may be less public open space, a less attractive environment, more nuisance from bad neighbours or children playing, more crime and vandalism, and so forth. The general literature on the economics of urban size (Richardson 1973; Walker 1981: ch. 8) tends to assume that larger, denser cities generate a whole range of costs or disamenities for their residents. However, this perspective carries the dangers of confusing the coincidence of social problems and urban scale with causation, which raises complex questions, including what specific role residential density plays. It reflects a pervasive anti-urbanism that characterizes Anglo-Saxon attitudes to urban planning (Glass 1970). The traditional negative view of high density may be misplaced in certain circumstances (Verbrugge & Taylor 1980, Rosenberg 1982), as high density may be appropriate in parts of cities for certain groups. High density may create more social problems when it takes particular forms, in conjunction with patterns of occupancy. For example, high child density has been a focus of criticism in the past (Shankland et al. 1977) and again more recently (Page 1993), but this is as much an issue in the management and allocation of social rented housing as a planning issue.

In a useful recent study of larger new private housing estates Winter et al. (1993) draw attention to the increased density characteristic of recent developments and the contrasting evaluations of the resulting environments by planners and residents. They argue, interestingly, that higher densities have resulted from both deliberate planning policies (Best 1981) and pressures from developers reflecting market forces. Planners were critical of features of these new estates associated with their high density, including issues of garden size and appearance. Residents tended to display high overall satisfaction and choices to purchase had been more influenced by internal features, financial factors and location. However, they displayed considerable dissatisfaction with some specific features associated with density, including privacy, parking, landscaping and children's play facilities. The study suggested that developers had succeeded in producing designs and layouts that mitigated the general perception of crowding, partly under the influence of negotiations with planners, who had themselves been much influenced by the movement since the 1970s towards explicit design guidance.

There is no doubt that density is a sensitive planning policy issue in contemporary Britain. Complaints about "town cramming" have become commonplace, and mature suburban housing estates have become targets for infilling and extensions (Evans 1991, Whitehand & Larkham 1991, Gosling et al. 1993). But policy conveys mixed messages about whether higher densities are good or bad, as we explain further below.

Design and public policy

Planning as a discipline grew first out of architecture (and engineering), and only subsequently became more orientated to the social sciences (Hague 1993). Yet paradoxically it is probably true to say that planning control was less concerned about design in its earlier years (the 1950s and 1960s) than it has been since the 1970s. There was a definite reaction against the style of developments that characterized those post-war decades in Britain, both the large conventional suburban estates of semi-detached houses and the high-density schemes (residential and commercial) that typified the reconstruction of central and inner areas of cities. This was the period when urban conservation arose as a cause, when large-scale public sector redevelopment fell out of favour, and when overtly "modern" architectural styles found less favour than styles that attempted to recapture elements of past informal, vernacular styles. With private housing for owner-occupation becoming the predominant tenure, development control became the only significant channel of influence from public policy over housing design.

This is the context in which some local authorities sought to introduce more self-conscious policies about housing design, intended broadly to raise quality and in some cases to fit new housing in more harmoniously with the appearance of the existing fabric. The best known and most influential attempt of this kind was the *Essex design guide* but there were many other examples. Such policies were controversial when first developed and were not allowed to operate completely unchallenged by the DoE or the development industry. Nevertheless, they appear to have had a lasting impact on the layout, style and appearance of typical new private housing schemes in many areas (Winter et al. 1993). Part of the reason for this impact may be that the features the design guides were promoting were features of a kind that the market was moving towards favouring anyway: higher density, smaller schemes with more diversity, curving cul-de-sacs rather than straight grid roads, traditional materials (e.g. brick) and forms (e.g. pitched roofs). One could interpret some of these changes as part of broader cultural shifts from modernism to postmodernism, with a considerable harking back to tradition. Alternatively one could explain the changes in simpler terms as reactions against previous forms based on experience. Either way, the housing and local environments produced may well have been seen to generate higher sales and resale values and greater development profits, especially after allowing for density changes.

Some local authorities in areas noted for a distinctive urban heritage, for example the city of Bath and its neighbouring area of the Cotswolds, have attempted to apply much stricter controls on the design detail of new developments. For example, the materials used for external cladding may be specified as being in a particular stone or artificial equivalents. This could be seen as a more extreme form of the American practice of zoning. The aim is to ensure that an area retains its present overall character and appearance. In the example of Bath quoted above, this could be said to have been successfully achieved. It is likely that such requirements add to costs and reduce flexibility in many cases. On the other hand, they also create benefits which at least some people appear to value and which may be reflected in property values.

Although some of the attempts at design guidance in planning over the past 15 years may have blended well with market forces, this cannot be assumed always to be the case. In general, attempts to prescribe design forms and features through development control represent a considerable incursion into the realm of private ownership rights and market forces. There are obviously dangers of imposing costs on development (and hence on consumers), of imposing aesthetic judgements that many consumers do not share, and of stifling diversity and choice. How can such interventions be defended?

One defence may be the view that many developers and consumers of new housing do not have such well developed aesthetic sensitivity as the planners producing the design guides. This seems a very elitist and paternalistic view, and not in itself a justification for imposing costs on those developers and consumers. A better argument may be that some developers and consumers are unaware of the range of potential creative design solutions, tailored to local environments, that within the same budget might represent better, ultimately more valued, choices. This is an argument about educating providers and consumers and it may have more validity. Another line of argument may be that housing is very durable and that either (a) we have a duty to future generations to bequeath them a good quality stock or (b) standards and expectations will rise over time and we should aim above what is minimally acceptable now. Persuasive though this is, it assumes we can rank what is better than what, and if it costs more that we take a long enough view to justify incurring that cost now. Finally, of course, there is the "neighbourhood externality" argument introduced in Chapter 3. The external appearance of housing may be a key influence on the amenity enjoyed by nearby residents, and this effect may be reflected in house prices. The benefit is a market externality, in that it accrues mainly to people other than the new house-buyer. This implies that the design controls may be economically efficient (benefits outweigh costs) but that the policy has some redistributional effects, favouring existing residents relative to new buyers.

Is planning inflexible?

Planning may be open to criticism for being inflexible, not just about the number of houses to be built but about their type, quality, density, layout and other aspects. As argued in Chapter 3 and above, rigid planning norms on density could lead to loss of welfare as a result of people being forced to consume more or less space than they would prefer and possibly having to travel farther to workplaces and other urban services. Such norms could also reinforce the kind of bland uniformity of urban areas which was part of the basis for design intervention. Similar comments could apply to highly prescriptive policies on size and type mix, materials and standards, and other matters.

Our impression is that, overall, the current British planning system is less inflexible than it was in the past and less so than the systems in some other countries. Early post-war approaches to planning, perhaps influenced by engineering approaches, often applied fairly rigid numerical norms to density and related matters (e.g. open space). These appear to have fallen out of favour in the profession and in the guidance given by the DoE. More typical now are general statements of concern, with a great deal of discretion and negotiation about individual schemes in particular areas. Recent research on Hertfordshire and Cambridgeshire (areas of significant restraint and concern about environmental quality) showed that, while density was clearly an issue generating considerable tension between developers and the local authorities, this was resolved through negotiation and the policies were not expressed or applied rigidly (Jackson et al. 1994). These areas are similar to Berkshire, as described in Short et al. (1986). Our own work in Avon revealed a picture of density not being much of an issue between developers and planners (see Ch. 5).

The overall characteristic of the British system, that it emphasizes discretion rather than rigid rules, has been reiterated by other authorities (Grant 1992). This should be tempered by a recognition that the scope and coverage of the British legislation is more all-embracing than many other systems. In other words, developers can negotiate, but they may have to negotiate over many things.

This issue of flexibility may be associated with the housing market cycle. It has been suggested (see Ch. 5 and Lambert 1990) that the housebuilding industry has a tendency to move up-market in boom conditions and down-market in slump conditions. This implies that part of the supply response is a quality one in the broad sense, and that a flow-of-units measure of response understates the overall response in terms of value added or investment. This pattern of behaviour, if true, would also have implications for policies relating to affordability and need; the need for affordable or social housing might actually rise in booms, or be higher in boom areas. It assumes that demand for trading up, demand from high-income groups, and demand for housing as a luxury or investment good (as opposed to a necessity) are forms of demand that are more elastic and fluctuate more sharply with the cycle.

A partial test of this proposition can be undertaken using the cross-sectional data we have on the mix and value of new-build output, comparing high- and low-demand districts. In fact, it appears that the cross-sectional pattern is the opposite of what has just been suggested. The elasticity of supply in value terms is less than the elasticity in volume terms. In other words, high-price areas produce a less valuable product, assessed with reference to the price of a standard modern second-hand house. This is another way of looking at the "more means worse" phenomenon mentioned in Chapter 6. It is not evidence of planning inflexibility, but if anything evidence of a willingness to accommodate market adjustments to high land values. This evidence is cross-sectional, however, and the qualitative evidence in Chapter 5 suggests that the opposite tendency applies over time across the cycle. Furthermore, other elements of the cross-sectional evidence discussed later in this chapter do not support the view that the system is particularly flexible.

Table 8.4 towards the end of this chapter shows that changes in the type mix of new housing output over the past decade were broadly consistent with the hypothesis that developers shift up-market during booms. However, one countervailing tendency was the growing importance of flats, which are in part a response to high demand and land values. The movement of the price of new houses relative to the standardized price of all houses (Nationwide) shows a slight upward movement in the relative value of new houses between 1981 and 1988, but only by about 8%.

Size mix, demography and affordability

Traditionally, new housebuilding in both public and private sectors concentrated mainly on family-size housing. The assumption was that the priority need and the effective demand was for new housing of this type. Any demand for small units and small households was more likely to be met within the existing stock. This picture has now changed, both as a description of what is being built and as a perception of what is required. Local authorities built a good many small units intended primarily for housing elderly people in the 1970s and 1980s, and housing associations also built a high proportion of small units. Private developments became more diverse, and increasingly included proportions of units as small as one bedroom.

Demographic change has encouraged planners and developers to think more about the possible diversity of size and type requirements. The number of elderly people has grown considerably and the number of households headed by a person over retirement age is projected to grow from 5.5 to 6.2 million between 1991 and 2011. A further rise in the proportion of elderly people is expected in the early part of the twenty-first century, rising from just over 18% of the population in the 1990s to 26% by 2031 (Rolfe et al. 1993: 12, 19). Other changes have increased the apparent need for smaller dwellings (Ermisch 1990). Family formation is often deferred for some years, partly because of the greater workforce participation of women, which makes for more couple households. Relationships are breaking down more frequently, giving rise to more lone-parent and single adult households. More young people are leaving home before marriage (or the establishment of a relatively permanent relationship) and living singly or sharing with other young people. Figure 8.1 shows the household type structure in 1991 compared with that prevailing 20 years before. This shows that the changes just mentioned have been quite far-reaching.

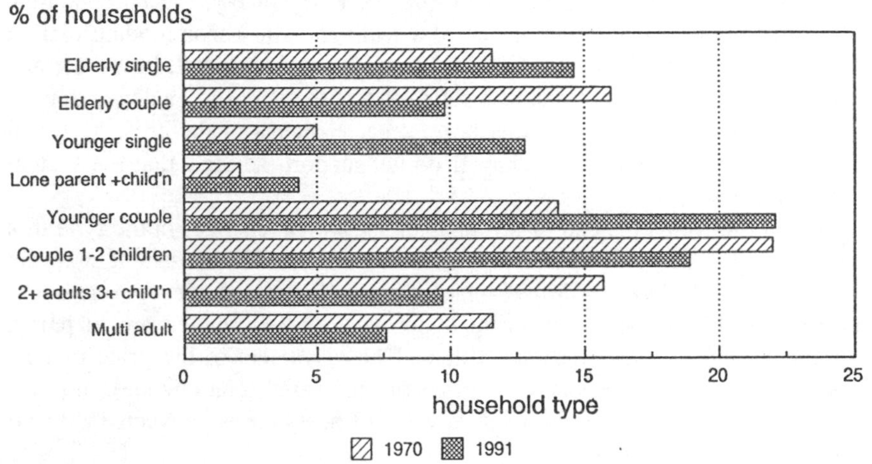

Figure 8.1 Household type in 1970 and 1991 (% of households).

Planners and housing providers would be mistaken to assume there is necessarily a direct relationship between some of these changes and housing size requirements. Life-styles and expectations change, with experience and higher incomes. Retired householders may wish to have one or two spare bedrooms to accommodate visiting relatives, whereas couples may want to provide not just for future children but for present study or homeworking space. Single buyers may wish to have the option of taking in a lodger, for financial and social reasons. These aspirations have to be tempered by considerations of cost, but the marginal cost of extra rooms is generally less than proportionate.

Housing policy and debate in Britain has become increasingly concerned about issues of "affordability". There are several reasons for this, some more valid and less ephemeral than others (Whitehead 1991, Bramley 1994). The way in which affordable social housing provision has come to occupy an important and legitimate place in the planning system was described in Chapter 4. The demographic trends just described provide one part of the explanation for growing concern about affordability. The reason is that many of the household types

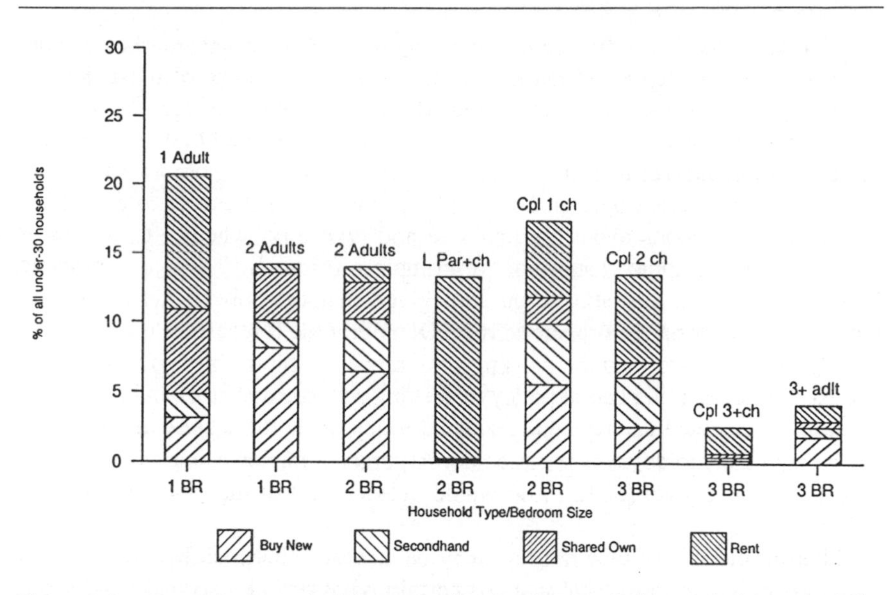

Figure 8.2 Access by household type, England, 1990 (% of all households under 30).

that are becoming increasingly common, for example single-person and lone-parent households, tend to have relatively low buying power in the market. At the same time, other groups (particularly couples with two earners) have considerable buying power. These differences are illustrated graphically by Figure 8.2, drawn from a detailed study of housing affordability in 1990 (Bramley 1991a). For each household type, very different proportions can afford to buy new, second-hand, or under a shared ownership arrangement.

These demographic changes are part of what underlay a widening of inequalities of income in Britain in the 1980s, although other factors such as higher unemployment played a part. Between 1979 and 1989 the bottom tenth of households saw their net incomes fall from 35% to 29% of the average; at the same time the top tenth increased their relative income by 24% (*Family Expenditure Survey*; see also Hills 1993).

The higher purchasing power of the households favoured by these trends may have both pushed up house prices in general and encouraged housebuilders to shift their product up-market. The most typical product of the late 1980s was the four-bedroom detached house; in earlier decades it was the three-bedroom semi. The 1980s house was also better equipped in terms of kitchen equipment, central heating and other features. At the same time, some housebuilders were also finding markets for smaller units, including flats and retirement homes. Recent official research in the South East confirmed that new private housing tended not to be purchased by moderate-income locals in housing need or buying for the first time, but that some of the demand from second-time buyers was for trading down as well as trading up (Forrest et al. 1993).

"Starter homes" for first-time buyers were developed and marketed quite extensively in the depressed market of the early 1980s. Some of these designs were criticized for low standards and high density, but others offered more scope for gradual enlargement. In the recession of 1989–92, some builders attempted to develop this market further.

The policy question here is, how far is it sensible for planners to attempt to intervene in decisions about housing size and type mix, whether to reflect or anticipate demographic change, or to promote affordability? It is questionable how far intervention should be pushed, given that developers themselves are increasingly offering a more varied mix. Demographic forecasting itself is not a wholly exact science, and the housing preferences of future households may be less easy to predict. A general policy of seeking a mixture of sizes and types may be more defensible than any rigid size mix policy or, at the other extreme, leaving it completely to developers to decide. Arguments for social and demographic mix at the estate level (Page 1993) would provide part of the rationale for such policies.

Altering the mix of new housing may be at best a marginal benefit in terms of affordability. In most local markets certain types of older second-hand property provide the main entry route to owner-occupation, and any new-build unit may prove to be more expensive or give poorer value in terms of space for the same price. For the majority of households excluded from owner-occupation by high prices, the appropriate solution is likely to involve rented housing, or perhaps an intermediate form of tenure such as shared ownership.

Energy standards and sustainability

Concern first arose in the 1970s about how far current patterns of living, consumption and production in Britain and other Western countries could be sustained in the longer term, allowing for finite resource supplies and the ecological consequences of human activity. At the end of the 1980s these environmental concerns became a major political issue and received official recognition in government policies (DoE 1990). A central part of this wave of concern has been a desire to limit the risk of global warming associated with wasteful and growing use of fossil fuels. This has been followed through in the form of recent planning policy guidance to local authorities, while the planning profession have in general taken up the theme of environmental sustainability with enthusiasm. Two specific issues affecting new housing are drawn out for discussion here: energy efficiency and insulation standards for new homes, and the interaction between planning for new housing and transport emissions.

The British housing stock in general exhibits rather low energy efficiency. This reflects past building practices, cheap fuel and a moderate climate (in comparison with northern European and Nordic countries where standards are much higher). *Ad hoc* improvements in the existing stock (e.g. loft insulation, double glazing) have been promoted through publicity campaigns and a scheme of small grants for insulation. For new housing, standards have risen somewhat, although Britain still lags behind continental leaders in this area. Housing associations have taken the issue particularly seriously because of a realization that fuel bills may be more critical for affordability than rents for low-income tenants.

How far should policy intervene in this area? It can be argued that the government should not impose prescriptive building regulations on issues such as this, but rather rely on market forces, aided perhaps by better information. Energy-saving features in homes do not just create a nebulous feel-good factor; they do save money in future fuel bills for the individual consumer. If buyers are aware of these future savings, they should pay more for the house that offers them, and this will mean that developers get their money back for including the energy-saving features in their products. This virtuous circle may work to some extent, but it does depend upon good, impartial information being generally available to consumers. It also depends upon an expectation that future energy costs will rise progressively in real terms, either because of depletion or because of environmental taxes. At the time of writing, a controversial imposition of VAT on fuel in Britain is having this effect. The market solution works less well for consumers who are cash or credit constrained. Marginal first-time buyers may be at the limit of what they can afford in terms of capital outlay, and may be forced to ignore future running costs when finding somewhere to live. Developers catering to this market may well compete by cutting standards to the minimum in several respects. There is a reasonable concern about the regressiveness of wholesale reliance on market processes as a mechanisms of energy-conservation policy.

As with other standards issues, it may be a great deal cheaper to design and install the desirable features at the new-build stage, rather than install them later in the life of the dwelling. If we (collectively, through the State) have good grounds for foreseeing a growing need to conserve energy, as is implicit in the government's recent white paper (DoE 1990), there is a case – on grounds of efficiency linked to information and foresight – for regulating to include these features in all new housing.

The relationship between planning and transport has always been recognized as important in a general sense, but official recognition that planning can help to reduce the amount of car travel and emissions has come rather belatedly. In the 1980s, car ownership and use grew rapidly, and the share of transport in total CO_2 emissions grew from 13% to 20% (Jones 1993). Government-sponsored research (DoE & DTP 1993) suggests measures that could help; the striking feature of these is the extent to which they represent a reversal of the *de facto* policies (or *laissez-faire* trends) of the 1980s: counter-urbanization, out-of-town shopping centres and business parks, car-dependent leisure facilities. The perspective of reducing car use leads to a more critical stance towards housing development in villages and small settlements, support for containment, higher residential densities in urban areas close to public transport or service nodes, and support for more mixed uses. Clearly, transport policies and planning policies for other uses, especially commercial uses, are very important, but housing plans can play a part. Overall, the research suggests that appropriate policies could reduce CO_2 emissions by 10–15% over 20–25 years.

Accessible lifetime housing

Another aspect of the design standards of new housing is the way it provides (or fails to provide) for people whose personal physical mobility is limited owing to age, disability, or ill health. In the past two decades, social housing providers did provide or adapt a few homes to facilitate use by people with mobility problems or wheelchair users. More recently, it has been argued that there is a good case for incorporating certain design features to aid mobility in all, or a high proportion of, new housing (Lewis 1992, Access Committee for England 1993). The argument is that:

(a) a surprisingly large proportion of households already contain a member with some degree of limiting long-term illness or disability (OPCS 1988)
(b) the population is ageing and more people may have to face this situation
(c) people with disabilities wish to lead a normal life, including the possibility of visiting friends and relatives
(d) policies of Care in the Community and individual preferences both point to "staying put" in their own home as the preferred option for most people when age and illness start to limit activities; furthermore, it is argued that the cost of incorporating a few simple design features (e.g. level access, and larger toilets and doorways) is not necessarily high at the new-build stage.

Again, the issue for policy is whether to go beyond promoting these principles as good practice and actually to require their incorporation in building regulations, or to include them within local planning policies but subject to negotiation. As with energy and other design standards, there is likely to be some cost involved, and some uncertainty about where this cost would fall. Suppose the desirable extra features cost £1000 per new house. Our model of new housebuilding output suggests that imposing such an extra cost on all new housebuilding would reduce output by 1.4% in the medium term, and raise prices by 0.65%, or about £312. These results suggest that nearly 70% of imposed costs of this sort would fall on the landowner or developer, and only just over 30% would fall on the consumer. This calculation does not allow for the imposed standard actually raising the value of the houses, which is likely to happen to some extent, although possibly less in this case than in the energy efficiency case discussed above.

As with size and type mix and affordability issues, there may be a better case here for the planning system seeking a proportion of new homes that meet accessibility standards rather than imposing a completely blanket requirement.

8.2 Density elasticity in one city

Role of density adjustment in theory

One method of expanding the supply of housing is through increasing the quality or the stock of housing capital on land already used for housing. As we saw in Chapter 2 this can take the form of building extensions, infill, converting attics into rooms, or demolition of whole blocks and replacing the former housing with higher-density stock. According to the theory examined in Chapter 2, this type of activity is likely to be stimulated by rising land prices. When land prices rise, owners and developers have an incentive to pack more housing capital onto a given land area. The ease with which this can be done is in part determined by the existing pattern of land use and the existing type of housing stock in an area, and partly by the planning regulations in force which limit the type and extent of conversions that may be made. We have already referred to the degree to which housing capital can be "substituted" for land, in response to an increase in the relative price of land, as the "elasticity" of substitution. The easier it is to make this substitution (the more elastic is the supply of housing on a given plot), the greater will be the response of developers and owners to increases in the relative price of land, which will be bid up in times of housing boom. Consequently, the elasticity of housing supply in response to price increases is closely linked to the elasticity of substitution between capital and land in any given housing area.

In this section we utilize this insight to develop a measure of the housing supply elasticity in the City of Bristol. To do this we carried out an empirical study of the relationship between housing density and land prices using primary data gathered from individual houses in the city based upon details supplied by local estate agents.

The purpose of the study was to estimate the elasticity of substitution between land and housing capital in the Bristol housing market. This elasticity can be measured as the coefficient relating relative amounts of housing capital used per unit of land to the relative price of land and housing capital (see Ch. 2 and Koenker 1972). As explained above, this elasticity shows how the density of housing varies as relative prices change.

The approach used was to estimate this relationship on a cross section basis. The advantage of using a cross section approach across a single-city housing market is that we can consider the unit price of housing capital to be the same for all housing units, since the forces of competition will equalize the return to capital within the housing area. On the other hand, we can expect to observe spatial variation in both density and land prices. Therefore, the parameter we wish to estimate can be uncovered by an empirically estimated relationship between density and land price per unit area.

Empirical study of Bristol

Data were assembled for a sample of 585 properties sold through 105 estate agents offices in the Bristol area in 1991, including detached, semi-detached and terraced housing across the city. Flats were not included owing to the greater difficulty of estimating their capital value. Unfortunately, their absence may impart a downward bias to the estimates of the elasticity of substitution. This is because these types of property are often created through conversion of family homes in response to the sort of changes in relative prices of capital and land, and their absence from the sample means that we are missing an important component of the changing structure of density in the city.

The density of housing for each property was calculated as the ratio of the gross internal floor area of each dwelling to the size of the plot on which the dwelling is situated. The plot size was determined from records in the city planning department. Table 8.1 shows that plot size is highest in the outer suburban areas such as the southern fringe (4354 sq. ft) and lowest in the inner-city areas such as the inner south (2042 sq. ft). As expected, the density (measured by plot ration, i.e. floor area over plot area) varied across areas, being highest in the inner city (in the inner north area it was 0.74) and lowest in the outer city areas (in the southern fringe it was only 0.36). Density also varied with the age of the dwelling, being highest among houses built before 1920 (0.63) and lowest for houses built between 1920 and 1945 (0.34) (as predicted in Ch. 3). It also varied across different types of property, being highest for terraced properties (0.61) and lowest for bungalows (0.23).

Table 8.1 Variations in density in Bristol travel-to-work area.

Sector	Plot size (sq. ft)	Density (plot ratio)
Inner north	2337	.74
Inner east	2267	.62
Inner south	2043	.58
Outer northwest	3373	.41
Outer northeast	2158	.56
Outer south	2464	.41
Kingswood Urban	2616	.43
North fringe	2781	.38
Southern fringe	4354	.36

The price of land was calculated as the residual difference between the selling price of the property and the reconstruction cost of the dwelling. This reconstruction cost was determined by a two-stage process. First, an estimate of the reconstruction cost was determined by using unit prices derived from the Building Cost Information Service (BCIS) of the Royal Institution of Chartered surveyors (RICS 1991). This provides estimates of the unit reconstruction costs for dwellings in £ per sq. ft based upon various discrete characteristics of the dwelling, such as the type of dwelling (detached, semi-detached, terraced) and its size (large, medium, small). Reconstruction costs for the newest types of dwellings were used to reflect contemporary cost of capital. The BCIS tables do not include flats among their property categories, and for this reason these types of dwelling were excluded from the survey. The total construction cost was then calculated as the product of the unit cost and the gross internal floor area.

The next stage was to smooth the data by running a regression of the estimated cost against actual characteristics of each dwelling in the sample, such as actual age and actual size. This gave a predicted reconstruction cost that effectively "filled in" the gaps in the BCIS table. The predicted land value was calculated as the residual of selling price minus predicted reconstruction cost. Finally, the predicted land price was calculated as the ratio of the predicted land value to plot size. Quite large differentials in the price of land emerged from this process, as shown in Table 8.2. For example the price of land was three times greater in the inner north of the city than in the northern fringe area.

Table 8.2 Rebuilding costs, house prices and land values in Bristol (£).

	Rebuild cost	Sale price	Land value	Land value per sq. ft
Inner north	62775	127433	64658	34.63
Inner east	53312	73340	20027	9.46
Inner south	40634	49885	9511	5.48
Outer northwest	52192	84772	32580	11.56
Outer northeast	40750	50109	9359	4.25
Outer south	40604	57390	16786	7.89
Kingswood Urban	44924	64139	19214	9.01
Northern fringe	47098	73168	26069	9.59
Southern fringe	51953	87523	35569	10.98

Notes: Values in cols 1–3 in £ per house; col. 4 land value in £ per sq. ft.

However, the pattern of land prices does not seem to follow the "concentric city" model of pure theory referred to in Chapter 3. Prices are relatively low in some inner-city areas such as the inner east and the inner south, and relatively high in the southern fringe and the outer northwest. To some extent these reflect features of the topography of the city (the inner south is separated from the city centre by the river Avon for example). But it also reflects demand patterns that arise from the linkage of local housing markets to the social class structure of various neighbourhoods in the city (the definition and characteristics of the nine sectors of Bristol used in Tables 8.1 and 8.2 are discussed in Bramley et al. 1990 19–22).

The final estimating equation related the log of density (plot ratio) to the log of predicted land prices using regression analysis as follows:

$$\text{LDENS} = -1.30 + 0.18\ \text{LPREDLP}$$
$$(23.27)\quad(7.30)$$

$r^2 = 0.09$; $F = 53.3$; $N = 526$

The regression analysis shows that the density of housing is positively related to the level of land prices. Judging by the high value of the t statistic ($t = 7.3$), the relationship is statistically highly significant. The estimated elasticity of substitution between housing capital and land is 0.18. It indicates that a 1% increase in land prices relative to the price of housing capital is associated with a 0.18% increase in density. This is rather low, certainly compared with estimates in the range 0.5 to 1.0 common in American studies.

From this, and the estimate for the ratio of housing capital values to land values (which is 1.98), we can also estimate the elasticity of supply of housing. This turns out to be around 0.35 (=1.98 - 0.18). On average, therefore, a price increase of 10% can be expected to result eventually in an increase in housing capital in the city (through an increase in density) of around 3.5%.

In principle, these cross-section results should reflect the long-run process of adjustment that takes place when capital stock is fully flexible, and after changes in the structure of relative prices within the city worked themselves through into changes in the structure of the stock of capital. In practice however, it is likely that there will inevitably be a mixture of more or less fully worked-out changes in structure. Over time, some dwellings will be undergoing conversion, and others will be in a stage where relative price changes are not yet great enough to warrant an act of new investment (see Ch. 3). The section of the housing stock where changes are most likely to be felt rapidly are those that have been more recently built. Changes to longstanding stock may be more difficult and costly to engineer. We therefore expect the elasticity of substitution to be greatest in dwellings of more recent construction.

This proposition can be tested by focusing attention on the subset of more recently constructed houses in the sample. In order to do this, we examine the relationship between density and price for the 72 houses built after 1980 for which complete data is available from the study. A simple regression of density against the unit price of land gives:

$$\text{LDENS} = -1.99 + 0.38\ \text{LPREDLP}$$
$$(8.06)\quad (4.15)$$
$$r^2 = 0.20;\ F = 17.23;\ N = 72$$

This result shows that the elasticity of substitution for new housing is 0.38, over twice as high as for the sample as a whole (and again the relationship is statistically significant at the 1% level of confidence). Nevertheless, although the elasticity of substitution is higher for new-build houses, this does not establish that there is any difference in the housing supply elasticity. To calculate this we also need to take into account the ratio of factor shares for these dwellings. Land values are on average greater for new dwellings than for older dwellings, mainly because newer dwellings in the suburbs tend to have larger plot sizes than older dwellings in the inner city (see Table 8.1). In the sample as a whole, the average land value was £23776, whereas for the subset of newer dwellings it was £34587. Correspondingly, the ratio of factor shares (capital value divided by land value) was lower for new dwellings at 1.40, compared to a ratio of 1.98 for the sample as a whole. However, even accounting for higher average land shares, the implied elasticity of housing supply for these newer dwellings is still greater than for the whole sample. For new dwellings the supply elasticity turns out to be 0.53 ($=1.40 \times 0.38$), compared to a value of 0.35 for the sample as a whole. As expected, this indicates that for new-build housing the supply response to price changes is actually more elastic than in older more established existing housing stock.

Nevertheless, whether we look at newer housing or the housing stock as a whole, the most important point to emerge from this examination of the density adjustment process within one British city is that the elasticity of supply is very low. Chapter 2 quoted mainly American studies which suggested that long-run elasticities could be expected to be of the order of 5–10. This new evidence confirms our hunch that, in typical British conditions, supply adjustment through intensification of land use is relatively limited. The specific results just quoted probably do somewhat exaggerate the extent of this inelasticity, because of the exclusion of flats from the sample. In addition, Bristol may be a city that shows lower flexibility, because of its large stock of older housing, topographical limits on development and, in recent years, fairly restrictive planning and conservation policies. These qualifications are only partly borne out in the next section, though, where we undertake a roughly parallel exercise looking across different districts.

8.3 Density and mix variations across the country

Density data

The data we have available to us to explore density variations and relationships across the districts in our inter-urban sample are limited in scope and reliability. We have a single estimate of density in housing units per hectare for prospective new housing sites, derived from planning land availability monitoring returns of variable accuracy. The DoE (1991a) study of *Rates of urbanization* provides some data on implicit gross residential density at county level. This is used as a check on the planning data, both to fill in missing values and to scale the results, county-by-county, for consistency. The NHBC data give us a type mix breakdown for completions in one year (1988), and a corresponding set of average prices for the same year. It is possible to compute some indicators from these data, but their limitations should be obvious.

Elasticity of substitution

Chapter 2 explained the theoretical background to the argument that the response of density to price is one of the main ways in which supply adjusts to demand in the long run. The §8.2 applied this model within one city, to both new and existing housing stock. We are able to use the data described just above to extend our

British application of the model to the inter-urban scale. This model provides an indirect estimate of supply elasticity based on the key parameter of the elasticity of substitution between land and construction inputs. This elasticity is defined as the proportional change in the land:construction ratio resulting from a unit proportional change in the ratio of the price of these inputs. We use the "standard new house" defined earlier for the purposes of standardizing prices and estimating construction cost, which this time varies between different locations. We are assuming that the average house in each district corresponds in size to the standard house. This model gives a good fit (the r^2 of 0.85 cannot be compared with the model in the previous section, which refers to individual houses). The elasticity of substitution is 0.25. Fitting an alternative version of the function, using quantity rather than value ratios, gives a poorer fit but a slightly higher value for the elasticity of substitution of 0.30.

These values are higher than the Bristol estimate for all housing, but lower than the figure of 0.38 for new housing in Bristol. These are again very low values compared with figures from American studies, which tended to be in the range 0.5 to 1.0. Errors in some of the underlying data (especially density) might impart some bias, but probably not of this magnitude. They imply low values for the elasticity of supply even in the long term. The magnitude of this elasticity will vary (inversely) with the relative share of land, but an average value for our dataset might be 0.4–0.5. This is the same sort of result as we found within Bristol. The inter-district dataset may be more biased by the very high land values prevalent in 1988; under more typical conditions the land value share would be less and the supply elasticity rather more.

Even making some allowance for new land brought into housing use, using the model described in Chapter 6, this implies a relatively low overall supply response even in the long run, probably under 2.0. This is much lower than the figures discussed in Chapter 2.

The density elasticity is lower than in the American studies partly because British residential densities are much higher than those in most American cities. It is easier to boost the density of the very low-density American suburbs than the typical British suburb. This situation is arguably at least in part a consequence of the general planning policy of containment. Even making allowance for this factor, the low propensity of density to adjust with market prices suggests that the British system is more inflexible than the American. It suggests that the planning process in Britain does have the effect of restricting variations in density. From our earlier discussion of this issue, we observed that British planning had moved away from rigid density norms in favour of more discretionary negotiation. However, we must conclude from these findings that the system as a whole does appear to inhibit the classic form of flexibility, namely varying density with land prices.

Planning policy and density

The model we have just applied is solely concerned with the relationship between prices and density. Can we use our inter-urban data to identify systematic statistical relationships between density and other factors, particularly varying local planning policies and constraints? Table 8.3 presents the results of applying a general regression model, rather similar to the models used for supply in Chapter 6, to the task of explaining variations in the density of new housing development between districts. The model is intended to be a general exploration of the range of factors associated with density, rather than a highly specified theoretical model, unlike that described above. We therefore just use a linear form of model including the range of variables that we would expect to have some influence. We compare the application of the model to the whole sample with the results of applying it separately to two subsamples: districts with more and less restrictive planning policies (based on the subjective dummy variable PPD2). The rationale here is that different processes may operate in these different environments; for example, we might expect prices to have more effect where planning was weaker.

Table 8.3 Regression models for density of new private housing by district in 1986-8, distinguishing more and less restrictive planning policies (dependent variable: dwellings per hectare).

Explanatory variables	(1) Whole sample model	(2) More restrictive	(3) Less restrictive	(4) Reduced
Constant	5.56	49.6	42.4	19.42
	(2.9)	(2.2)	(2.3)	(13.5)
Demand factors				
G7LN dist London	−4.17	−5.68	−5.47	
	(−2.0)	(−1.8)	(−1.9)	
Z3 high soc class	−0.095	−0.268	.138	
	(−0.7)	(−1.3)	(0.8)	
PCS8 price/profit	.011	−.010	.05	0.207
	(0.1)	(−0.1)	(0.5)	(2.5)
Policy & supply factors				
DW ward density	0.54	0.567	0.195	−3.93
	(5.0)	(3.7)	(1.3)	(−2.7)
CONST1 lack of constraints	5.56	3.79	0.65	−2.99
	(2.9)	(1.2)	(0.6)	(−1.8)
PPS1 planning policy	−4.78	−4.51	−4.78	4.82
	(−3.3)	(−1.4)	(−2.0)	(2.0)
POL3 Labour council	2.29	1.38	5.67	
	(1.1)	(0.4)	(2.4)	
Adjusted r-squared	0.508	0.619	0.199	0.243
F	14.1	11.0	2.6	8.1
N	89	43	45	89

Some of the effects in this model are as one would expect. Densities fall with distance from London and are lower in areas of high social class (although this effect is of marginal statistical significance). Densities tend to reflect the existing density of the adjacent urban areas, giving a significant positive relationship with the ward density indicator (DW).

The effect of price is generally very weak and insignificant in the extended models, once allowance is made for other influences. Price is expressed here as development profit or land value (PCS8), for consistency with the supply models and general urban economic theory. This finding is surprising. There is a partial explanation for it in the fact that price/profit is correlated with other spatial and demand-side variables included in the model. Excluding these correlated variables in the reduced model (column 4) suggests that price may have the positive effect predicted in theory, although we cannot fully separate this from the spatial influences, some of which may be mediated through planning policy. The coefficient of 0.207 on price in this reduced model implies that a 10% price rise (just over £5000) would increase the density of new-build by just over one dwelling per hectare, or 4.6% on average. Given the doubt about how much of this could be interpreted as a price response, this reinforces the conclusions of the preceding analysis, namely that in the British system the responsiveness of density to price is weak.

Planning policies appear to have a consistent effect in the way one would expect. More positive, less restrictive planning policies (measured by PPS1) tend to be associated with lower densities. One standard deviation of policy difference would lower densities by 4.7 dwellings per hectare, whereas the difference between the most and least restrictive district would be associated with a difference of 11 dwellings per hectare, about 30% of the mean value. The effects of planning policy are also seen by the comparison between the results in columns 2 and 3 of the table. Density variations are more predictable in the restrictive areas, although it is interesting to note that the policy variable is not less significant in the less restrictive subsample. The effect of policies is about one-third weaker in the reduced model, but still significant.

The constraints variable seems on the face of it to have the "wrong" effect in some models; areas with less severe constraints on land supply have higher densities. This effect appears in the overall model and for more restrictive policy areas, but disappears in the areas with less restrictive policies, and reverses in the reduced model. Model 3 gives a clue that this variable may be suggesting that, in areas with tight constraints (including green belt), councils may tend to try to apply upper density limits more rigorously. Model 4 shows a reversed effect because existing ward density now operates through this composite indicator.

The inclusion of a political control dummy variable (POL3) in alternative model forms sheds some further light on local variations in density policies. In general, Labour councils are associated with higher densities of new building, other things being equal, whereas Conservative councils tend in the other direction. The effect is consistent in direction, and statistically significant in two of the four models shown. Why might this political effect occur? Labour councils may be more concerned with maximizing housing output and development generally, and with issues of affordability. Conservative councils are probably more concerned with protecting suburban residential amenities, resisting town cramming, and applying an element of what the Americans would term exclusionary zoning.

In this section we have used a rather blunt instrument to measure some broad influences on residential densities. Planning may affect density both through broad policies on the amount of land released and through specific density policies in development plans and development control practice. Our statistical approach is mainly geared to identifying the first kind of effect. We do not have systematic data from our sample on any specific density policies applied. On the whole, one needs to look at case studies in more depth to clarify the nature of such policies. We commented on some case study evidence earlier in this chapter and in Chapter 4, observing that in general such policies tend to have moved away from rigid quantified norms. Nevertheless, the statistical work hints at some of the kinds of effects at work. In particular, it suggests that, while in general releasing more land is associated with lower densities, in some cases very restrictive overall policies may be combined with attempts to keep densities down.

Type mix and density

The proportions of output in certain house types may be taken as indicators of quality. Detached houses (including bungalows) indicate higher-quality, or more up-market, housing; flats (including maisonettes) indicate lower-quality or more down-market housing.

Density is in part a direct function of the mix of house types, although the causality can run either way. We examined the NHBC data on mix and its relationship with density. Rather less than half of the variance in density could be accounted for by type mix, but this may be exaggerated by errors or lumpiness in the density data. There is a particularly strong relationship between the density in dwellings per hectare and the proportion of flats in new private output.

Table 8.4 shows the proportion of three common types in three years at different points of the housing market cycle, and Table 8.5 shows the composition of 1988 completions by county for our sample. Flats have become quite common within the overall mix of private housebuilding output, especially in the South East as well as London. At the same time, the detached house became the most common form of new private output, particularly in the boom period of the 1980s. Evans (1991) comments on the way developers have evolved design and layout features to combine "linked detached" houses with high density.

Table 8.4 partially confirms the tendency of the output mix to move up market during the boom (1982–8) and down market during the recession (1988–92). This tendency accounts for the swings between semi-detached and terraced houses, as the down-market examples, and detached houses as the up-market

Table 8.4 House type mix over the 1980s (percent of starts in England).

Year	Detached house	Semi-detached house	Terraced house	Flat/maisonette
1982	27	21	22	17
1988	37	12	15	24
1992	30	20	24	21

Source: NHBC *Private housebuilding statistics*

Table 8.5 House type mix by county in 1988 (percent of completions).

County	Detached house	Terraced house	Flat/maisonette
South East			
Berkshire	41	20	31
Hampshire	40	22	28
Oxfordshire	36	21	25
South West			
Avon	45	18	22
Dorset	44	18	28
Gloucestershire	39	28	16
Somerset	45	21	13
Wiltshire	47	20	13
West Midlands			
Hereford & Worcester	54	20	12
Shropshire	63	11	8
Staffordshire	85	4	3
Warwickshire	58	11	11
West Midlands	57	8	13

Source: NHBC data supplied to the authors of this book.

examples. However, the proportion of flats does not fit this pattern, if we take flats to represent a down-market (lower-quality) form. Rather, the data suggest a secular upward trend in the share of flats, with a tendency for flats to become more important in the boom. The secular trend could be accounted for by (a) demographic change, smaller households and the emergence of the trade-down market for older households, together with (b) any long-term tendency for land to become scarcer (Evans 1988a,b). The cyclical effect could reflect the land-price density effect in operation together perhaps with the fact that in 1988 output boomed most in the South East, where flats have become a more common form.

Flats formed nearly a third of output in Berkshire in 1988, compared with only 3% in Staffordshire. This contrast suggests that land scarcity and price are indeed a key factor in accounting for variations in the share of flats. The proportion remains fairly low in most rural counties. There is a strikingly high share of detached houses in the new output in Staffordshire. This county represents those areas of the country where the economy is less strong, demand and prices are low, and where there is a substantial and cheap second-hand supply of terraced houses. In this situation, new building may be catering more for a trading-up demand.

8.4 Conclusions

In this chapter we have considered aspects of the quality of the housing produced by the housebuilding industry and the extent to which these are or should be matters for planning policy or intervention. Many of these issues affect or revolve around density, which itself plays a key role in urban economics and the theory of housing supply. Other issues tend to raise questions of cost, for example design standards, energy and accessibility. We can refer to our models to comment on the market impacts of imposing costs through planning or regulation.

Density clearly is important and the British planning system undoubtedly does have major impacts on residential densities. We caution against simplistic judgements about the adverse welfare effects of high density, and note that concern about sustainability and transport emissions provide a further rationale for urban containment. Developers, in conjunction with the planning system, have produced layouts and designs that seem to make moderately high densities quite acceptable for many consumers. Part of the context for this is a market in which the type of housing being sought and built is becoming more diverse.

The effects of the planning system on density may be divided into at least two parts. First, there is the effect of restraining the overall release of land for housing development, which inevitably tends through the market process to lead to higher densities. Secondly, there are more specific policies for density that are applied in local development plans and development control decisions. Here the effect might be to put ceilings on developers' options in some cases, and floors in others, and there may be considerable local variation. Our impression is that such policies are nowadays relatively flexible and negotiated, and are rarely applied as rigid numerical norms. Nevertheless, we believe that such policies do still operate, in different directions according to the local context, including political predisposition. Thus, in some cases policy may encourage town cramming, whereas in other cases it may seek to defend low-density suburban environments.

Overall, we believe the existence of the planning system must restrict the extent to which development can respond flexibly to market forces. We have demonstrated a low elasticity of density response to prices statistically, both within one major city and across the country. We have also demonstrated a general relationship of density to broad planning policies. If the housing environments produced are broadly what people want, then this may not be a bad price to pay for local democratic control over the process of land development.

CHAPTER 9

Taxes, subsidies and the housing market

9.1 Introduction

Planning is probably the most important way in which government policies affect the private housing market in Britain. However, governments can affect markets through a wide variety of different policy instruments. Broadly speaking, these fall into the classes of regulatory interventions (legal rules), fiscal interventions (taxes and subsidies), and direct State participation in the provision of goods and services (Le Grand et al. 1992). Governments employ elements of all of these strategies of intervention in the case of housing, although the recent trend has been to reduce direct government involvement in provision. Planning falls broadly into the first class of policy instrument, the regulatory. With the moves towards privatization in the 1980s, regulation has become a more important issue in general. In housing, however, the regulation represented by the planning system, together with building control and environmental health, was already well established. In this chapter, we turn our attention to the second class of intervention, the fiscal, which is also a very important way in which government policies may affect the housing market.

Taxes and subsidies may affect housing both in ways that are deliberate and clearly related to housing policy goals, and indirectly in ways that are not necessarily intended, as a by-product of other policies. In this chapter we will consider examples of both of these effects. Mortgage interest tax relief (MITR) is a major form of general subsidy to house-buyers, motivated in part by the government's goal of promoting wider home ownership. Local property taxes, such as the former British Domestic Rating system and the new Council Tax, are taxes intended to finance local authorities and the local public services they provide. The fact that changes in these taxes might impact on the housing market is an incidental by-product of the fact that they are levied, mainly for reasons of practicality, on domestic property.

The effects of taxes and subsidies are not ultimately independent of the planning system. As we go on to explain in the next section, the effect of a tax or a subsidy on a particular commodity depends among other things on the way that the supply of and demand for that commodity change in response. Earlier in this book we have shown both theoretically and empirically how planning can modify this supply response. As was mentioned in Chapter 1, we initially became involved in the research projects around which this book is based through a concern with trying to assess the impact and incidence of the housing finance system in Britain.

Planning has a more intimate relationship with aspects of taxation than even the rather general statement above would suggest. From the outset of the modern British town and country planning system in the 1940s, it was recognized that planning was inextricably linked with questions about "betterment" and "compensation". This is because it was clear that planning directly and indirectly had major impacts on land values, enabling some landowners to make spectacular gains whereas others might make unexpected losses. Since planned development also generated considerable public costs for infrastructure provision, there was perceived to be a strong case for applying special forms of tax to development gains. Yet three general legislative attempts at applying specific measures to deal with this issue (in 1947, 1967 and 1976) all failed, for a combination of administrative and political reasons. Although uniform, top-down legislation has failed, gradually from the bottom up, a partial and very variegated solution to this problem has emerged. It is the planning agreement (or obligation), which we have already discussed in earlier chapters. It is a typically British instrument, emphasizing negotiation and discretion. But there should be no mistake about its function: it is to use the lever of planning permission to obtain from developers contributions in cash or kind to the provision of infrastructure and local beneficial amenities for communities. In the last part of this chapter we discuss planning agreements from this point of view, and compare them with the alternatives as a mechanism for funding infrastructure and local services. For a discussion of this issue in an American context, see the colourfully entitled *Windfalls for wipeouts* by Hagman & Misczynski (1978).

9.2 Economic theory and the incidence of taxes and subsidies

In this section we briefly summarize the standard economics textbook analysis of the impact of a tax or subsidy on a specific commodity, and go on to develop some particular implications for housing. It should be emphasized that we are considering here *specific* taxes or subsidies and their effect on one specific market, housing, rather than general changes in overall tax rates (e.g. VAT, income tax) and their overall effects on the state of the economy. In other words, we are looking at the *microeconomic* rather than the macroeconomic effects. This is not to belittle the importance of macroeconomic (i.e. whole-economy) effects of changes in the housing market, or vice versa. We also touch on these later, particularly when discussing mortgage tax relief.

Figure 9.1 encapsulates the standard analysis in the familiar framework of a demand and supply diagram (this presentation builds on the very helpful analysis in Ermisch 1984). The horizontal axis measures the quantity of housing demanded or supplied; the vertical axis measures the price of housing per unit. The vertical axis can also be interpreted as the "marginal value" of housing per unit (see Le Grand et al. 1992: 29–32). So the demand curve D_0 shows the quantity of housing (Q) that people are willing to buy without a subsidy at different prices (P); at the same time and equivalently, it can be interpreted as a measure of the marginal value of an extra unit of housing consumption. In a free market system people will consume just that quantity of housing (Q_0) at which the marginal value to them equals the price they have to pay (P_0). If the market is functioning correctly (technically if it is in "equilibrium"), this quantity will equate to the quantity of housing that suppliers are willing to provide. While the marginal buyer values her house at an amount equal to the price, other (non-marginal) buyers value their homes at more than they have to pay, in the sense that (according to the demand curve) they would have been willing to pay more. This difference is known as the "consumers' surplus" and it can be measured by the sum of all the vertical distances between the D_0 line (between E and K) and the horizontal line FE, that is by the area of the triangle KEF.

What happens if we introduce a subsidy to help housing consumers? Basically, this has the effect of lifting the demand curve upwards, from D_0 to D_1, because the subsidy is augmenting the spending power of consumers. The amount of the subsidy per unit is measured by the distance CI, which is equivalent to P_1s, the new price times the rate of subsidy. Consumers now pay a net

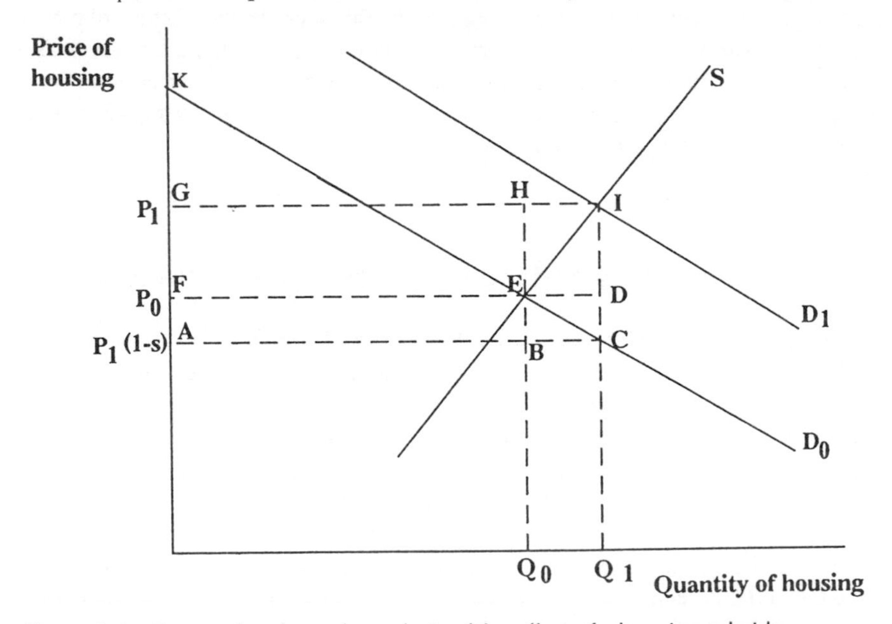

Figure 9.1 Demand and supply analysis of the effect of a housing subsidy.

price of P_1.(1–s), which is less than the old price of P_0. However, the new actual market price (P_1) is higher than the old price. Price rises when demand is shifted upwards so long as the supply curve (S) is upward sloping. In other words, unless supply is completely elastic, a subsidy will raise prices. From all of the discussion earlier in this book, we may safely assume that housing supply is not completely elastic. Therefore, the general pattern illustrated in Figure 9.1 applies.

What about a specific tax on housing? This will have an analogous but opposite effect. The effective demand for housing will fall, and actual prices will fall, but consumers will have to pay more including the tax.

Figure 9.1 can be used to identify the main gains and losses to different groups in society from the subsidy. First, *existing housing consumers* gain from a reduction in their housing costs. This effect is measured by the area AFEB, the quantity consumed times the cost saving per unit. Secondly, *new marginal consumers* are enabled to consume some housing which they previously could not. This is measured by the smaller triangular area BEC, corresponding to the increase in consumption from Q_0 to Q_1. (If we were discussing a tax, this would be a negative benefit associated with marginal consumers priced out). Thirdly, the *producers* of extra housing (landlords, builders) obtain a so-called "producers' surplus" in the form of development profits or rents, measured by the area EDI. Fourthly, the *owners* of existing housing (who might be landlords or owner-occupiers) gain an amount equal to FGHE. These are all benefits, but in economics there is rarely a free lunch and we have to consider also the costs of the subsidy to *taxpayers*. The cash cost of the subsidy is measured by the rectangular area AGIC, namely the subsidy per unit (s.P_1) times the quantity of housing consumed (Q_1). There may be an additional cost to the economy, allowing for the effects of the extra taxation needed to finance the subsidy, but we do not consider this here.

There are several points that emerge from this analysis which are worth drawing out more explicitly. First, the analysis suggests that the overall cost of the subsidy exceeds the sum of its benefits. The difference (loss) is measured in Figure 9.1 by the triangle EIC. Another way of putting this is to say that the subsidy is *economically inefficient*, or incurs a "deadweight loss". This is a standard result in economics, which relates to any subsidy to a specific commodity (Culyer 1980, Le Grand et al.1992). The argument is that the subsidy "distorts" consumer decisions away from what they would have chosen and that this is a less than optimal policy. General housing subsidies have attracted considerable criticism over the past two decades for distorting consumption and investment decisions in favour of housing, and this is really another way of making the same point. This of course assumes that there are no other policy reasons for giving a subsidy, for example to correct for externalities or to deal with distributional issues (see below).

The subsidy has *distributional* as well as efficiency effects. Distributional effects are concerned with who benefits and who loses from the subsidy, and may be judged against general criteria of equity or fairness (Le Grand et al.

1992). The analysis in Figure 9.1 identifies five distinct, although possibly overlapping, groups: existing and new consumers, existing owners, new providers, and the taxpayer. It suggests that all the specific housing groups gain at the expense of the general taxpayer, but that some groups gain more than others. In particular, existing owners of housing make a large gain, whereas marginal new consumers make quite a small gain. This perspective may modify the perceptions of those involved in the policy process, who might have believed that the main purpose of the subsidy was to help new consumers. Once allowance is made for tenure differences, the distributional effects may be even more dramatic. For example, if the subsidy is given to owner-occupiers but not private tenants, the private tenants will be much worse off because they will be paying the higher rents (relating to the new price P_1) while their landlords enjoy the benefit. Even if the rents of social tenants do not change with market prices, they will have to pay for the owner-occupier subsidy through their taxes.

Inelastic supply

Figure 9.2 shows the effect on the analysis of assuming that housing supply is highly inelastic. This may be a more realistic case, particularly for Britain and in the short to medium term. It is also indicative of some of the impact of a relatively tight planning system. Inelastic supply is represented by a steeply upward-sloping supply curve *S*. In this situation it is clear that most of the effect of the enhanced demand created by the subsidy goes into higher house prices (and market rents), and relatively little goes into higher housing production and consumption.

Is this good news or bad news? Paradoxically, it is good news in one sense. The economic efficiency or deadweight loss effect is proportionately smaller, shown by the compressed triangle to the right of the supply and demand lines. In other words, if supply does not respond very much, then the subsidy does not create much distortion of real economic activity into the housing sector. However, if there were other policy reasons for having a subsidy, such as external or social benefits that justified more housing consumption (see below), then the subsidy will clearly have failed. Looking at the distributional effects, the news looks pretty bad. The main gainers are existing owners of housing property, landlords and established owner-occupiers. On the whole we would assume that these people are among the better off in society. Housing consumers make a relatively small gain, because the subsidy is almost completely wiped out by higher prices. The gain for marginal new consumers is negligible. Thus, for example, if supply is inelastic we would expect general subsidies such as mortgage tax relief to be of little benefit to marginal first-time buyers.

The underlying assumptions made about supply and demand elasticities can have important implications for the analysis of housing finance policies. American studies tend for example to assume that supply is very elastic, whereas some

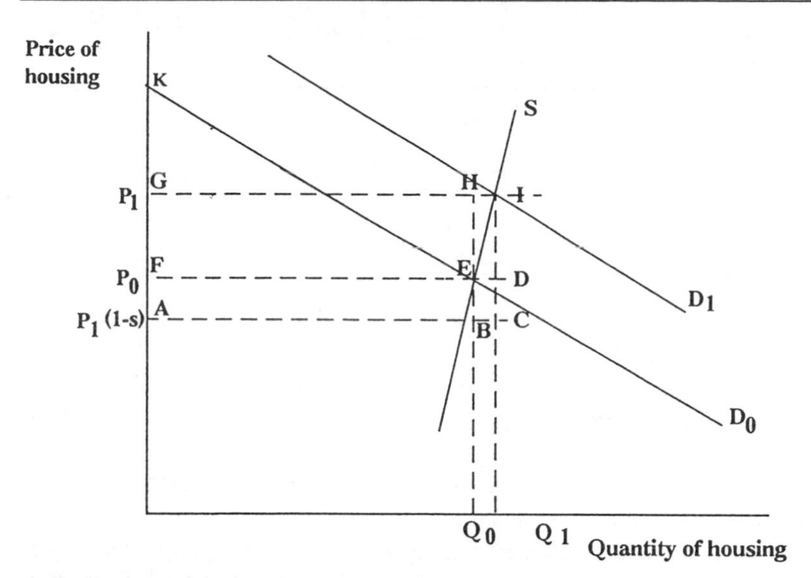

Figure 9.2 Demand and supply analysis of the effect of a housing subsidy with inelastic supply.

British studies of the effects of subsidies assume that supply is completely inelastic. For example, as White & White (1977) have shown, the assumption of an infinitely elastic supply of housing services led both Laidler (1969) and Aaron (1972) to overestimate the deadweight loss effect of income tax subsidies to owner-occupation and to underestimate the transfer loss to renters attributable to the induced increase in the price of housing services that they purchase (since the mortgage interest tax relief subsidy is available only to mortgaged owner-occupiers). White & White refer to the latter effect as the renters' distributional loss (RDL). It works in the opposite direction to the gross deadweight loss effect, since an increase in the price of housing services redistributes welfare away from renters (and new owner-occupiers) towards existing owner-occupiers.

The extent of these welfare changes depends crucially upon the magnitude of the supply elasticity of housing services. White & White provide estimates of the changing effects from a $10bn subsidy programme in the USA for various values for the elasticity. These estimates are shown in Table 9.1, which assumes a (rather high) value of –1.5 for the demand elasticity. They show that deadweight losses fall but renters' distributional losses rise as the supply elasticity falls.

Benefit incidence and income

A related area of policy analysis is provided by the use of household level survey data to provide estimates of the distribution of welfare gains and losses across the income distribution associated with specified changes to the housing subsidy

Table 9.1 Deadweight and distributional losses for different supply elasticities ($billion).

Supply elasticity	Gross deadweight loss	Renters' distributional loss
infinity	1.11	1.29
2.0	0.80	1.29
1.0	0.68	1.74
0.5	0.58	2.15
0.0	0.30	2.82

Source: White & White (1977).

regime. The result of this type of study is again crucially dependent on the assumptions made concerning the supply elasticity for housing services; and there has been little agreement on the appropriate values to choose. For example, King (1983a) in his study of the effects of the abolition of mortgage income tax relief assumes a perfectly elastic supply, whereas Brownstone et al. (1988) assume a completely inelastic supply elasticity in their study of the effects of the recent Swedish tax reform. In the absence of firm support to back up any particular value, King (1983b) seems wise to make separate calculations for a variety of assumed values for the elasticity.

The different forms of subsidy used for different tenure groups in Britain show very different distributional patterns by income. Figure 9.3 shows the patterns in the Bristol area (which is fairly typical of England as a whole) for owner-occupiers and council tenants, using two different definitions of subsidy, (a) a cash flow measure including MITR and Housing Benefit (HB), and (b) an economic measure including differences between actual and market rents and the non-taxation of investment returns from housing (similar analyses are to be found in Hills 1991, Nicholson & Willis 1991, Hancock & Munro 1992, Walker & Marsh 1993). It should be stressed that these patterns reflect the "initial incidence" of the subsidies, before any adjustments in supply, demand and prices. The pattern is very striking. Low-income groups can receive a high level of subsidy in rented housing through the HB system, but this subsidy is withdrawn very rapidly as incomes rise above the minimum. As incomes rise, it quickly becomes more favourable to be an owner, and the advantage of owning rises with income. (Changes since 1989 have slightly lessened the advantage of higher income mortgagors, but further reduced the general element of subsidy to council tenants.)

The tendency of subsidies to affect house prices rather than housing output or consumption is sometimes referred to as "capitalization" – the subsidy is capitalized into the house price. O'Sullivan (1984) speculates about the possible effect that differential capitalization rates for different subsectors of the housing market might have for our conclusions about the ultimate distributional impact of housing subsidies. His argument is that higher-income consumers tend to have more elastic demand, so that they respond more to a subsidy, and to operate in parts of the housing market where supply is more elastic, i.e. on the edge of the city rather than in the inner city. Thus, for higher-income groups the subsidy is

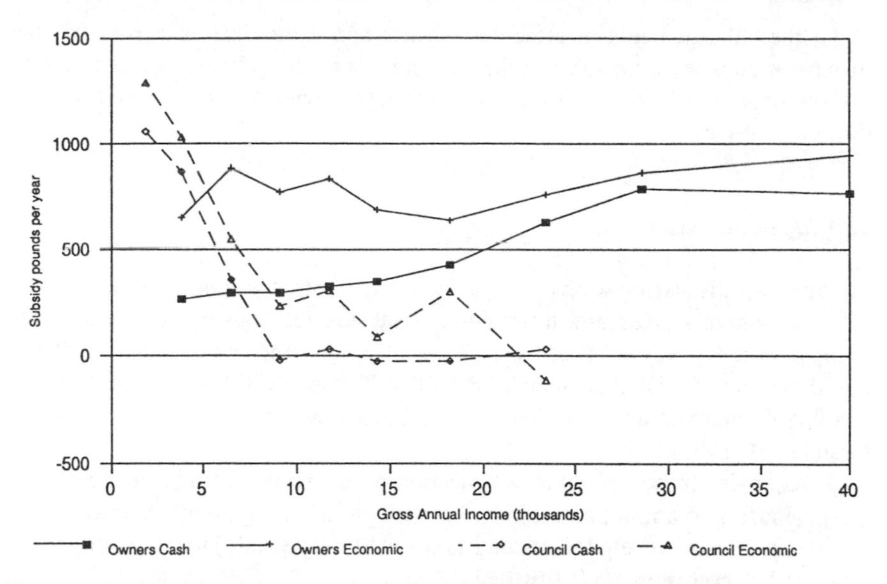

Figure 9.3 Subsidy and income broadly defined, Bristol area, 1988/9.

much more effective in enabling them to realize higher consumption of housing, and indeed it encourages trading up. For lower-income groups the subsidy is more likely to be capitalized, and consequently fails to be effective in improving housing consumption. If these groups are renters rather than owners, they lose out directly; if they own their homes, however, this analysis suggests that they would benefit from the subsidy, in the form of a capital gain.

This analysis is consistent with the simple urban economic model discussed in Chapters 2 and 3. O'Sullivan concedes that there may be circumstances where some high-income consumers occupy (and own) housing which has unique attributes and which cannot be increased in supply, referred to by Hirsch's (1977) term of "positional goods". Cottages in the Hampstead or Chelsea districts of London might be examples. In this instance they experience capitalization rather than expanded consumption. For our purposes, perhaps the question to ask is, what difference does planning make? Chapter 3 suggested that the common planning policy of urban containment would limit supply and raise prices in the outer suburbs and in satellite settlements. These are typical residential areas for the better off, and this suggests that planning would have the effect of increasing capitalization for higher-income groups. But it should be remembered that these groups are already overwhelmingly owner-occupiers, unlike the lower-income groups. Chapters 3 and 8 suggest that planning would lower the supply response of density to demand, as a general tendency, but also especially in attractive, high-status, low-density residential suburbs. Again, this would have a similar effect, reinforcing capitalization of subsidies at the top end of the market. From these *a priori* arguments it is not at all clear what conclusions could be reached about the balance between effective subsidy and capitalization across income groups. It does seem though that the way one approaches this is to examine supply response in different types of area, and this is what we have been trying to do in our research.

Subsidy policy goals

So far in this discussion we have tended to make implicit assumptions about what the government's goals are in providing a subsidy for housing. Perhaps at this point it would make sense to consider briefly what the main goals might be, based both on official statements (e.g. DoE 1977, DoE 1987) and on the writings of other commentators (O'Sullivan 1984, Gibb & Munro 1991, Hills 1991, Le Grand et al. 1992).

Three main strands of policy justification for subsidies seem to be important:

(a) Housing to a minimum standard constitutes a "merit good" or basic need, and subsidy to help low-income households (especially) to attain this standard of consumption is justified.

(b) There are certain external or social disbenefits from bad housing, for example health and amenity effects, that justify subsidy where this can ameliorate the problems.

(c) Owner-occupation is the ideal tenure for most households (and for society) and a subsidy to buyers can help more households to realize this position.

It is not our purpose here to debate these objectives at great length, but merely to try to highlight some of their implications for our analysis of the impact of housing subsidies in a system where supply is significantly influenced by planning. The first argument is probably the most important and enduring rationale for housing subsidy: it is a restatement of phrases such as "a decent home for all families at a price within their means". The merit good concept has a slightly uneasy relationship with mainstream economics, because it seems to suggest that somebody other than the individual household is making a judgement about how much housing (or health, or education) that household should have; in other words, it can be criticized as paternalistic. A better restatement of the argument would be to say that many people in our society agree with statement (a) and are willing to pay something through taxes to see it carried out by a government they elect to do it. It can then be seen as a particular kind of external benefit, in the sense that person A derives a benefit from knowing that person B is adequately housed. This rationale may be particularly important where certain groups such as children, elderly or disabled people are concerned, for reasons connected with their lack of choice about their situation and the more severe or pervasive effects of inadequate housing on their lives. It is almost a matter of taste whether this rationale is counted under the banner of economic efficiency (i.e. an externality) or a specific form of redistribution (for further discussion see Culyer 1980, Musgrave & Musgrave 1980, Le Grand et al. 1992, Bramley & Smart 1993; for more specific evidence on people's attitudes to minimum housing standards see Mack & Lansley 1984).

The second argument refers to more specific and tangible disbenefits that flow from bad housing or lack of housing, often concentrated in local neighbourhoods. Examples might include public health risks, visual amenity, or security from crime and disorder. Such arguments were undoubtedly powerful in the original development of housing policy in the 19th century, and remain significant in the arena of policy concerned with the maintenance and renewal of older housing areas. Some of the issues about quality, density and design discussed in Chapter 8 provide examples of neighbourhood external effects, and to that extent this rationale may still apply to aspects of planning and regulatory policy. It is generally accepted that this argument is less than sufficient to justify the whole gamut of housing subsidy in today's conditions.

The third argument is clearly important in the real world politics of housing policy, and has tended to take on more importance over time. Some academic analysts have argued that subsidies should be "tenure neutral", but it is increasingly clear that the politicians have been far from neutral in their approach. Recent evidence shows that, except for lowest-income groups, the subsidy incentives strongly favour owner-occupation (see Bramley et al. 1990, Maclennan et al. 1991, and Fig. 9.3 above).

While arguments (a–c) above provide some rationale for subsidizing housing in some way, it is far from clear that they justify a general, open-ended demand-side subsidy to house-buyers. Each of the objectives stated above seems to suggest that only certain groups or areas should be targeted for subsidy: low-income and/or vulnerable groups, run-down areas, and marginal/potential first time buyers. An across-the-board subsidy seems very wasteful of scarce public money, and this argument for targeting is used with increasing force in the reform of housing finance for the social rented sector, as it is more widely in debate about the Welfare State. If, as seems to be generally the case, supply elasticities are low, the case against general demand-side subsidies is almost overwhelming, because this means that most of the subsidy will disappear in the form of increased house prices, and little benefit will be achieved in terms of real housing consumption by the poor or marginal groups. There is in fact a significant strand of argument in housing in favour of providing subsidies linked to supply, rather than demand, which reflects a concern about supply inelasticity as well as a general perception that more housing is needed (Robinson 1981). This was part of the rationale for the way council housing was provided and funded in the past, and housing association development still attracts significant supply subsidy. However, partly because of arguments for less public involvement and bureaucracy, and more consumer choice, such subsidies are eschewed in relation to owner-occupation in Britain (and increasingly so in other European countries).

9.3 Effect of mortgage tax subsidy

We examine the impact of changes to MITR because this is the most obvious, widely recognized tax subsidy to owner-occupation in Britain. A full economic definition of subsidy to owner-occupiers would recognize the subsidy implicit in the non-taxation of the return on investment in housing assets, in the form of both imputed rental income and capital gains (see O'Sullivan 1984 or Hills 1991 for explanation and discussion). But in the light of recent policy debates (Hills 1991, Joseph Rowntree Foundation 1991, MacLennan et al. 1991, Pearce & Wilcox 1991) it would seem to be much more technically feasible and politically comprehensible to reduce or remove MITR, rather than to try to introduce either capital gains tax or imputed rental income tax (especially given the re-introduction of a property tax for local government, as described below). It also appears to be becoming more politically acceptable, in a context of budget deficit and fiscal stringency, to move towards a phasing out of this relief.

What would the effect of this reform be on the housing market? Elementary theory as set out above suggests that the impact would be to cause house prices to fall, by some amount less than the proportional value of the subsidy. We would also expect prices to fall more initially, because of the low short-run elasticity of supply. In the longer run, supply will adjust more and the price effect will be moderated. We are in a position to put more flesh on the bones of this description by using the simulation technique described in Chapter 6 to test out this question on our pseudo-national database.

Simulating MITR abolition

A rather crude attempt is made to model the abolition of MITR. The assumed route to abolition is a reduction in the maximum eligible loan, which currently stands at £30000. We have modelled both phased and immediate withdrawal: model 1 phases MITR out in three annual steps between 1988 and 1990, while model 2 phases it out in one go in 1988 (i.e. hypothetically rewriting recent history). A somewhat short, sharp phasing is convenient for our computations rather than a judgement about a realistic choice of reform phasing. It can be argued that an announced change would be fully capitalized in house prices at the time of the announcement, regardless of any phasing, if people believed that the Government was firmly committed to the change.

The model deals in averages; we assume that, because "a house is a house", everyone buys at the average standardized second-hand price with a 66% mortgage (this is the national average for mortgaged purchases, the vast majority). The immediate effect of the withdrawal of relief is modelled by assuming that the "post tax relief" price paid by consumers remains the same after the change (in terms of Fig. 9.1, we move initially from point I to point G). To achieve this, the actual market price must fall by an appropriate amount; how much depends

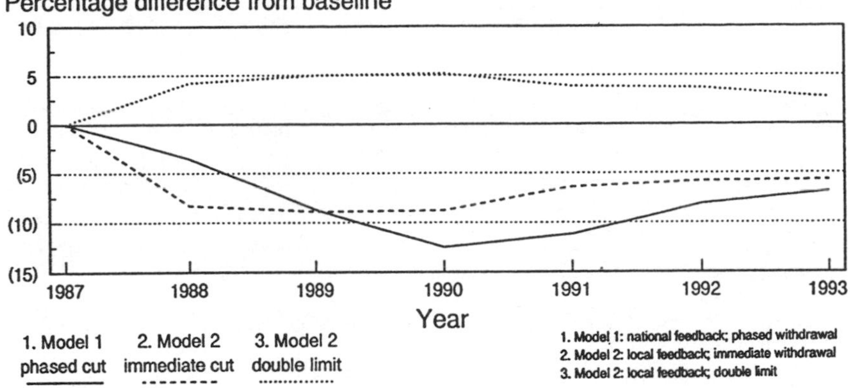

Figure 9.4 Price effects of mortgage tax subsidy changes over the medium term.

on where the operative upper MITR limits bite in the local housing market.

If P_1 is the market price before the change, and P_2 after, M_{1*} and M_{2*} are the respective MITR limits before and after the change, then

Case (a) $0.66(1-0.25)P_1 = 0.66(1-0.25)P_2$ where $0.66P_1 < M_{1*}$
i.e. $P_2 = P_1$ and $0.66P_1 < M_{2*}$

Case (b) $P_2 = P_1 + 0.25(M_{2*} - 0.66P_1)$ where $0.66P_1 < M_{1*}$
and $0.66P_1 > M_{2*}$

Case (c) $P_2 = P_1 + 0.25(M_{2*} - M_{1*})$ where $0.66P_1 >= M_{1*}$
and $0.66P_1 >= M_2*$

This general statement of the model can cope with phasing or indeed increasing the MITR limit, as well as instant withdrawal ($M_{2*}=0$). The initial effect of the MITR withdrawal on prices is quite direct in our model, with the effect of each phase of withdrawal being as given by the above expression. In districts where the average price is above £45000, so bringing the upper MIRAS limit into play, the reduction will be 25% of £30000, or £7500. In districts below this level the reduction will be 25% of 66% (i.e. 16.5%) of the price. The sample average value of the loss of subsidy is £6400, or about 11.8% of baseline 1988 prices. The interesting issue is what then happens to supply, and what this means for prices in the longer term.

A fall in price causes, after a lag, a fall in new-build output, for any given land supply, according to the output model described in Chapter 6. It also leads to some reduction in the flow of new planning applications, which themselves will affect output. As output falls, the price feedback mechanisms come into play at local, regional and national level, putting some upward pressure on prices. This begins to moderate the process; the price reductions initially recorded begin to fade as supply falls off progressively. In terms of Figure 9.1, the system gradually converges on a point such as E.

Figure 9.4 and Table 9.2 summarize the results of this crude simulation. Sure

Table 9.2 Simulations of mortgage interest tax relief changes (1988–93).

	1988	1989	1990	1991	1992	1993
"National" price (second hand £)						
MODEL 1						
– baseline	54100	53800	51100	48400	49200	51900
– MITR abol.	51800	49100	44600	43000	45200	48300
– % diff.	−3.5	−8.7	−12.5	−11.2	−8.1	−6.9
MODEL 2						
– baseline	43850	44570	44420	44820	45410	45980
– MITR abol.	40230	40610	40490	41950	42780	43340
– % diff.	−8.3	−8.9	−8.8	−6.4	−5.8	−5.7
– £60k MITR % diff.	4.2	5.0	5.2	3.9	3.7	2.7
Output (comps/1000 owners)						
MODEL 1						
– baseline	17.6	19.7	22.0	21.5	19.4	17.4
– MITR abol.	17.6	19.1	20.7	19.0	16.5	15.2
– % diff.	0.0	−3.1	−5.7	−11.3	−15.2	−12.4
MODEL 2						
– baseline	15.35	15.97	18.38	16.35	15.78	15.21
– MITR abol.	15.35	15.97	18.17	14.45	13.98	13.93
– % diff.	0.0	0.0	−1.1	−11.6	−11.4	−8.4
– £60k MITR % diff.	0.0	0.0	0.6	7.0	7.4	5.4

Note: Model 1 uses national price feedback based on demand elasticity of −0.7; Model 2 uses local price feedback as described in this chapter, using information on demographics, affordability, vacancies and queues.
Model 1 phases MITR abolition over 3 years, Model 2 applies it in first year. Model 1 baseline set around norm price at 1988 levels, Model 2 at 1987 levels. Model 2 local price floor set at 80% of construction cost.

enough, the price of housing falls sharply and progressively as the abolition of MITR is implemented. But it should be noted that at no stage does the price fall reach the level of 16.5% that might theoretically have happened if all mortgages attracted relief. The maximum attained is 12.5%, which is what would be expected given that in 1988 the average mortgage would have been above the limit. What is most interesting is the fact that this price fall is not sustained, but diminishes quite significantly. In three more years it is down to 6.9%. The extent of this effect does depend in part on the externally imported value of the national elasticity of demand, with more elastic demand increasing the price fall, and vice versa.

We do not know how appropriate this national demand elasticity is and this aspect of the model does not shed much light on local and regional variations. We have therefore experimented with an alternative approach to modelling price adjustment at the local level, which is described in more detail below. This makes more use of information on migration, affordability and the other components of demand and supply, to provide a plausible account of price adjustment at the local level. The overall results of this alternative approach are also shown by the broken line in Figure 9.4. It suggests that the order of magnitude of the price effect of MITR abolition is similar to that just quoted, but slightly less overall. Over the six years of the simulation, prices would be 7.3% lower, compared with 8.5% under the first approach.

The effect on output builds up more gradually, but towards the end of the period it has reached significant proportions. Completions could be 15% below the baseline level in year 5, but then the gap seems to narrow again. Under the alternative price feedback mechanism, the output fall is less, peaking at 11.6% and averaging 5.4% rather than 8.0% over six years. This seems, superficially at least, quite a large output effect, but it is rather what our elasticity estimates (including induced land supply) would lead us to expect. It should be remembered that the proportional change in net flow supply resulting would be about a quarter to one third of this. In the longer term, with the price fall moderating, the output gap should also gradually close. But a significant cumulative amount of investment in the stock would not have happened.

Other national estimates

The results of Pearce & Wilcox (1991) may be directly compared. They use a version of the Treasury model of the British economy to simulate various MITR abolition scenarios, emphasizing that the results depend crucially upon the way the authorities do or do not compensate in fiscal or monetary policy (our model implicitly assumes some form of compensation). They find that, with the most favourable option of constant money supply/lower interest rates, immediate abolition would lower prices by up to 10% in years 1–2, falling to 7% in years 3–4. For a phased withdrawal the figures are 4% and 6%. With the least favourable option of non-compensation prices would fall by 17% in years 1–2 and 26% by years 3–4. As we would expect, our results are closer to the former scenario, and indeed are very similar in magnitude.

Local variations in impact

The model enables differential local and regional effects to be studied. However, the version of the model described in Chapter 6 that relies mainly on a national price feedback effect is inherently limited for this purpose. We have therefore experimented with an alternative approach that tries to model the market adjustment process at the local level, using a range of additional information and a set of plausible assumptions. The assumptions of this approach are as follows:

- Local house prices depend on three factors, the price in the previous year, the predicted price based on underlying demand factors, and the balance between the net flow of households seeking to buy and the net supply of units in the year in question.
- Net flow demand comprises new household formation (constant for each

district, based on demographic structure), net migration, and a proportion of households queuing for housing (based on adjusted waiting lists).

- Net supply of units comprises new-build completions, turnover in the owner-occupier stock (constant, depending on demographic structure), and excess vacancies above the initial level.
- Effective demand from new households and queues depends upon the ability to buy (affordability), estimated separately for each district using a model developed in Bramley (1991a) of local income distributions and the house prices generated within the simulation.
- Net migration is modelled using the regression equation described in Table 6.2 as a function of local attraction factors (constant) and price and new-build output generated by the simulation; migration flows are controlled to maintain a given rate for the whole multi-region system.
- Excess flows of demand and supply are absorbed by changes in vacancies and queues.
- Downward movements in prices are limited by a floor set at 80% of construction costs (this slightly arbitrary assumption does limit adjustment in low-price areas).

This modified simulation does seem to generate reasonably stable adjustment processes, partly because prices are dampened by the use of the lag and predicted prices in the first assumption. It is consistent with the approach of the overall model in working with net flows of households and dwellings, but enables us to use a wider range of information available. The insight that local markets are very open is retained, but now modelled explicitly through net migration. We can now offer a plausible story of how the market adjusts without having to import an arbitrary external value for the demand elasticity. In doing so, we also generate additional information about the local dimension of impact of policy changes.

On the basis of the first simulation model (with mainly national price feedback), at the end of the period analyzed (year 6) output would have fallen by 15–16% relative to baseline in some West Midlands counties, but only by 7.5% in high-demand Berkshire (see Table 9.3). The price falls associated with this are similar in absolute terms (£3000–4000), but much lower in percentage terms in high-priced Berkshire (–4.4%) than in the West Midlands conurbation (–10.7%). The main reason for uniform absolute price effects is that local markets are very open, with high local price elasticities of demand in this version of the model. In percentage terms, price changes range from minus 4% (Windsor, Wokingham) to –11% (Birmingham). These figures may be interpreted as the capitalized value of MITR. They show that the capitalization of this subsidy is if anything more pronounced, in relative terms at least, in lower-price areas. But the £30 000 limit on MITR plays a major role in bringing this result about.

However, when we use our alternative model as described above, with more explicit local market adjustments, the pattern is rather different. Percentage price falls are higher in some of the counties in the South East and South West, gen-

Table 9.3 Impact of mortgage interest tax relief changes on prices and output by county (after six years; diff. %)).

County	Abolition of MITR			Double MITR limit
	Model 1 output	Model 1 price	Model 2 price	Model 2 price
South East				
Berkshire	−7.5	−4.4	−7.2	8.4
Hampshire	−10.0	−5.3	−8.8	5.9
Oxfordshire	−10.0	−4.8	−4.8	−1.4
South West				
Avon	−13.8	−6.7	−9.1	3.3
Dorset	−12.3	−6.8	−8.7	1.2
Gloucestershire	−14.0	−6.8	−10.0	2.1
Somerset	−12.4	−8.0	−4.3	1.3
Wiltshire	−12.6	−6.1	−7.5	3.8
West Midlands				
Hereford & Worcester	−15.1	−8.5	−6.2	1.9
Shropshire	−15.7	−9.7	−2.7	1.2
Staffordshire	−13.0	−9.4	−2.3	0.3
Warwickshire	−15.0	−8.5	−2.3	1.3
West Midlands Met	−10.2	−10.7	−0.6	0.6
Whole sample	−12.4	−6.9	−5.7	2.7

erally areas with higher demand and prices, but significantly lower in the areas of the West Midlands characterized by lower demand and prices. This effect may be slightly exaggerated by the last assumption in our modified model, but it is not unreasonable to expect construction costs to place some sort of floor on prices. This version of the model generates more local variation in the estimated price effect of MITR abolition, which may be interpreted as the capitalization of the subsidy. The effect is greatest in affluent suburban and resort areas and least in declining industrial and major city areas. Capitalization of subsidy is positively correlated with price levels and with the underlying structural demand factors. It is only weakly associated with planning policy and land availability factors.

The effect of raising the MITR limit to £60000 was also tested. This time both versions of the model give similar results. Under the simplified assumptions of this model the effect is mainly confined to higher-price areas, where typical buyers are affected by the £30000 limit. Prices may actually fall slightly in lower-price areas because of the national supply-price feedback in the first version of the model. Price changes range from +8% in Berkshire (both models) to −2% (first model) or plus 0% to 1% (second model) in much of the West Midlands. Capitalization of this form of subsidy increase is even more strongly correlated with the structural demand factors. The districts with the greatest price increase are notably affluent areas (Wokingham, Bracknell, Winchester in the South East,

Cotswold and parts of Wiltshire in the South West, and Stratford, Solihull and South Herefordshire in the West Midlands). Thus, the overall impact of MITR with a higher limit would be greater in affluent high demand areas.

The particular form of policy change examined in these simulations is not the only way in which tax subsidies to owner-occupiers might be changed; for example, the rate of tax relief might be changed rather than the capital limit. But it serves to illustrate the effects quite well, and reminds us that the present £30000 limit significantly modifies the pattern of subsidy from the simple proportional case that textbook presentations tend to assume. The pattern of capitalization revealed is somewhat sensitive to the way price changes are modelled, although our more refined approach gives a consistent picture for both subsidy reduction and increase. The pattern is rather different from that suggested by O'Sullivan (1984), although it should be remembered we are looking here at an inter-urban comparison rather than within one city. The simulations also bring out the point that abolition of tax relief would have effects on output as well as on prices.

9.4 Effect of local property taxes

Local taxes and the housing market in theory

In §9.2 we explained how a subsidy on the consumption of a specific commodity, housing, would normally be expected to have a significant effect on the market for that commodity, changing both the price and the quantity produced and consumed. The same is true, but in reverse, if a tax is levied on a specific commodity. For example, the special excise duties on tobacco and alcohol both raise the price that consumers have to pay and reduce the consumption of these commodities. So, if a special tax were levied on housing, we would expect this to (a) raise the cost to consumers, causing them to (b) reduce the amount of housing they consume, while (c) reducing the net-of-tax price received by housing producers, causing them in turn to (d) reduce the supply of housing. The balance between price reduction and quantity reduction would depend, as in the subsidy case, on the supply and demand elasticities, and would generally be different in the longer run from the short run. In the short run, the price effect would be more important, while in the longer-run quantity adjustments might be greater.

The major subsidies affecting the private housing market in Britain, as in many other countries, tend to take the form of exemptions from taxes that would normally apply to other commodities or assets. There are taxes that affect housing either specifically or disproportionately (e.g. stamp duty) or which housing has some degree of exemption from (e.g. VAT in relation to new building). For a fuller discussion of the taxation of housing see Hills (1991) or O'Sullivan (1984). But there is one type of tax which is of special interest here, and that is the local property tax. Apart from the brief period of the ill fated Community Charge ("Poll Tax"), Britain has had a system of local domestic property taxation for a very long time and for most of this period the tax in question (known as Rates prior to 1990, and now known as the Council Tax) has been quite a significant element of the overall tax structure.

Local property taxes are of special interest for two reasons. The first is the point that these taxes are levied specifically on some measure of the value or quantity of *housing*, and as such have the characteristics of a specific tax as described above, with strong effects on the housing market. The second point is that these taxes are *local taxes*: they fund local government services and have variable local tax rates set by autonomous local councils. In other words, this specific tax affecting the housing market may weigh more or less heavily in different localities, and interact with the operation of local housing markets.

In simple terms, we would expect districts that have higher local tax rates to see that reflected in somewhat lower house prices. The extent to which this is so depends on the elasticities of supply and demand. However, in the typical British situation (especially in the short run) of inelastic housing supply and elastic demand (because of migration and the openness of local markets), we would expect a large part of tax differences to be capitalized. People shop around and in choosing which district to live in they take account of local tax rates.

This simple proposition needs to be modified somewhat to take account of other aspects of the situation. Local taxes are used to finance local public services. This means that higher taxes may correspond to higher expenditure giving better quality services. If these services are valued by existing and potential residents, they may be willing to pay the higher taxes for them. This assumes that the extra expenditure translates into higher standards of service, rather than into inefficient bureaucracies, and that the standards of service can be clearly perceived by potential residents, both of which assumptions are questionable. The balance between local taxes and service expenditures is affected by other variables, particularly grants paid by the central government to the local authorities and access to other sources of funds (e.g. asset sales, non-domestic taxes, tourist revenue, etc.). In Britain the grants are supposed to compensate for local differences in spending needs and resources (Bramley 1990), but it is always arguable how effective this "equalization" is. In general, when testing statistically for any relationships between local taxes and house prices, it is desirable to include measure(s) of local service provision or expenditure as well.

In the economic literature on local government, this interaction between local fiscal situations, the housing market and planning controls is of some importance. For example, Oates (1972), in his important work, *Fiscal federalism*, examined the influence of local fiscal variables on property values. Later work developing or commenting on this issue pointed out that the extent of capitalization depends upon the inelasticity of the supply response (Edel & Sclar 1974, Hamilton 1975, Foster et al. 1980: 225–7). Barnett & Topham (1980) argue that capitalization of fiscal disparities between localities may negate the case for equalization grants. King (1984: 146–7) and Bramley (1990: 54) question this on various grounds, including housing tenure structures, the degree of potential mobility, and differences between what grants are trying to equalize and what determines housing demand.

A particular version of the "shopping around" view of local government is provided by Tiebout's classic (1956) article. This sees many small local jurisdictions competing with one another for residents by offering different packages of services and tax rates. Although this model has many limitations, again more especially in a British rather than a North American context, it contains some insights which should not be forgotten. One way in which this idea has been taken forward by some authors (e.g. Hamilton 1975) has been to link it to planning control, particularly American-style zoning, where localities try to maintain a particular niche in the market by operating mutually supportive tax, service and zoning policies. For example, a suburban municipality may try to use zoning to restrict residence to households able to afford very large plots, who generate low demands for local public services and welcome low tax rates.

Whether or not we find this perspective helpful, it is certainly clear that planning controls will affect the supply elasticity of housing and as such affect the extent of any capitalization of local fiscal differences. We have shown in previous chapters how the supply elasticity does vary and how this is affected in various ways by planning. Thus, we would expect differential degrees of capitalization as a general result.

Recent British reforms

Local government finance in Britain has undergone considerable upheaval over the past decade or so. The most important reform took place in 1989–90, based on proposals set out in a 1986 Green Paper (DoE 1986). The replacement of Domestic Rates with an adult Poll Tax, officially known as the Community Charge, was the best-known element of the package, but there were other important changes in the grant system and the effective "nationalization" of the Non-Domestic (business) Rate. There are many comments that could be made on this reform, most of which go beyond the scope of this book (see Bailey & Paddison 1988, Bramley 1990b, Smith 1991, Wilson 1991). But one particular aspect that attracted attention has been the impact on the housing market.

Superficially, it might be thought that replacing a tax called Rates, amounting to, say, £500 per year for an average household, with another tax called a Community Charge, amounting on average to the same amount per year, would not make very much difference. Some people would be better off and some worse off, but on average there would be no difference, and consequently there would be no impact on the housing market. However, microeconomic theory says that this view is *too* simple. Taxes on a specific commodity alter the price of that commodity relative to other commodities. If the price rises with a tax, consumers therefore find it worthwhile buying less of that commodity and more of others; they "substitute" other forms of consumption for housing. So the replacement of a tax related to the quantity and value of housing consumed, the Rates, by an equal tax *not related to housing consumption*, the Poll Tax, would be expected to increase the demand for housing, because of this substitution effect.

Suppose (as happened in 1991) the general level of the Poll Tax is reduced; does this affect the housing market? If the tax reduction is not offset by changes elsewhere (e.g. in VAT, as in the 1991 example), the answer is that it will have an effect, but only a relatively slight one. This is because relative prices are not changed, so there is no substitution. Instead there is just an "income effect"; people have more disposable income and they will spend more, but not just on housing. Housing is likely to attract only about 20% of this extra spending, as this is roughly the proportion of their incomes that households typically devote to housing. Even this change might not be apparent immediately, as it takes time to adjust housing consumption (e.g. through moving or improving one's house).

The general point to make here is that tax changes can have price/substitution effects and/or income effects, and that generally the former are more potent in their effects on specific markets, such as housing. In the case of the original introduction of the Poll Tax, the income effects were not significant on average because the average tax bill was supposed to remain the same (in practice, it increased). However, income effects may be more significant once allowance is made for changes in the distributional incidence of the taxes. For example, the poll tax increased burdens on lower income and larger households, whose spending patterns and housing market situations might tend to differ markedly from the gaining groups (smaller, better-off households).

The main point about the Poll Tax is that it did not relate to the amount or value of housing consumed, whereas Domestic Rates did, at least in principle. In practice, because of the administrative procedures used in undertaking rating valuations, in a context where there was very little unregulated private rented housing to observe, rates were rather poorly related to current market values (Foster et al. 1980).

Some studies attempted to assess the impact of the local tax reform of 1990 on house prices and the housing market generally, including DOE (1986: Annex E), G. Hughes (1988) and Spencer (1988) and these are helpfully reviewed in Gibb & Munro (1991: 200–3). DOE estimated, in a rather back-of-an-envelope fashion, that prices might rise by 15% in the short run but only 5% in the long run. Hughes argued for rather larger effects in the medium term, ranging from 11.5% in London and Wales to 23% in Scotland, differences stemming mainly from inherited differences in the burden of Domestic Rates relative to private sector housing costs.

The average Domestic Rate bill per household in 1987 was £410 per year for our sample areas, whereas in 1990 the average Poll Tax bill per household nationally was about £675. These figures for annual local tax costs may be compared with the annual value of MITR on a £30000 mortgage of between £650 and over £1000, depending on the interest rate. This comparison suggests that the abolition of Domestic Rates could have had quite a significant effect on the housing market, although not quite as great as the effect of abolishing MITR.

Gibb & Munro (ibid.) comment on two more specific aspects of the impact of the Poll Tax on housing. First, it was expected to increase demand and prices most at the top end of the housing market. The reason is that removing a tax related to housing value increases the incentive to trade up (or improve), and the occupiers of larger, more valuable houses experience the largest increase in income. If we combine this with the finding from our work that capitalization may be greater in higher price areas, then the windfall gains by this group are reinforced. Secondly, the shift to the Poll Tax reduced the incentive for single adults to live with other households, since under the new tax they would have to pay wherever they lived. This could be predicted to lead to an increase in separate household formation, boosting housing demand this time more towards the bottom end, including in the rented sector. This effect might have been moderated to some extent by attempts by quite large numbers of young adults to evade the tax by "disappearing" from all official registers.

The introduction of the Poll Tax created serious problems for the government, and it was soon decided to replace it with another new type of local tax, the Council Tax. This reform was implemented from 1993. The Council Tax is best seen as a hybrid form of tax, containing elements related to property value, households, number of adults, and income (Hills & Sutherland 1991). The property value element is represented this time by capital rather than rental values, but grouped into eight broad bands. The relationship between tax bill and property value is less than proportional; in fact the proportional rise is about half the rise in average value across the main bands. There is a discount for single adult households and certain other discounts may be collected. Income affects the net tax liability through a rebate scheme very similar to that applying to both the Poll Tax and Rates. The average level of Council Tax bills is lower in real terms than the Rate bills of the late 1980s, thanks to a rise in the proportion of local expenditure financed by grant. Local spending is now more tightly controlled through a system of capping, so that spending and tax variations are less than they would otherwise be.

What are the effects of this change likely to be on the housing market? Broadly speaking we are dealing with a change back towards the old system, but the new system is not identical, as indicated above. So a reversal of some of the price gains of the end of the 1980s, which could have been attributable to Rates abolition, is likely to have happened. Prices in the early 1990s have certainly fallen, but several other important influences have been at work, notably the state of the economy.

Capitalization of local fiscal disparities

How far are fiscal variations between different local authority jurisdictions capitalized in house prices in practice? This question has attracted more attention in

North America than in Britain, partly perhaps because the conditions giving rise to this possibility have been seen as more common there. Perhaps the most thorough attempt to examine this question in a British context is to be found in the work of Topham & Ward (1992). This study involved modelling a large dataset of individual house purchase transactions in one metropolitan region, Greater Manchester, including Rates bill and local authority expenditure indicators in their explanatory models. Like others, they argue that capitalization is most likely in a metropolitan area where many households exercise choices about which neighbourhood and which local authority to live in. They find that both local taxes and expenditure levels affect house prices, with expenditure relative to the official measure of needs performing better in the model than expenditure per se. Quite a large part of the fiscal differences seem to be capitalized. Some inferences are also made from the data about the efficiency of local service provision.

The influence of planning and housing supply elasticity is not discussed in detail in the above study. While in general one would expect supply elasticities to be lower in a metropolitan area such as this, as in our West Midlands sample, there are still areas of considerable private development potential within Greater Manchester. At the same time, it is a region of generally low house prices and residual land values that might be expected to lessen the scope for capitalization.

It is possible to use our inter-urban dataset to test for evidence of fiscal capitalization at a slightly broader scale. We test the inclusion of relevant variables in our house price regression models, including the average Domestic Rate bill or the rate poundage (i.e. tax rate) in 1987 and the percentage difference between local authority expenditure and the official needs assessment known as Grant-Related Expenditure (GRE). Without reporting all the detail, the results are rather mixed. The Rate poundage has a positive effect on second-hand prices, of marginal statistical significance, when included, which is the opposite of the effect expected. The average Domestic Rate bill per household has a negative effect that is significant in some models, using composite demand indicators, but not in some other models using many individual variables or on new house prices. This negative effect is as expected, but may be affected by interactions with other factors. Finally, the expenditure relative to GRE generally has a negative sign, which is not expected, but is often not statistically significant.

How do we interpret these results? The tax rate and tax bill variables give contradictory messages. The results using tax bills suggest that it may be the arbitrary nature of rating valuations under the old system that was being capitalized, rather than the fiscal behaviour of the local authorities. The negative effects of expenditure are consistent but not very significant. They suggest that higher expenditures are not valued by consumers in the housing market. But higher expenditures might be a proxy for social and environmental problems not adequately reflected in the official needs assessments (GREs). It is difficult to separate out the effects of spending on different services, some of which might be valued more, and to deal with the fact that the major services in most of our districts are provided by the upper-tier county authorities. Overall, the results can only be described as inconclusive. There are some signs that local fiscal variables have some effect on house prices, but without further investigation it would be unwise to make too categorical an assertion about the strength of such effects.

9.5 Planning agreements and infrastructure charges

In Chapters 4 and 5 it was pointed out that planning agreements under s.106 (formerly s.52) of the Town and Country Planning Acts have become increasingly common as a means of financing infrastructure or local community facilities. In the introduction to this chapter we suggested that these agreements are the latter-day successor to past attempts to tax betterment. Their use is very *ad hoc* and it depends on local authority initiative and negotiations (Healey et al. 1993). In some other countries, more standardized methods, including specific taxes, exist to achieve the same purpose. Such charges can be seen as one solution to the growing problems in financing local government or the improvement of urban infrastructure.

The model developed in our research can be used to estimate the impact of such a use of planning powers on the economics of development and hence on housebuilding and prices. Two simple, polarized views would be (a) that infrastructure charges would be added to house prices in full, or (b) that infrastructure charges would fall wholly on land values, leaving house prices unchanged. The model exemplified here suggests that the outcome would lie between these two extremes, once allowance is made for changes in supply decisions by developers and demand/price feedback effects.

To illustrate the effect in a general way, it is assumed that all planning authorities apply a standard planning agreement requiring a contribution to infrastructure and local facilities equal to 10% of construction cost (i.e. roughly equal in real terms of what it would buy in different areas). This is on average £4000 per house in 1988 values, implicitly in addition to whatever was typically being charged at that time (Lambert 1990 (p. 22) cites interview evidence of £3000–5000 per unit in the Bristol area at that time).

Figure 9.5 shows the impact over time on new-build output of this extra infrastructure charge. The average effect under the first simulation model is a fall of 5.4% in completions, ranging from a maximum reduction of 9.3% in the second year to only 1.8% by the sixth year. Under the alternative simulation model, with local feedback mechanisms, these figures are 6.3%, 9.5% and 3.2%. The mechanism involved is simply the fact that the infrastructure charge eats into the gross profit margin of housebuilders, which is a significant determinant of their output levels; some particular sites may switch from viable to non-viable. The decline in output resulting is greater, in the longer term, in the more marginal geographical areas such as Staffordshire and Shropshire, whereas there seems to be a slight increase in Berkshire and a very small fall in the other South East

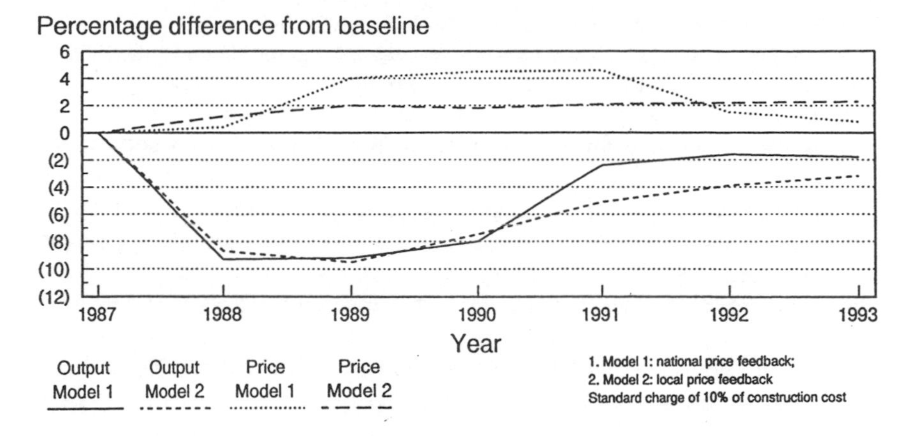

Figure 9.5 Price and output effects of infrastructure charges.

counties (attributable to prices being higher). On the whole this pattern seems plausible.

Figure 9.5 also shows the price impact over time; as generally in this model, price effects in proportional terms are considerably smaller than the output effects. Using the first version of the model, the average price rise is 2.6%, with a range from 4.6% (year 4) to 0.8% (year 6). Using the modified simulation, the average price rise is less, at 1.9%, and the pattern over time is more static. The largest proportional price rises are in some Staffordshire and Shropshire districts, but even these are only around 4.5%. Correlations reveal that the extent of the price penalty would be greater in districts with much land available for housing and those where the elasticity of demand related to affordability was smaller.

One could interpret these results as suggesting that the penalty for such a policy on infrastructure financing would not be too severe. The effect on house prices of a £4000 infrastructure charge is only about £1000. The answer to the question of who pays for this kind of planning obligation or tax is that consumers only pay about a quarter of it, while landowners and developers pay the other three-quarters. It might turn out to be a more favourable scenario, if the charge enabled more infrastructure constraints to be overcome and more land to be effectively released, in which case there would be more output and lower prices. Alternatively, the charge might be used as a substitute for local tax revenues. In this case local taxes (rates/community charge/poll tax) would be lower. The theory of fiscal capitalization discussed above suggests that this might have a further upward effect on house prices.

The policy implications of this finding are to lend support to those who argue in favour of the reasonable use of planning agreements or obligations to obtain contributions from developers. The penalties in lost output and higher prices are generally modest in most cases, although they might give slightly more cause for concern in areas of low prices and land values where there is a wish to promote development. There is a strong case for having arrangements that link contributions to the provision of infrastructure that enables sites to be developed sooner or more fully than they otherwise might. Although slightly more controversial, there is also a case for allowing contributions for other kinds of beneficial community facilities, insofar as this is likely to motivate local planning committees to look more favourably on the planning application or proposed local plan allocation. These outcomes, which are associated with a virtuous circle of more usable land being released giving more output and lower prices, can be achieved where agreements are negotiated locally. It is much more questionable whether such benefits would flow from standardized development charges where the revenue was pre-empted either by the Treasury or by utility undertakings. Charges being used to lower local tax rates might also be less helpful in their market effects.

Other kinds of local property taxation, particularly site value taxes, have also been mooted as a mechanism to encourage allocated land to be developed (MacLennan 1993). Such mechanisms have rather different properties, and require further consideration as to how they might interact with the new plan-led system for bringing land forward.

9.6 Conclusions

We have shown in this chapter that there are connections between, on the one hand, taxes and subsidies affecting housing, and, on the other, planning and housing supply. Taxes and subsidies impact on the housing market, and where supply is inelastic, because of a tight planning system or for other reasons, these effects are mainly on price rather than output or consumption. The extent to which this is true may vary from location to location, and may affect different demographic, tenure or income groups differentially. Because of both its distributional impact and its tendency to be capitalized into house prices, mortgage tax subsidy has been increasingly criticized as a wasteful and ineffective arm of housing policy.

Fiscal measures impacting on housing include both deliberate housing policy measures, and measures serving other purposes, such as funding local government, but with an indirect effect on housing. Planning is a regulatory form of intervention, but it too redistributes gains and losses, and in this sense it resembles taxation and subsidy. The conscious use of planning agreements to provide a flexible form of development taxation to fund infrastructure and local services is one of the most important developments of recent years. Our model results suggest that the majority of the cost of such agreements falls on landowners and developers rather than housing consumers.

CHAPTER 10
Planning and housing in perspective

10.1 Introduction

In this chapter we try to draw together the main arguments and conclusions developed in this book. Most of the research evidence drawn on in the preceding chapters, both our own work and that of others, has referred to Britain in the 1980s. In this chapter, we try more consciously to look forward to the 1990s and beyond, and speculate a little about how the system may evolve. Although we are not in a position to offer thoroughgoing comparative material, we also refer to the different models of planning and development that appear to operate in different countries.

The discussion is structured around some major themes that reflect broader currents in thinking about public policy and planning. The first of these themes is the concept of *market failure*, which has traditionally provided the underpinning for public policies in general and land-use planning in particular. In the light of our studies, what do we regard as the main potential forms of market failure in the private housing development sector, and how important are these in practice? In recent years, the arguments of the New Right in politics and the public choice school in economics have suggested that State interventions can also systematically fail. In what ways is housing a case of *planning failure*? Is planning for a private housing market inherently flawed or limited in what it can achieve, and does it exhibit particular biases? What are the effects of such failures on the efficiency, equity and quality of outcomes?

It is clear, particularly from international comparisons, that although land-use planning is very widespread the *style of planning* can differ quite markedly. We have shown, for example, that the British planning system is characterized by comprehensiveness accompanied by considerable discretion and negotiation. Other systems differ by placing more emphasis on legalistic regulation and zoning, often more partial in their coverage of issues or areas. If there are failures in the British planning system, to what extent are these caused by aspects of its style of operation? The system is in any case changing; how is the new style of district-wide local plans likely to perform? Should planners be more aware of and responsive to market and financial conditions? Can good planning be reconciled with local democratic control?

If there is a single theme that permeates current planning thinking, it is probably the notion of *sustainability*. Does this imply major shifts in the substantive content of plans for housing development, for example in relation to the key issue of density? Does it argue for new elements of regulation in a wider context where government is pursuing an agenda of deregulation?

Where does all this leave the *UK housebuilding industry* in the 1990s? Housebuilding has to recover from a very severe recession under what is likely to be a less privileged fiscal regime. It is likely to face increasingly diverse markets, some with limited buying power, against an overall background of demographic downturn, rather than a situation of buoyant demand for a standard suburban product. The scope for easy development profits will be less as planning authorities try to exploit planning agreements more fully. How well will this fragmented industry respond to demands for better quality?

10.2 Market failure

At various points in this book, particularly in Chapters 3 and 9, we have drawn attention to some of the potential ways in which unfettered market forces might fail in the case of housing. Housing is clearly not a case where the market fails comprehensively, in contrast with some other areas where State activity is important, for example health care. Housing provision and consumption are predominantly organized through a market mechanism. For the majority of households who attain owner-occupation, this mechanism provides choice, information and incentives that are on the whole beneficial. The supply of housing is relatively competitive and producers must generally strive to produce efficiently what people want. Even the procurement of social rented housing is organized in an increasingly competitive fashion (Bramley 1993). Mortgage finance is highly developed, competitive and relatively efficient in Britain (Diamond & Lea 1993).

Nevertheless, sources of potential market failure remain. Some of these have long been recognized and provide much of the basis for planning control and regulation. Externalities, particularly local neighbourhood effects, are always important in urban development, although the nature of these and their relative importance may change over time. The traditional public health problems associated with bad housing are perhaps less of an issue now that general standards have risen, and basic regulations governing building standards are probably the main check on such problems. The use of zoning to separate land uses that would make bad neighbours is a central function of planning, although the decline of traditional dirty heavy industries may make this a less pressing issue. Planning is used routinely to deal with some of the problems of traffic generation and parking associated with development, although sustainability arguments discussed below may suggest that this intervention may be failing at a more strategic level. Rising environmental awareness has given greater weight to arguments about the adverse external effects of certain types of development on environmental quality, and the planning system is the main conduit for political lobbying on these issues. A wide range of types of development raise environmental concerns and, although some of the most sensitive are not directly housing-related (e.g. minerals extraction, motorway building), there are important examples that do directly relate to housing – new settlements, town cramming.

The need to co-ordinate development with the provision of infrastructure remains a crucial issue where planning is necessary for the effective functioning of the market. The growing difficulty of funding infrastructure publicly both reinforces this point and explains the growing importance of planning agreements.

Housing policy analysts have often pointed to supply inelasticity in the housing market as a form of market failure, in conjunction with other factors such as demand-side booms or indiscriminate subsidies. We have given considerable attention in this book to the analysis and measurement of supply elasticity. On the whole, our findings concur with the view that housing supply is relatively inelastic in Britain. We have demonstrated this in relation to both of the main mechanisms by which supply may be augmented, the bringing forward of new land for housing development and the adjustment of density on existing housing land. However, this conclusion should be qualified in two ways. First, the supply is not completely inelastic, as it is sometimes portrayed. New housebuilding does respond to prices in a significant and positive way. Secondly, the inelasticity of response is connected to the existence and character of the planning system. While planning is undoubtedly attempting to deal with certain market failures, as just described, it may be creating or exacerbating another. We have shown for example that planning is relatively unresponsive to market forces in the way that it supplies new planning permissions. We have also shown that planning tends to inhibit density adjustment, although it would be wrong to portray planning approaches to density as rigid. These comments should be balanced against the observation that housing supply is not highly elastic, even where the planning system allocates large amounts of land, a point developed theoretically in Chapter 3 and empirically in Chapters 6 and 7.

Supply inelasticity is more of a problem if the demand for housing is unstable over time. This means that demand surges, initiated by monetary conditions for example, will feed quickly into prices, and there is then likely to be speculative behaviour that causes prices to overshoot. By the time the supply of housing has fully responded, the market is likely to be entering a recession, which may then be deepened by an overhang of supply. The importance of housing for the stability of the economy as a whole has received increasing recognition (Muellbauer 1990, Maclennan et al. 1991, Meen 1993, Wilcox 1993). For example, housing asset values relative to debt have strong effects on saving, and housing moves and transactions are associated with a wide range of consumption spending.

Booms and slumps in housing can also adversely affect mobility and labour supply, for example by making interregional moves difficult or, as in current conditions, by locking households in through "negative equity" (Dorling 1994). The British housing market has experienced three major booms in the past two decades (see Fig. 5.1), which underlines the importance of this issue. What is of particular concern is the view that the demand side may have become more unstable during the 1980s, because of the effects of financial deregulation in Britain and other countries (Bartlett & Bramley 1993).

Demand instability is a severe problem for the housebuilding industry itself, arguably the most severe problem it faces. Chapter 3 discussed this in theoretical terms, and Chapter 5 examined the strategies housebuilders adopted in the face of uncertainty, often with limited success. Ball (1983, 1988) has argued that such uncertainty has led the industry into a mode of operation that emphasizes flexibility (e.g. through subcontracting) at the expense of quality and technical progress. Training provision by the construction industry is widely recognized as a major area of weakness, and demand instability is one factor lying behind this. Another form of market failure is also involved here, the problem of poaching and the disincentive to investment in training that this represents.

If, for the above reasons, the housebuilding industry has a certain tendency to generate problems of quality, this places a greater premium on the mechanisms of regulation, including self-regulation, and on the information available to consumers. Although there have been improvements in this area, for example through the standard forms of house-buyers' reports promoted by the professional body RICS, the traditional economic assumption of "perfect information" remains a poor description of most people's experience of the housing market.

We have portrayed the housebuilding industry as generally competitive, and this is certainly our general impression from both qualitative evidence and hard data on the structure of industry. Therefore, we would not place too much emphasis on the theoretical possibility of local monopoly stemming from concentrated ownership and control of key development sites. As mentioned in Chapter 3, this could give rise to the speculative withholding of land from development, particularly in boom conditions. There is some danger that this possibility becomes more serious under a tight land-use planning control system; indeed, this could be more serious under the new style of development plans which are mandatory in the 1990s. A countervailing factor, though, is the openness of local markets revealed in Chapter 6, which means that competition between districts places a further limit on local monopoly.

The final aspect of market failure we would mention is a long-standing argument for State intervention in housing, as we suggested in Chapter 9. The argument that a minimum standard of housing consumption for all or some types of household is a "merit good" that people should have access to, regardless of ability to pay, is one that most would probably subscribe to. Despite rising average incomes, living standards and housing consumption, it remains true that significant minorities of households cannot gain access to adequate housing. Evidence for this is seen in the high levels of homelessness and waiting lists for social rented housing. In part, these problems reflect widening inequalities of income, as mentioned in Chapter 8. Up to the end of the boom in 1988–9, the tendency of house prices to rise ahead of the general price level, and in some periods faster than earnings, is another factor. Very high interest rates have exacerbated affordability problems at some points in time. At the time of writing, conventional affordability measures for owner-occupation are much more favourable, but problems of access to savings for deposits and credit-worthiness are more important. Clearly, many of these factors originate outside the field of planning and the housing market. However, there is some reason to be concerned that the housing system may exacerbate inequalities of real income, wealth and access. In particular, booming house prices may greatly enhance the differences in wealth between existing owners in favoured areas and others less favourably placed. The planning system may share some of the responsibility for this situation, to the extent that it reduces supply responsiveness. But, in the 1990s the planning system also offers new possibilities for offering affordable housing solutions to some of the households excluded from the mainstream owner-occupier market.

10.3 Planning failure

A balanced view of the role of planning would recognize the potential for planning in practice to fail, either in terms of its own objectives or in relation to some wider social goal (efficiency, growth, choice) which it gives too little attention to. Awareness of potential State failures has grown in recent years, particularly under the influence of the public choice school (Wolff 1988, Mueller 1989). In a recent restatement of the general theory of government failure, Le Grand (1991) grouped potential failures according to whether their impact was mainly on efficiency or equity, and according to the type of government involvement, whether in direct provision, subsidy/taxation, or regulation. Within this framework, land-use planning is primarily a regulatory form of government involvement, although it has some indirect implications for subsidy as we saw in Chapter 9.

Le Grand (1991: 15–16) identifies five general efficiency problems with regulation. The first is that it is difficult for the regulatory bodies to obtain the relevant information. This is clearly a real problem for planning authorities, for example in relation to future housing needs and demands, the significance of external effects, or the viability of particular schemes. In discussing the way that planning authorities assess future needs, we observed that there was perhaps an excessive and sometimes misleading emphasis on rather mechanistic demographic projections. It is desirable that planners should develop more awareness of market demands, prices and costs, not necessarily so that all demands are slavishly met but rather as background information to inform decisions, for example on affordability and social housing targets. To make this point is not to belittle the difficulties in deriving robust information in this area, let alone in making forecasts. Meaningful house price measures, for example, require adequate samples and standardization for size and type mix, condition and location. National professional organizations and economic forecasters find it difficult to forecast the housing market reliably.

A second general problem is the danger of "regulator capture", whereby continuous close contact with the regulated industry leads to a pattern of regulation that closely reflects the interests of the industry. This is plausible as a general scenario, although, in the case of planning, the local democratic accountability mechanism provides a counter, as does the fact that planning has to regulate a wide range of industries. It should also be noted that the optimum degree of land-use regulation, from the housebuilding industry's point of view, is unlikely to be none; the industry will want to reduce its uncertainty about infrastructure availability, future development patterns and potential external effects.

These problems can lead to a further danger, that of regulation restricting entry to, and competition within, the market. This can be a significant danger with land-use planning, because the act of zoning restricted parcels of land for development gives the owners of those sites potential monopoly power, which may be exploited by higher prices and slower development. Not only is this inefficient but also it provides inequitable rewards to individual landowners. It is important to be aware of this danger, although our evidence from the 1980s suggested that housebuilding was a fairly competitive activity. The new-style planning system of the 1990s, discussed further below, may create more dangers of local monopoly, and the lack of adequate public information about landownership and development options contributes to this problem. On the other hand, as mentioned above, the openness of local markets limits the monopoly power of landowners.

Le Grand's fourth problem only really arises when regulators try to control prices, creating excess supply or demand. This problem can arise with social housing provision, including low-cost home ownership schemes, but is not really a function of planning powers. Lastly, excessive regulation may stifle innovation and hence limit the dynamic efficiency or growth of the economy. This could be a potential problem with forms of regulation relating to building standards, design, energy and the like, as discussed in Chapter 8. Some of the technological backwardness, if that is a fair description, of British housing might relate to the way the building regulations are set out (e.g. why houses for many years had cold-water tanks in their roof spaces). However, the conservatism of buyers and financial institutions may be equally at fault.

Le Grand also reminds us that regulation may create perverse redistributional impacts; for example, rent controls to help the poor may end up benefiting well housed people on middle incomes and denying housing to poor homeless people. We argued in Chapter 3 that planning policies such as containment could redistribute welfare, spatially and socially. Chapter 9 went on to discuss the way in which some of these redistributions may be translated into wealth, through being capitalized into house prices. In Chapter 7 we argued that the restriction of land supply by the planning system does raise house prices somewhat, which re-distributes in favour of existing owners and against tenants and potential new buyers. However, we went on to suggest that the fuller use of planning agreements for affordable social housing could more than compensate in terms of access to housing.

When discussing subsidy policies, Le Grand (1991: 13–14) identifies some features of democratic majority voting procedures that give rise to potential failures or biases in public decision-making, based on the classic works of Downs (1957) and Buchanan & Tullock (1962). In fact, these problems could well apply to regulatory planning decisions as well, particularly where planning is subject to local democratic control. Voting mechanisms do not necessarily produce a rational, consistent way of aggregating individual preferences; particular groups (floating or median voters, pressure groups) may have undue influence; strength of preferences are not necessarily reflected; and representative democratic institutions with party systems mean that issues are packaged together in ways that suit the politicians. Decisions may not be made in a way equally informed about the costs and benefits.

Evans' (1991) discussion of the political economy of planning may be seen as a case study of the way some of these failures or biases arise. He argues that planning policy in South East England has led to a concentration of high-density development in or adjacent to urban areas, because of an excessive protection of rural areas. This has happened partly because it is what the general public appear to want, although he suggests that people's judgement is based on a false perception of the existing extent of urbanization. Partly it reflects the effectiveness of rural and agricultural interest groups. Finally, it reflects the weighting of a planning system operated by elected local authorities in favour of the interests of existing residents, who generally favour the status quo; potential in-migrants are given no weighting in local decision-making. Evans goes on to describe the process of actual land release in this context as one where the DoE tells the local authorities how many dwellings must be provided for and the local authorities then try to accommodate these in ways that minimize local political opposition. This generally involves cramming them in at high densities, using environmentally unattractive sites (e.g. next to transport routes), and concentrating development on a few very large sites. Although this picture may be slightly exaggerated, our own examination of the process in Avon, as well as other studies discussed in Chapter 4, do confirm that these tendencies are observable in practice. If the regulators have been captured, it is more by the rural lobby and suburban residents than by the housebuilding industry.

It can be argued that the spread of owner-occupation has worsened this problem. Most voters now have an equity stake in their local environment, which often represents the main part of their personal wealth. Most greenfield development, as well as suburban infill and intensification, will be perceived by the immediately adjacent residents as a diminution of their amenity, and is likely to be perceived as having some negative impact on house values.

A common practical complaint about the planning system is that it creates delay in the development process; delay is generally costly for developers, if any capital has been committed to a scheme, and it further reduces the responsiveness of supply. Delay in planning permission, and the associated uncertainties, are mainly a function of the style of planning, discussed further below. The same is probably true to some extent of the administrative cost of operating the planning system, and also the cost of "rent-seeking" activity by developers (Cheshire & Leven 1982), as discussed in Chapters 3 and 5. Devoting many real resources to the task of obtaining planning permissions would suggest a degree of failure in the system. This is a strong argument for a clearer plan-led system with less discretion.

Our own research has thrown up another general ground for concern about the success or failure of the planning system. This is what we termed in Chapter 7 the "implementation gap"; that is, the weak relationship at local level between structure plan housebuilding targets and actual planning permissions and completions. On a fairly basic measure of outcome, the system did not seem to be performing very successfully in the 1980s. Several reasons were put forward for this. Reasons which have to do with the nature of the planning system include the generalized, non-site-specific nature of the targets, the fact that some targets might be unrealistically high in low-demand areas, delays, and the fact that the system is essentially responsive so far as private sector development is concerned. Other important reasons include the growing importance of windfall sites, delays attributable to infrastructure problems, and the decisions of individual key landowners or developers regarding the timing of development. A better match of targets and output could probably be achieved by more realism in some cases, including allowances for probable windfalls, and avoidance of delay. There may be a case for more clearly distinguishing targets which are upper limits (e.g. in areas of containment) from targets that might function as forecasts, or aspirations. In other words, this problem is to some extent created by the planning system and its particular style of operation. If it is a problem for the real world, as opposed to being just a problem for planners, then practical solutions might involve more public intervention rather than less; more of what used to be called "positive planning".

At present the key change is from a reliance on structure plans and development control to a general reliance on site-specific local plans. This does appear to represent a step in the direction of more planning, although there may be compensating savings in terms of negotiations and appeals later on. However, it falls short of direct public involvement in the provision of development land. Previous British legislative attempts at giving public authorities a larger role in the ownership and supply of development land have foundered, politically and administratively. This is more true of the national legislation; in particular local contexts, including the new and expanded towns of the 1950–80 period, public sector land-banking and supply has been very successfully managed. Some other countries have been more successful in this regard, including the Netherlands (Needham 1992), Sweden (Barlow & King 1992, Barlow 1993) and parts of Australia (Cardew & Cuddy 1987). One of the traditional objections to public land-banking is the high cost of forward acquisition and holding of land. However, the private development industry could be imitated here, with the land banking agency simply buying options; small-scale examples of this model are being tried in rural areas, as Options Landbank Trusts.

10.4 Styles of planning

Some of the comments just made about possible planning failures draw attention to the importance of the style of planning policy and its implementation. The British planning system is distinguished by several features which give it a particular style. First, its coverage is very comprehensive in terms of the kinds of development it can control. Secondly, the range of material considerations it can take account of in reaching decisions is potentially very wide. Thirdly, there is no general presumption in favour of development with narrowly prescribed grounds for refusing planning permission. Each case must be considered on its merits and local planning authorities have great discretion over how they do this. Fourthly, planning decisions are conditioned by a hierarchy of plans, regional guidance, structure plans and local plans, which may not all be fully up-to-date and consistent. Fifthly, planning is very professionalized, in the sense that all planning authorities are staffed by professionally trained staff exercising considerable discretion and applying a host of norms and concepts of good practice. Increasingly, developers employ professionals with a similar background in order to work with this system. Sixthly, the features just described, together with other elements such as the growing importance of planning agreements, give rise to a great deal of negotiation between planning authorities and developers. Conversely, the scope for legal challenge to planning decisions is limited mainly to procedural rather than substantive matters. Recourse may be had to the quasi-judicial planning appeal process, but this is still an element in the same process subject to many of the same intrinsic features.

Many British planners would probably wish to defend this system and emphasize its virtues. It enables a wide range of considerations to influence planning decisions, which should hopefully improve the quality of those decisions. It offers great flexibility, which is important when market conditions can vary greatly over time and space and when local circumstances, and preferences, can make the rigid imposition of standards inappropriate (Healey et al. 1993: 40). The process of negotiation and the possibilities of planning agreements arguably facilitate development, within an overall framework of constraint, by unlocking infrastructure problems and by motivating local planning committees to overcome their natural reluctance to approve new housing developments in many areas. More than any uniform system of development charges or taxes, this negotiated system is more sensitive to circumstances and contains incentives that promote development. At the same time, it is more defensible than simple auctioning of planning permissions.

Other aspects of the British system can also be argued to be beneficial. The comprehensive and professionalized system generates a great deal of information, much (although not all) of it in the public domain. Excessive reliance on expensive legal processes dominated by a professional group not specialized in land-use planning is avoided. Britain may be, in comparison with the USA, somewhat "over-plannered", but at least it has the compensating advantage of not being so "over-lawyered".

Defence of the present style of British planning tends to involve certain implicit assumptions. First, planners are relatively knowledgeable and make intelligent use of a range of good information. For example, they can assess the range of external costs and benefits associated with a development, as well as shrewdly judge the net private gains to developers/landowners. This assumption may be optimistic. Secondly, planners act broadly in the public interest. Alternative views about the nature of planning and in whose/what interests it acts were rehearsed in Chapter 3, whereas in Chapter 7 we evaluated these against some evidence on the responsiveness of planning. On the whole we believe that, although planning is not simply captured by the housebuilding industry, there are signs that it may be captured in some localities by dominant local pressure-groups that emphasize some aspects of the public interest at the expense of the others. Having a professionalized planning system is an attempt to structure in a systematic concern for broader public interests, but it inherently carries in it the danger that to some degree the profession will act in its own interest. Thirdly, it is assumed that the planning system is not in general corrupt. On the whole, we have traditionally felt comfortable about such an assumption in relation to British public administration, whereas one would not necessarily make such an assumption in all other countries. Nevertheless, there are considerable opportunities for corruption in planning. The local democratic control and accountability of the system in some ways act as safeguards but in other ways opens up alternative channels for corruption.

What then of the negative side of the British style of planning? Some of these points have just been rehearsed, in the discussion of possible planning failure. A major criticism is that the discretionary system inherently increases rather than reduces uncertainty, a key issue identified in Chapters 3 and 5. Our evidence from the 1980s of an implementation gap in the case of structure-plan housing targets may be regarded as supporting this general contention. A counter argument might be that unambiguous plans would have been over-rigid in the face of an inherently unpredictable market and land supply situation (with its high level of windfall sites). A second general area of criticism is that discretion/negotiation are generally costly, in terms of the input of the planning side, rent-seeking expenditures by developers, speculative applications, and delay. There is some evidence that at least some of these costs are growing, giving genuine cause for concern. These features of the process also contribute to the overall low responsiveness of housing supply to changes in demand.

There are some grounds for concern about the lack of accountability associated with the essentially private process of negotiation around planning agreements and development control (Healey et al. 1993: 38–41). Other aspects of the planning system involve substantial public participation opportunities, not itself without cost. Much of the argument for this is the point that development tends to involve local external effects, which give third parties a legitimate interest in planning decisions. Yet in practice the rights of third parties may be limited, if they cannot influence the local political decision-making process. Lack of accountability may contribute to inequities and inconsistencies in the outcomes of negotiations. These may also arise from an ignorance or naïvety among planners about the economic and financial aspects of development proposals, in part a result of many years of planning practice guidance from government, which steered them away from such issues and urged them to concentrate on "pure" land use issues.

Reforming the style of planning

Is it possible to envisage reforms in the planning system that modify its style of operation, in such a way as to overcome or reduce some of the adverse features identified above? We can at least identify an agenda of possible changes, some more radical than others. Some of these are already being applied to some degree, at least in some areas.

- Structure plan targets for housing could be made more sophisticated, for example by specifying different levels of target (minimum, expected, maximum, aspiration), by expressing targets as contingent on relevant conditions (e.g. housing market), and by a more conscious and informed approach to windfall land.
- Local plans, which are district-wide and site-specific, are supposed to be being approved in all areas by the mid-1990s; this should greatly increase certainty and improve implementation, but there are some dangers of rigidity and lower responsiveness, the bolstering of local monopoly, and the pushing back of negotiations to an earlier stage in the process.
- To counter problems just mentioned, some have suggested that local plans should have a longer time horizon than ten years, so that more land is effectively allocated to give flexibility, subject to some phasing policies.
- Another approach might be to identify reserve and contingent sites; these could be brought forward subject to (a) demand exceeding expectations, or (b) the supply of windfall sites falling short of expectations.
- A public sector body could act as a land bank of last resort, holding some

potentially developable land (perhaps on option) and releasing it when required by pressure of demand in the private market (and need in the social sector) relative to the supply of private sites; this could be the local planning authority (in practice many do this with substantial inherited landholdings) or a special-purpose body, such as the Land Authority for Wales.

- Public/private partnership could become a more normal mode of development; this has been happening to an increasing extent, and the enhanced possibilities of planning agreements give more scope for this; one feature of this approach should be more overt and systematic accounting for development costs and profits, and their distribution (this is also an issue within the consortia of developers and landowners involved in larger sites).
- There should be a clearer framework of ground-rules for planning agreements, as argued by Healey et al. (1993).
- Consideration should be given to appropriate forms of taxation of development gains and/or land with prospective development value, with an emphasis on forms of taxation that promote rather than stifle development where planning has indicated that this is appropriate.

10.5 Planning and sustainability

"Sustainability" has almost become the watchword of planning in the 1990s. Planning is closely associated with environmental protection and enhancement, and so it is perhaps not surprising that the renewed emphasis since the late 1980s on environmentally sustainable development has been taken up enthusiastically by the planning profession. Chapter 8 briefly identified two specific ways in which one central aspect of sustainability, energy conservation, might impact on the planning and regulation of new housing. However, the sustainability slogan has much wider ramifications. What implications would there be for housing in a planning system that took sustainability seriously?

Sceptics might argue that government environmental policies are more symbolic than real, intended to give the right image for electoral and diplomatic purposes but not intended to be too radical, costly or challenging, either to important economic interests or to the average voter's life-style. This sceptical view may have some substance, but clearly environmental issues are politically quite important and contestable. The political process may turn a symbolic policy into something more substantial. One of the routes by which this may happen is through local democratic control of planning authorities. In addition, international pressures and agreements, including the European Union, are increasingly influential in this area. Finally, environmental policies are likely to be taken up more seriously when market prices and taxes convey a consistent message. For example, were the real price of petrol clearly seen to be rising and likely to rise further in the future, planning to limit car use might seem more urgent.

It could be argued that the sustainability issue is more critical in other areas of planning policy: transport, retail and commercial development, rural development and agriculture, minerals extraction, and settlement pattern. Nevertheless, some of these may have indirect implications for housing.

Let us take first the central issue of reducing energy consumption and CO_2 emissions. Chapter 8 suggested that the most important single policy area at issue here is transport, although energy efficiency in the home remains important. Environmentally sensitive transport policy has implications for planning, in the longer term, that cut right across some of the trends of recent years. These trends have included: more reliance on private road transport, a predominance of road-building over public transport investment or subsidy, counter-urbanization, out-of-town retail and commercial development, separation of housing and workplaces, and keeping densities down in some areas. From this point of view, the sustainability perspective suggests a radical change in urban strategy, and to this extent one must express some caution about its political realism, despite official statements giving some support to the new approach. Having said this, it should be recognized that some aspects of the existing planning policy could be seen as supportive of this perspective: urban containment (although this may have promoted more longer-distance commuting) and urban regeneration probably fall in this category. To this extent the new policy is not a complete departure.

Density is central to the economics of planning and housing supply. Planning orientated to a sustainable transport strategy implies higher densities, less scattered development in smaller rural settlements, and fewer low-density suburbs. This implies that the (mainly private) welfare that households enjoy from living at lower densities (e.g. larger gardens) will be restricted, and that compensating improvements in housing design and quality, and in (public) open space and recreational facilities, may be called for. Furthermore, acceptance of this strategy implicitly means that a low supply elasticity for housing must be expected to feature even more strongly in the future. The arguments of some economists to reduce or remove planning control become even less realistic. If this is a problem for macroeconomic policy, other measures to provide compensating supply response (tax incentives, public land banking, etc.), or to control the fluctuations in demand, may be called for.

Sustainability may reinforce the case for regulating standards of new housing more strongly, especially in relation to energy efficiency. At the time of writing, there is a strong thrust within government to reduce regulation throughout the economy, and this may be a case where different strands of policy simply conflict. As Chapter 8 pointed out, though, energy efficiency does at least provide occupiers with a pay-off, and a reliance on good information and advisory standards might be almost as effective. The problems are likely to arise at the bottom end of the market, where poorer, credit-constrained purchasers may feel forced to buy a cheaper, energy-inefficient house where alternative accommodation options are very limited.

The sustainability concept could be applied to other aspects of the quality of new housing in a more general and direct sense, as durability. Environmentalists would probably argue that it is wasteful to spend many resources building a house that is only going to last, say, 20–40 years, when for a modest extra cost the life could be extended perhaps indefinitely. Some at least of the resources used in housebuilding are non-renewable (e.g. energy) or carry considerable environmental cost (e.g. forest products, aggregates). It is salutary to remember that the annual rate of new building in Britain is equivalent to only 1–2% of the stock, which implies that housing is expected to last 50–100 years. Current rates of demolition in Britain are remarkably low, and simple extrapolation would imply that British houses are expected to last more like 600 years. Many building professionals would question whether these figures are sustainable indefinitely, and they could suggest a danger of a major problem of housing obsolescence accumulating for future generations to deal with.

Experience with housing renewal programmes in Britain has shown that it is difficult to manage processes of demolition and replacement of older private sector housing in ways which are acceptable to residents, communities and the local political process, however poor the quality of the housing. One key reason for this is the development of owner-occupation as the predominant tenure, even in the older urban areas and among people on moderate or low incomes. Another is the negative experiences associated with past clearance programmes and the replacement housing provided by local authorities. Experiences in other countries differ somewhat. For example, in the USA, housing has traditionally not been expected to last so long, and this is reflected in methods of construction and the significant role played by mobile homes. Factors associated with this different tradition include the greater mobility of the population and the larger role played by private renting. Land supply and planning also clearly play a part. The British emphasis on containment and urban regeneration imply that the existing housing stock is more likely to be retained. Insofar as housing is being demolished, it is increasingly likely to be the least popular public sector stock that is taken out, a trend also apparent in other countries. The fact that this housing is often relatively modern is less important than the fact that it is the most socially stigmatized and also very often suffering from major structural defects.

In Chapter 2 we pointed out that expenditure on repair and maintenance was an important element in the overall supply of housing, acting as it does to counter obsolescence. Repair and maintenance, together with investment in major renewals and upgrading, now account for a similar volume of investment as new building (Bramley et al. 1990). This is the reason why, despite the low rate of demolitions, the overall condition of the housing stock is not deteriorating, although it is not improving very much either (DoE 1988, 1993a). The major concern here is perhaps not so much with the amount of expenditure as with aspects of its effectiveness, efficiency and distribution. Public spending constraints on the availability of grants and subsidies for repair and improvement make this issue one of growing concern (Leather & Mackintosh 1993). This raises issues beyond the scope of this book, but serves to remind us that the sustainability of our housing stock is as much to do with repair and improvement as it is to do with new building.

10.6 The housing industry in the 1990s

In looking to the future, what trends and changes in the housebuilding industry can be anticipated on the basis of our analysis of experience over the past decade and our review in this chapter of the evolving character of planning for housing? Some important themes can be discerned, and it is worth spelling these out somewhat at least as a focus for debate within and about the industry. These themes relate to stability, structure, diversity, quality, profitability and its sources, and styles of housing promotion.

Stability

Between the early 1970s and the early 1990s the housebuilding industry suffered from extreme instability, in Britain and some comparable countries. This instability stemmed primarily from the sensitivity of housing investment demand to macroeconomic and monetary conditions. This instability was exacerbated in the 1980s by the move towards deregulation of the mortgage and financial markets and the coincidence of the housing cycle with equally extreme cycles in commercial development (Bartlett & Bramley 1994). The problems for the industry were further exacerbated by the major cutback after 1976 in the public sector housing programme, which had previously acted to some extent as a counter-cyclical source of demand. Following the recent boom, macroeconomists and policymakers became much more sensitive to the adverse feedback effects of housing market instability on the behaviour of macroeconomic variables such as consumption and saving. This is one key reason why we may expect the immediate future to be less like the immediate past, and predict that there is unlikely to be a repetition of the 1980s boom. The Treasury may be expected to act earlier to prevent this and to support policies geared to stabilizing the market. The progressive withdrawal of mortgage tax relief is one tangible element of such policies, as are attempts to revive private renting and the willingness to use public housing investment counter-cyclically, as in 1992–3.

Other factors reinforce our view that another boom in housing demand is unlikely, particularly the major demographic downturn associated with the age structure of the population (fewer young couples forming new households, as explained by Ermisch 1990). We could add to this a view that owner-occupation may be approaching a saturation level and that, in the short term, experiences of house price deflation, negative equity, mortgage arrears and repossessions will act to deter confidence and investment demand.

A future in which housing demand may be less unstable has implications for the industry that may be regarded as broadly positive. These are developed further below, and include the possibility that the performance of housebuilding firms may be more related to activities in housebuilding per se than to their engagement in speculative land development. The discussion in Chapter 5 drew attention to some of the problems in the structure of the industry, for example relating to subcontracting, training and labour supply, and the rapid entry and exit of firms, which seem to be closely related to its instability (a theme much emphasized in the work of Ball 1983 and 1988). In considering apparent trends in the industry and its output over the past decade or so, it is easy to confuse the effects of cyclical change with longer-term secular changes. In Chapter 8 for example we looked at the changing mix of house types produced in this light. If the coming period is one of more stability, the secular changes may emerge as more important.

Structure

The structure of the housebuilding industry has clearly changed, but as Chapter 5 illustrated there are some contradictory or confusing elements in the picture. While some commentators have suggested that the longer-term trends are towards greater concentration and dominance by the large-volume housebuilders, the picture in the late 1980s was one characterized by intense competition and considerable new entry (albeit often complemented by frequent exit). Housebuilding is still much less concentrated and more competitive than many sectors of industry, although markets are more localized and less globalized than in most of manufacturing and some services. There does seem to be a longer-term trend whereby medium-size independent firms specializing in housebuilding for a local/regional market have declined, often being taken over by larger firms motivated in part by the acquisition of land banks with planning prospects. The predominant firms now are regional housebuilding subsidiaries of large corporations with wider interests in allied sectors, for example civil engineering, building materials, commercial development or leisure industries. Small local firms may still find a niche, for example in building more up-market homes in small volumes, although such activity is sensitive to the state of the market, access to finance and land. Such firms may be more active in repair, improvement and conversion work.

It can be argued that the planning system has reinforced these structural trends and will continue to do so. We argued in Chapter 5 that larger firms can spread their risks between sites across a wide area, and may have better financial backing to engage in forward acquisition of sites or options and land trading. They may be better able to afford to engage the level of professional input to maximize their chances of getting enough planning permissions to continue operations at a reasonable level, although one should not understate the importance of local knowledge and contacts, which may still favour locally based firms. Another feature that emerges strongly from this and other studies is the important role played by a few very large sites, a consequence of the political economy of planning. Large firms are better able to manage such developments or engage in consortium approaches with adequate bargaining power. Large firms may also be better able to exploit the opportunities for negotiating planning agreements involving social housing and other community facilities, under the new policies set out in PPG3 (DoE 1992), for example by having the range of house types to offer or the ability to finance cross-subsidy. As the housing association sector itself becomes more concentrated and more interested in volume and package deals, this tendency may be reinforced.

One of the striking features of housing production in recent years has been the extent of reliance on subcontracting. This accounts for the continuing statistical picture of a very fragmented industry. It has also been argued to contribute greatly to problems of quality control, training and working conditions in the industry. Subcontracting is clearly in part a response to the problem of unstable demand. If the future is characterized by more stability, this trend may reverse itself to some extent. However, subcontracting offers other advantages in the management of production, and it is worth pointing out that this style of industrial organization has been very much on the increase in many sectors other than building. Although the technology of house construction is not subject to very dramatic change, it has not been completely static. For example, greater use is made of mechanical equipment and prefabricated components. These trends seem to be compatible with a continuing heavy reliance on subcontracting. As in other sectors, housebuilding firms may strive to devolve and disperse everyday management and responsibility, particularly for employment, while increasing their overall control of the process, using whatever technical aids are available. An example of this is the growing tendency to use design-and-build package deals when contracting to supply housing to social landlords, achieving efficiencies by taking control of the design process so that priority is given to ensuring that the housing is easy to build.

Diversity and quality

Diversity may be an increasingly important theme in the 1990s. In Chapter 8 we discussed some aspects of this trend, which reflects both demographic changes, leading to demands for a wider range of types and sizes of new housing, and tastes. One could set this in a broader societal context by referring to concepts of postmodernism, which entail a move away from mass production and mass consumption towards more specialized but flexible production for consumers who exhibit more diversified tastes relating to differing lifestyles and ways of using the home, with differing cultural priorities and points of reference. Many of those who buy new homes are not motivated by an urgent need to find somewhere to live, but are making a discretionary move to improve their quality of life or adapt to changing circumstances, for example those associated with the maturing of families, ageing or relationship changes. Such consumers are likely to be more discriminating and may be strongly concerned with issues of quality and user cost. Investment motives for house purchase may still be important, but informed by recent experiences that emphasize that house prices are not certain to rise by large amounts in real terms. Homes thought likely to hold or gain value because of their intrinsic qualities may be at more of a premium. Housebuilders who can tailor products and market them successfully in this more discriminating market are likely to be more successful than those who simply try to sell large volumes of a uniform product, or those who concentrate on land development at the expense of addressing the nature and quality of the product. The amount of land development gain in the total price of housing and in the profit of housebuilding firms is likely to remain smaller, because of the probability that prices will not rise dynamically and also because of the greater claim on these gains that planning obligations are likely to represent.

Social housing represents a diversification of output for some builders, although others have always worked with local authorities and housing associations as clients. The detailed specifications required by housing associations usually differ from nominally equivalent private sale housing, although associations may compromise on these when offered a favourable package deal or buying "off the shelf". In Chapter 5 we noted that the interest of private housebuilders in social housing increased between the mid-1980s and the early 1990s, some firms setting up subsidiaries specializing in social, partnership or low-cost housing, and some in the related field of urban regeneration. Such a move seems a rational response to the slump in the private market and the recent expansion of the housing association programme (in 1992/3 the scale of the housing association programme was approaching half the size of private new-build output, compared with about one-sixth in 1988). This move may have a cyclical element, and some observers believe that when the market recovers there will be less enthusiasm for social housing in the industry. Others suggest that some firms will make a more permanent commitment to this sector because it is a form of diversification that reduces demand-side instability, risk and selling costs.

Specialized housing, such as sheltered housing for elderly people provided with such facilities as alarms, common rooms and warden support, was originally developed in the social sector but has subsequently emerged as a private market. Certain firms have developed this specialism, although the recent slump showed that operating in this sector could be risky; moves into private sheltered housing tend to be discretionary and sensitive to price appreciation and ease of sale in the mainstream owner-occupation market. Housing associations operate leasehold (shared ownership) schemes for the elderly which are intermediate between private and social housing, and these have also shown similar market sensitivity.

We argued above that housing consumers may become more discriminating and concerned with quality. How far this is true depends partly on the quality of information and advice available to consumers. In the past it is probably fair to say that many buyers were more swayed by location, space and amenities and by relatively cosmetic features of the appearance of houses, inside and out, than by the intrinsic quality of materials, workmanship and design. Ease of mobility and ever-rising prices may have meant that less attention was given to the latter features. In the second-hand market, the tradition has been one of letting the buyer beware, with little regulation or standardization of the information provided by the "exchange professionals" (surveyors, real estate agents), although this is beginning to change. Only when clear systems of accreditation and documentation of standards become more widespread and understood are the more intrinsic quality attributes of housing likely to be reflected more clearly in resale values and in the demands for new housing.

To the extent that this happens, the industry will face more of a challenge on quality. This will put to the test how far the structure of the industry created in the 1970s and 1980s, to maximize flexibility, will be able to deliver quality in the late 1990s. Quality depends on many things, but adequate skills, supervision and motivation of the workforce would be among those which one would expect to be present. These are areas which the current system of subcontracting may well not be delivering.

The promotion of new housing

We are arguing that the profitability of housebuilding may be rather more stable in the future, but that the opportunities for large-scale profit from the development gain in land values will be significantly less. Ability to manage the relationship with the planning system will continue to be important to the ability of firms to operate successfully, but this process will require real investment in infrastructure, community facilities and social housing. Profits will also be earned from successfully targeting, producing for and marketing to particular segments of the market, without becoming overspecialized and hence vulnerable. Developing a reputation for quality may also become an important element in some firms' strategies.

Because the speculative mode of promotion of new housing is so dominant in Britain, it is sometimes taken for granted as a necessary and unchanging feature of housing supply. Yet comparisons with other European countries show that this is far from universal. Other models include self-promotion, sometimes in more organized and large-scale forms, as well as promotion by public or non-profit agencies and co-operatives (Barlow & King 1992, Duncan & Rowe 1993). Britain in the 1980s had 82% of output produced speculatively for owner-occupation and only 6% was self-promoted, whereas in some countries including France and Italy more than 50% of completions were self-promoted (Duncan & Rowe 1993: 1335). Public or social housing agencies may also promote new housing, not only for rent but also through various forms of building for sale or low-cost home-ownership. The model of promotion is often bound up with the means of financing house construction and purchase. Thus, in other countries that have less highly developed mortgage lending arrangements than in Britain, special forms of credit often linked to specific supply subsidies and particular forms of promotion (e.g. co-operatives) have been common. In the long run, with financial deregulation and supply subsidy cutbacks, a degree of convergence toward the British model may be observable.

The planning system may also affect the scope for different forms of housing promotion. In the early post-war years in Britain, for example, the planning system undoubtedly gave positive support to public sector housing development, and contributed to the rapid growth of council housing. It is argued that the planning system, with its strong emphasis on containment, actually militates against the significant development of self-promoted housing, which typically operates through the process of potential consumers buying small plots of land and then either building a house themselves or purchasing one from a catalogue. The generally hostile attitude of the planning profession to past self-build efforts – for example, the bungalow developments in certain seaside areas – continues to be reflected in development control responses to self-build proposals (Duncan & Rowe 1993: 1343–4).

Recent changes in the ways in which social housing is promoted (Bramley 1993), emphasizing the role of housing associations, partnership approaches, and planning policy targets and agreements, are significant in their own right. They introduce more diversity and ambiguity into the promotion process; which agency is taking the lead in promotion: the housebuilder, the housing association or the local authority? Private housebuilders, with their entrepreneurial approach and their expertise, both in marketing and in dealing with the land-use planning system, may still have the decisive role here, but there are certainly examples of housing associations or local authorities taking more of a lead. The current tendency in procurement for social housing is towards design-and-build package deals, often grouped in such a way that one overall contract may supply units to several associations, possibly across several sites. Proposals to make Housing Association Grant directly available to private developers, relegating associations to a management role, would if activated reinforce the role of those developers who have successfully adapted to the new-style social housing "market".

A continuing and related concern in government policy is a wish to see private renting revive on a permanent basis, with new building for private rent as well as use of the existing stock. Between 1987 and 1993 the Business Expansion Scheme used generous tax relief subsidies to generate some investment of this kind (Crook et al. 1991), but this scheme was inherently temporary and, at the time of writing, no more permanently sustainable form of subsidy has been established. Without such a subsidy, or a further cutback in owner-occupation subsidies, substantial investment in new provision for private renting seems unlikely to happen (Kemp 1993). Private renting seems fairly buoyant only in certain niche markets, particularly for students, and young and mobile workers. What may be more important in the longer term is a progressive blurring of the boundaries, both between ownership and renting (with the growth of shared ownership) and between social and private renting (with the forms of promotion described above, together with more contracting out of management within the social sector). In some other countries this blurring is more pronounced, for example in West Germany where social provision is effected through limited life subsidies to private providers.

10.7 The big issues

In this chapter we have examined themes about the relationship between planning, housebuilding and the housing market, drawing on recent experience in Britain and elsewhere, and looking to the future. Taking these ideas and speculations, together with the more firmly based conclusions from research detailed earlier in the book, what conclusions do we draw about the big issues in planning and housing? There are perhaps four overall conclusions we would want to emphasize.

The first is that planning does affect the housing market, raising house prices and densities and reducing supply responsiveness. This conclusion should be placed in perspective, however. An absence of planning, or a very liberal planning policy on housing land release, would not eliminate these problems, or even dramatically reduce them. We also believe that some of the ways in which the British planning system fails in its relationship with the housing market could be significantly ameliorated by modifications in planning's style of operation, for example in relation to structure- and local-plan housing targets.

The second key point is that planning is almost certainly here to stay. This conclusion emerges from our examination of both the rationales for planning, particularly its rôles in countering certain market failures, and of its political economy and the support it enjoys in the political system, not least at local level. The rise of environmental politics and the centrality of the issues of sustainability are bound to reinforce planning and regulation.

Our third conclusion is that the use of planning agreements to facilitate the provision of infrastructure and community facilities, and to overcome or compensate for the negative impacts of development, is a positive, permanent development to be welcomed, encouraged, but perhaps systematized. We favour the use of this approach to secure land and subsidy for social housing where appropriate and viable, suggesting that this could be quite significant in some areas but less so in urban and depressed areas. In our view, this approach, which is negotiated and bottom-up, is to be much preferred to uniform, top-down development taxes or charges, because the planning agreement approach is much more likely to promote development with local support.

Finally, we hope and believe that the future will be less characterized by dramatic booms and slumps in housing and property prices, although this does assume that governments have the will as well as the means to tame the deregulated financial markets. Land development profit will be less dominant, and private housebuilders may increasingly find themselves competing on quality for more diversified markets.

APPENDIX

Variable definitions, sources and summary statistics

This appendix defines the variables used in the cross-sectional modelling of local housing markets reported in Chapters 6–9. The units of observation are 90 local authority districts in 13 counties as shown in Figure 6.3. For each variable the definition is given below with the source given in parentheses, with variables grouped into broad categories (e.g. demographic). A table then shows summary statistics for each variable. Finally, the main data sources are identified with variables listed grouped by source.

A.1 Variable definitions

Demographic variables

NO1	Number of owner-occupier households in 1986, estimated (PHRG, CENSUS, HIP)
H3A	Gross new household formation per annum per 1000 households, inferred from demographic projection (PHRG)
H4	Household dissolutions per annum per 100 households (PHRG)
HDIS3	Household dissolutions per annum *c.* 1986 per 1000 households, mean of H3A and estimate based on elderly owner-occupiers in 1981 (PHRG, CENSUS)
NMIG	Net migrant households per annum per 1000 owner-occupiers, average 1981–6 (PHRG)

Economic & employment

E1	Total employment (by workplace) to resident population ratio, 1987 (CE, OPCS)
E3	Change in total employment per annum 1984–7, % (CE)
E10	Manufacturing employment as % of all employment, 1987 (CE)

U8 Resident unemployment rate, % of economically active (DE)
Y1 Median gross household income, estimated for 1989 (BAG)
Z3 High social class (professional, managerial, intermediate non-manual), % of economically active residents, 1981 (CENSUS)

Geographical

G2 Length of protected coastline in kilometres per 1000 population (GRE)
G7LN Natural logarithm of distance from central London in kilometres (MAP)
G8LN Natural logarithm of distance from the nearer of Bristol or Birmingham in kilometres (MAP)
G9 Latitude, measured in kilometres north of the Lizard point (MAP)
DW Population density, calculated as the population-weighted average of ward-level densities in persons per hectare for 1981 (CENSUS, via GRE)
DS Simple population density for whole district, persons per hectare, 1981 (CENSUS, via GRE)

Other housing supply & characteristics

QA1 Total lettings of social housing units per 1000 households 1986–7 (HIP)
WL87 Waiting list for council (social) housing in 1987, number (HIP)
N7 Private renting as % of all households, 1981 (CENSUS)
LSBATH Households lacking or sharing a bath in 1981, % (CENSUS)
VACS Estimated private sector vacancy rate in 1987 per 1000 (HIP)
DOMRB7 Average domestic rate bill per domestic hereditament, £ per year, 1987/8 (CIPFA)

Overall demand composite indicators

DEMANDS1 Structural demand composite index D_S, comprising unweighted standardized sum of Y1, Z3, –G7LN, –G8LN, –G9, N7, –LSBATH
DEMANDL1 Local/variable composite demand index D_L, comprising the unweighted standardized sum of H3A, –H4, E1, E3, –E10, –U8, –QA1, –DOMRB7

Land supply

LS7 Land with outstanding planning permission for private housing devel-

	opment in units per 1000 owner-occupiers, March 1987 (CPD, PS3)
LS6	As LS7, for March 1986
LA7	Land allocated for private housebuilding in approved local plan or by committee resolution but not yet granted permission, in units per 1000 owner-occupiers in March 1987 (CPD)
LF67	New planning permissions for private housing development, flow in units per 1000 owner-occupiers, average for two years 1986–8 inferred from stocks of permissions outstanding and completions data (CPD, LHS, PS3)
LSF7	Sum of stock (LS7) and flow of permissions (LF67) for 1987, in units per 1000 owner-occupiers (see LF7)
G18	Approved Green Belt area as % of all non-urban land (SERRL, CPD, MAP)
LTR2LN	Natural logarithm of total unconstrained land expressed in notional units per 1000 owner-occupiers (SERRL, CPD, MAP)
CONST1	Physical non-constraints index; composite indicator comprising unweighted standardized sum of -DW, -G18, LTR2LN

Planning policy

PPD1	Very restrictive planning policies dummy (CPD)
PPD2	Moderately restrictive planning policies dummy (CPD)
LP	Structure plan policy target for housing development in 1986–8 period, units per annum per 1000 owner-occupiers (CPD)
PPRAT	Weighted average success rate of planning applications for major and minor housing development 1986–8, % (PS2)
POL1	Conservative political control of district council in 1990, dummy (MY)
POL3	Labour political control in 1990 (MY)
PPS1	Planning policy stance composite index, comprising unweighted standardized sum of LP, PPRAT, –PPD1, –PPD2

Housebuilding output

QD6	Private completions in 1986 per 1000 owner-occupiers, from LA returns to DoE (LHS)
QD7	Private completions in 1987, as QD6
QD8	Private completions in 1988, as QD6
QN8	Private completions in 1988 per 1000 owner-occupiers, from NHBC records (NHBC)
QDN8	Average of QD8 and QN8
QD3YA	Average annual private completions over the three years 1986–8 per 1000 owner-occupiers, based on QD6, QD7 and QDN8

QD802 Total private completions over the three years 1980–81 per 1000 owner-occupiers (LHS)

DLS2 Density of new private housing sites with planning permission 1986–8 in dwellings per hectare (CPD)

House prices and costs

PS6 Price of a standard modern 900 sq. ft semi-detached house in 1986, £'000 (NABS)

PS8 Price of standard modern house in 1988, as PS6

PAH6 Price of all homes bought in 1986, £'000 (NABS)

PN8 Price of standard new house completed & sold in 1988, £'000 (NHBC)

PAV26 Change in average price of all sales between 1982 and 1986, % (NABS)

DCOSTIND Rebuilding cost index for housing, based on RICS (1991) with values interpolated by regression formula for districts (BCIS)

CS6 Estimated rebuilding cost for standard modern semi-detached house of 900 sq. ft in 1986 (BCIS)

CS8 Rebuilding cost for standard modern house in 1988, as CS6

CN8 Building cost for standard new house in 1988 (BCIS)

PCS6 Price (PS6) – building cost (CS6) for standard modern house in 1986 (NABS, BCIS)

PCS8 Price – cost for modern house in 1988, as PCS6

PCN8 Price – cost for new house in 1988 (NHBC, BCIS)

A.2 Summary statistics

Variable	Mean	Std dev.	Minimum	Maximum	N (non-missing
Demographic					
NO1	30446	24985	7522	216362	90
H3A	20.15	3.91	8.59	33.81	90
H4	.95	.30	.00	1.67	90
HDIS3	18.69	6.13	4.97	35.61	90
NMIG	7.35	12.51	−22.11	33.72	90
Economic & employment					
E1	.36	.10	.19	.73	90
E3	1.57	2.60	−3.10	12.87	90
E10	26.80	9.70	9.95	52.95	90
U8	7.18	3.07	2.3	16.3	90
Y1	246.6	34.1	194.6	347.1	90
Z3	33.35	7.80	15.1	54.8	90
Geographical					
G2	0.00	0.00	0.00	0.0104	90
G7LN	5.07	.43	3.69	5.69	90
G8LN	3.91	.78	1.10	4.95	90
G9	207.3	78.6	75	355	90
DW	19.47	12.33	1.51	53.71	90
DS	10.87	12.74	.34	46.58	90
Other housing supply & characteristics					
QA1	12.31	7.39	3.06	50.90	90
WL87	2433	2512	482	20664	90
N7	13.63	4.97	5.2	25.7	90
LSBATH	2.46	1.33	.4	6.2	90
VACS	35.67	13.21	10.02	71.14	81
DOMRB7	409	62.2	278	545	90
Overall demand					
DEMANDS1	0.0	.52	−1.28	1.14	90
DEMANDL1	0.0	.38	−1.44	.88	90
Land supply					
LS7	80.4	53.6	13.4	345.6	90
LS6	75.4	46.2	14.3	360.1	90
LA7	28.7	34.0	0	169.5	90
LF67	20.6	18.9	1.0	110.6	90
LSF7	101.5	63.4	18.3	426.6	90
G18	28.7	34.8	.0	100.0	90
LTR2LN	8.58	2.95	.33	12.57	90
CONST1	−.06	.63	−1.63	.82	90

Variable	Mean	Std dev.	Minimum	Maximum	N (non-missing
Planning policy					
PPD1	.14	.35	.00	1.00	90
PPD2	.34	.48	.00	1.00	90
LP	20.6	8.86	7.45	51.10	90
PPRAT	69.2	10.14	43.82	89.50	90
POL1	.52	.50	.00	1.00	90
POL3	.20	.40	.00	1.00	90
PPS1	.0	.52	−1.19	1.18	90
Housebuilding output					
QD6	15.7	7.97	.74	52.9	90
QD7	18.6	12.4	1.76	80.3	90
QD8	18.8	10.0	1.98	43.9	87
QN8	16.4	7.8	2.47	35.3	90
QDN8	17.6	8.56	2.66	36.7	87
QD3YA	17.2	7.39	3.30	38.8	87
QD802	36.0	16.7	5.8	95.6	90
DLS2	23.2	8.3	13.2	54.0	90
House prices & costs					
PS6	41.0	9.96	26.25	63.5	80
PS8	52.1	12.39	22.27	79.9	90
PAH6	39.3	9.7	19.5	66.5	90
PN8	74.6	21.49	41.25	151.4	90
PAV26	48.2	15.79	1.16	91.1	90
DCOSTIND	.98	.05	.874	1.128	90
CS6	35.5	1.96	31.72	40.95	90
CS8	39.8	2.20	35.52	45.85	90
CN8	38.4	2.12	34.33	44.32	90
PCS6	5.21	8.39	−7.58	23.6	80
PCN8	36.1	19.99	4.91	108.81	90

A.3 Data sources

The following list identifies the sources of data for the variables listed in this Appendix, in alphabetical order of the acronyms used in section A.1 above. The with the relevant variable names are given in parentheses.

BAG as estimated by the author for the *Bridging the affordability gap* study, Bramley (1991) (Y1)

BCIS RICS (1991) *BCIS Guide to house rebuilding costs for 1991* data on rebuilding costs of standard house types and on county-level construction cost variations (PCS8, PCN8, DCOSTIND, CN8, CS8, CS6)

CE	Department of Employment, Census of Employment data for 1984 and 1987 by workplace by district, accessed via the NOMIS database, University of Durham (E1, E3, E10)
CENSUS	1981 Census of Population, Office of Population Censuses and Surveys, published data for districts in *Key statistics for local authority areas*, together with certain indicators broken down by tenure from *Small area statistics* accessed via NOMIS database at Durham (NO1, Z3, N7, LSBATH, HDIS3)
CIPFA	Chartered Institute of Public Finance and Accountancy *Financial and general statistics 1987–88* includes data on average domestic rate bill (DOMRB7)
CPD	County Planning Departments were asked to supply a range of data broken down by districts on land with outstanding planning permission or allocated for housing, on planning policy targets and general planning policies (LS6, LS7, LA7, LF67, LSF7, PPD1, PPD2, LP, DLS2); also a secondary source on land use constraints (G18, LTR2LN)
DE	Department of Employment annual counts of unemployed people claiming benefit by district of residence, also accessed via NOMIS (U8)
DOERO	Department of the Environment Regional Offices, secondary source on Green Belt and AONB areas (G18, LTR2LN)
GRE	Society of County Treasurers (1989) *Block Grant Indicators 1988–89* includes indicators used for the former Grant-Related Expenditure system, including population weighted ward density (DW) and simple density (DS) and a coastline indicator (G2)
HIP	Local Authority "HIP1" returns to the Department of the Environment include annual data on the supply of lettings, private sector vacancies and council housing waiting lists (NO1, QA1, VACS, WL87)
LHS	Department of the Environment annual *Local housing statistics* data on private housing completions (QD802, QD6, QD7, QD8, QDN8, QD3YA, LF67)
MAP	Direct map measurement (G7LN, G8LN, G9; secondary source for checking G18, LTR2LN)
NABS	Nationwide (Anglia) Building Society data on average price and price per square foot of floor area of all houses purchased at market value with a Nationwide Anglia mortgage by broad age and type categories by district (PS8, PS6, PAH8, PAV26, PCS6, PCS8)
NHBC	National House Building Council returns compiled from registration-related inspection process of new private housing completions and estimated prices by type by district (QN8, QDN8, PN8, PCN8)
PHRG	Population and Housing Research Group, Anglia University (formerly Anglia Polytechnic), Chelmsford, England, who supplied a set of population and household projections for every district for five year intervals from 1981 to 2001 (NO1, H3A, HDIS3, H4, E1)
PS2	Department of the Environment annual returns from district councils

on planning permissions granted and refused for major and minor housing development (PPRAT)

PS3 Department of the Environment annual returns from district councils on land available for housing, as secondary source (LS6, LS7, LF67, LSF7)

SERRL South East Regional Research Laboratory GIS-based calculation of areas within each district which are urban (OPCS 1981 definition), approved Green Belt, or Areas of Outstanding Natural Beauty or National Park, using boundary data supplied by DoE (G18, LTR2LN)

MY *Municipal yearbook*, annual (POL1, POL3)

References

Aaron, H. J. 1972. *Shelter and subsidies: who benefits from federal housing policies*. Washington DC: Brookings.

Access Committee for England 1993. *Building homes for successive generations*. Access Committee for England, 25 Mortimer St, London W1N 8AB.

Adams, D. & H. May 1990. Landownership and land-use planning. *The Planner* **76**(38), 11–14.

Alonso, W. 1964. *Location and land use*. Cambridge, Mass.: Harvard University Press.

Ambrose, P. 1986. *Whatever happened to planning?* London: Methuen.

Amos, C. 1988. Testing time for new settlements. *Town and Country Planning*, November.

Arnott, R. 1987. Economic theory and housing. In *Handbook of regional and urban economics* (vol. II), E. S. Mills (ed.). Amsterdam: Elsevier.

Arnott, R., R. Davidson, D. Pines 1983. Housing quality, maintenance and rehabilitation. *Review of Economic Studies* **503**, 467–94.

Audit Commission 1992. *Developing local authority housing strategies*. London: HMSO.

Bailey, S. & R. Paddison 1988. *The reform of local government finance in Britain*. London: Routledge.

Ball, M. 1983. *Housing policy and economic power*. London: Methuen.

Ball, M 1988. *Rebuilding construction*. London: Routledge.

Ball, M. & R. Kirwan 1977. Accessibility and supply constraints in an urban housing market. *Urban Studies* **14**(1), 11–32.

Barlow, J. 1990. *Who plans Berkshire? Land supply, house price inflation and housing developers*. Working Paper 72, Centre for Urban and Regional Studies, University of Sussex.

—1993a. Controlling the housing land market: some examples from Europe. *Urban Studies* **30**(7), 1129–50.

—1993b. Paper presented at Planning & Environmental Training conference, London, 8 October.

Barlow, J. & D. Chambers 1991. *The impact of planning agreements on the provision of affordable housing*. Housing Research Findings 40, Joseph Rowntree Foundation, York.

Barlow, J. & D. Chambers 1992. *Planning agreements and affordable housing provision*. Working Paper, Centre for Urban and Regional Research, University of Sussex.

Barlow, J & A. King 1992. The State, the market, and competitive strategy: the housebuilding industry in the United Kingdom, France and Sweden. *Environment and Planning A* **24**, 381–400.

Barnett, R. & N. Topham 1980. A critique of equalising grants to local government. *Scottish Journal of Political Economy* **27**, 235–50.

Bartlett, W. 1989. *Housing supply elasticities: theory and measurement*. Housing Finance Discussion Paper, Joseph Rowntree Memorial Trust, York.

Bartlett, W. & G. Bramley 1994. *European housing finance: single market or mosaic?* SAUS Study, School for Advanced Urban Studies, University of Bristol.

Best, R. H. 1981. *Land use and living space*. London: Methuen.

Bishop, K. & A. Hooper 1991. *Planning and social housing*. London: Institute of Housing / National Housing Forum.

Boddy, M. 1980. *The building societies*. London: Macmillan.

Bogart, W. T. 1993. "What big teeth you have": identifying the motives for exclusionary zoning. *Urban Studies* **30**(10), 1669–82.

Bover, O., J. Muellbauer, N. Murphy. 1989. Housing, wages and UK labour markets, in Wages and House Prices Symposium. *Oxford Bulletin of Economics and Statistics* **51**, 97–162.

Bradbury, K. et al. 1977. Simultaneous estimation of the supply and demand for housing location in a multizoned metropolitan area. In *Residential location and urban housing markets*, G. K. Ingram (ed.), 51–86. New York: National Bureau for Economic Research.

Bramley, G. 1989a. *Land supply, planning and private housebuilding: a review*. SAUS Working Paper 81, School for Advanced Urban Studies, University of Bristol.

— 1989b. *Meeting housing needs*. London: Association of District Councils.

— 1990. *Equalization grants and local expenditure needs: the price of equality*. Aldershot: Avebury.

— 1991. *Bridging the Affordability Gap in 1990: an update of research on housing access and affordability* Birmingham: BEC Publications.

— 1993. The impact of land-use planning and tax subsidies on the supply and price of housing in Britain. *Urban Studies* **30**(2), 5–29.

— 1994. An affordability crisis in British housing: dimensions, causes and policy impact. *Housing Studies* **9**(1), 103–124.

Bramley, G. & G. Smart 1993. *Who benefits from local services? Comparative evidence from different local authorities*. Welfare State Programme Discussion Paper WSP/91. London: London School of Economics.

Bramley, G., W. Bartlett, A. Franklin, C. Lambert 1990. *Housing finance and the housing market in Bristol* York: Joseph Rowntree Foundation.

Breheny, M. 1993. Fragile regional planning. *The Planner* (January), 10–12.

Brindley, T., Y. Rydin, G. Stoker 1989. *Remaking planning: the politics of urban change in the Thatcher years*. London: Unwin Hyman.

Brisbane, W. 1985. Land supply for housing in urban areas. *Chartered Building Societies Institute Journal* **39**, 172–3.

Brown, R. L. & D. Achour. 1984. The pricing of land options. *Urban Studies* **21**, 317–23.

Brownstone, D., P. Englund, M. Persson 1988. Tax reform and housing demands; the distribution of welfare gains and losses. *European Economic Review* **32**(4), 819–40.

Brunsdon, C., M. Coombes, M. Munro, P. Symon 1990. *Housing and labour market interactions: an analysis of house price inflation in British LLMAS, 1983–7*. Centre for Housing Research Working Paper, University of Glasgow.

Buchanan, J. 1978. *The economics of politics*. Occasional Paper, Institute of Economic Affairs, London.

Buchanan, J.& G. Tullock 1962. *The calculus of consent*. Ann Arbor: University of Michigan Press.

Building 1993. Cheap land lures new buyers (12 February), 15.

Byrne, S. 1978. A public sector view. In *Releasing land for building development* [RTPI/RICS Seminar proceedings], G. Cherry & W. J. Plunkett (eds), 7–19. London: Royal Town Planning Institute.

Cardew, R. & M. Cuddy 1987. A comparison of the Land Authority for Wales (United Kingdom) and the Land Commission of New South Wales (Australia). *Habitat Interna-*

tional **11**(1), 97–111.

Cawson, A. 1982. *Corporatism and welfare: social policy and State intervention in Britain*. London: Heinemann.

Champion, A. G. (ed.) 1989. *Counterurbanization*. London: Edward Arnold

Cheshire, P. & C. Leven 1982. *On the costs and economic consequences of the British land-use planning system*. Discussion Paper in Urban and Regional Economics (Series C: 11), Department of Economics, University of Reading.

Cheshire, P. & S. Sheppard 1989. British planning policy and access to housing: some empirical estimates. *Urban Studies* **26**, 469–85.

Chiddick, D. & M. Dobson 1986. Land for housing: circular arguments. *The Planner* (March), 10–13.

Clapp, J. M. 1980. The elasticity of substitution for land: the effects of measurement errors. *Journal of Urban Economics* **8**, 255–63.

Clark, D. & K. Dunmore 1990. *Involving the private sector in rural social housing*. Cirencester: Action for Communities in Rural England (ACRE).

Coates, D. 1992. Affordable housing: a private sector perspective. *The Planner* (November), 57–9.

Coombes, M. & S. Raybould 1991. *Local trends in house price inflation*. Housing Research Findings 30, Joseph Rowntree Foundation, York.

Coopers & Lybrand 1985. *Land-use planning and the housing market*. London: Coopers & Lybrand

—1987. Land-use planning and indicators of housing demand. London: Coopers & Lybrand.

Couch, C. 1988. Aspects of structural change in speculative housing production: a case study in Merseyside. *Environment and Planning A* **20**, 1385–96.

CPRE 1988. *Welcome homes: housing supply from unallocated land*. London: Council for the Protection of Rural England.

Cronin, F. J. 1983. Market structure and the price of housing services. *Urban Studies* **12**, 91–9.

Crook, T., P. Kemp, S. Bowman, I. Anderson 1991. *Tax incentives and revival of private renting*. York: Cloister Press.

Culyer, A. J. 1980. *The political economy of social policy*. Oxford: Martin Robertson.

Curry, N. R. 1978. Public planning in land use – an economic perspective. In *Planning and the market*. Occasional Paper 9 (B. Pearce, N. Curry, R. Goodchild (eds), 49–78), Department of Land Economy, University of Cambridge.

Dahl, R. A. 1961. *Who governs?* New Haven, Connecticut: Yale University Press.

de Leeuw, F. & N. F. Ekanem 1971. The supply of rental housing. *American Economic Review* **6195**, 806–817.

Diamond, D. B., & M. J. Lea 1993. Housing finance in developed countries: an international comparison of efficiency. In Research Report SB:56 (*Housing finance in the 1990s*, B. Turner & C. Whitehead (eds)), National Swedish Institute for Building Research, Gavle.

Dildine, L. & F. Massey 1974. Dynamic model of private incentives to housing maintenance. *Southern Economic Journal* **40**(4), 631–9.

DoE 1977. *Housing policy review: a consultative document* (Cmnd 6851). London: HMSO.

—1978. *Circular 44/78: land for housing* London: HMSO.

—1980. *Study of the availability of private housebuilding land in Greater Manchester 1978–81* [joint report by DoE and House Builders Federation, vol. 1]. London: DoE.

—1984. *Circular 14/84: green belts*. London: HMSO.

—1984. *First report from the Environment Committee: green belt and land for housing*, vol. 2 (Cmnd 8345). London: HMSO.

—1985. *Circular 14/85: development and environment*. London: HMSO.
—1986. *Paying for local government* (Cmnd 9714). London: HMSO.
—1987a. *Evaluation of derelict land grant schemes* [Inner Cities Research Programme]. London: HMSO.
—1987b. *Housing: the government's proposals* (Cm 214). London: HMSO.
—1987c. *The future of development plans* (Cm 569). London: HMSO.
—1988. *English House Condition Survey 1986*. London: HMSO.
—1990. *This common inheritance: Britain's environmental strategy* (Environment White Paper). London: HMSO.
—1991a. *Rates of urbanization in England 1981–2001* [Department of the Environment Planning Research Programme]. London: HMSO.
—1991b. *Circular 7/91: planning and affordable housing*. London: HMSO
—1992a. *Planning Policy Guidance Note 3: housing*. London: HMSO.
—1992b. *The relationship between house prices and land supply* [Department of the Environment Planning Research Programme]. London: HMSO.
—1993a. *English House Condition Survey 1991*. London: HMSO.
—1993b. *Planning Policy Guidance Note 13: Transport*. London: DoE.
DoE & Department of Transport 1993. *Reducing transport emissions through planning*. London: HMSO
Downs, A. 1957. *An economic theory of democracy* New York: Harper & Row.
—1967. *Inside bureaucracy*. Boston: Little Brown.
—1973. *Opening up the suburbs*. New Haven: Yale University Press.
Drewett, R. 1973. The developers: decision processes. In *The containment of urban England* (vol. 2), P. Hall et al., 163–94. London: George Allen & Unwin.
Duncan, S. & A. Rowe 1993. Self-provided housing: the First World's hidden housing arm. *Urban Studies* **30**(8), 1331–54.
Dunleavy, P. 1991. Professions and policy change: notes towards a model of ideological corporatism. *Public Administration Bulletin* **36**, 3–16.

EIU (Economist Intelligence Unit) 1975. *Housing land availability in the South East*. London: HMSO.
—1978. *Land availability: a study of land with outstanding residential planning permission*. London: Economist Intelligence Unit.
Edel, M. & E. Sclar 1974. Taxes, spending and property values: supply adjustment in a Tiebout-Oates model. *Journal of Political Economy* **82**, 941–54.
Elson, M. 1986. *Green belts: conflict mediation in the urban fringe*. London: Heinemann.
Ermisch, J. 1984. *Housing finance: who gains?* London: Policy Studies Institute.
—1990. *Fewer babies, longer lives*. York: Joseph Rowntree Foundation.
Evans, A. W. 1973. *The economics of residential location*. London: Heinemann.
—1983. The determination of the price of land. *Urban Studies* **20**, 119–29.
—1988a. South East England in the 1980s: explanations for a house price explosion. In *Growth and change in a core region: the case of South East England*, M. Breheny & P. Congdon (eds), 130–49. London: Pion.
—1988b. *No room! No room! The costs of the British town and country planning system*. Occasional Paper 79, Institute of Economic Affairs, London.
—1991. Rabbit hutches on postage stamps: planning, development and political economy. *Urban Studies* **28**(6), 853–70.

Farthing, S., T. Coombes, J. Winter 1993. Large development sites and affordable housing. *Housing and Planning Review* (February/March), 11–13.
Feasey, R. 1992. The role of the planning system. *The Planner* (November), 59–62.

Follain, J. R. & S. Malpezzi 1980. *Dissecting housing value and rent: estimates of hedonic indexes for thirty-nine large SMSAs*. Paper 249-17, The Urban Institute, Washington DC.

Forrest, R. & A. Murie 1993. *New homes for home owners: a study of new building and vacancy chains in southern England* (report of research for the DoE). London: HMSO.

Forrest, R., A. Murie, K. Doogan, P. Burton 1991. *Labour mobility and housing provision: a review of the literature*. SAUS Working Paper 98, School for Advanced Urban Studies, University of Bristol.

Foster, C., R. Jackman, M. Perlman 1980. *Local government finance in a unitary State*. London: Allen & Unwin.

Garnett, D., B. Reid, B. Riley 1991. *Housing finance*. Harlow: Longman.

Gibb, K. & M. Munro 1991. *Housing finance in the UK: an introduction*. London: Macmillan.

Giussani, B., & G. Hadjimatheou 1990. *Econometric model of regional house prices in the UK*. Paper presented at the Housing Studies Association Conference, York, April 1990, Apex Centre Economics Discussion Papers 90/2, Kingston Polytechnic.

Glass, R. 1972. Anti-urbanism. In *The city: problems of planning*, M. Stewart (ed.), 63–71. Harmondsworth: Penguin.

Goodchild, R. 1978. The operation of the private land market. In *Land, planning and the market*, B. Pearce, N. Curry, R. Goodchild (eds), 11–48. Occasional Paper 9, Department of Land Economy, University of Cambridge.

Goodchild, R. & R. J. C. Munton 1985. *Development and the landowner*. London: Allen & Unwin.

Gosling, J., G. Keogh, M. Stabler 1993. House extensions and housing market adjustment: a case study of Wokingham. *Urban Studies* **30**(9), 1561–76.

Grant, M. 1992. Planning law and the British land-use planning system: an overview. *Town Planning Review* **63**(1), 3–12

Grieson, R. E. & R. J. Arnott 1983. The supply of urban housing. In *The urban economy and housing*, R. E. Grieson (ed.), 3–10. Lexington: Lexington Books, 3–10.

Grigson, W. S. 1986. *House prices in perspective: a review of South East evidence*. London: SERPLAN.

Grimley, J. R. Eve 1992. *The use of planning agreements*. London: HMSO.

Hagman, D. & D. Misczynski 1978. *Windfalls for wipeouts: land value capture and compensation*. Chicago: American Society of Planning Officials.

Hague, C. 1991. A review of planning theory in Britain. *Town Planning Review* **62**(3), 295–310.

Hall, P., R. Thomas, H. Gracey, R. Drewett 1973. *The containment of urban England*. London: George Allen & Unwin.

Ham, C. & Hill, M. 1984. *The policy process in the modern capitalist State*. Brighton: Wheatsheaf.

Hamilton, B. 1975. Zoning and property taxation in a system of local government. *Urban Studies* **12**, 205–11.

Hamnett, C., M. Harmer, P. Williams 1991. *Safe as houses: housing inheritance in Britain*. London: Paul Chapman.

Hancock, K. & M. Munro 1992. Housing subsidies, inequality and affordability: evidence from Glasgow. *Fiscal Studies* **14**(4), 71–97.

Harrison, A. J. 1977. *Economics and land-use planning*. London: Croom Helm.

Healey, P. 1992. The reorganisation of State and market in planning. *Urban Studies* **29**(3/4), 411–34.

Healey, P., A. Doak, P. McNamara, M. Elson 1985. *The implementation of planning policies and the role of development plans*, vols I and II. Department of Town Planning, Oxford Polytechnic.

—1988. *Land use planning and the mediation of urban change: the British planning system in practice*. Cambridge: Cambridge University Press.

Healey, P., M. Purdue, F. Ennis 1993. *Gains from planning? Dealing with the impacts of development*. York: Joseph Rowntree Foundation.

Henderson, J. V. 1977. *Economic theory and the cities*. New York: Academic Press.

—1986. Tenure choice and the demand for housing. *Economica* **53**, 231–46.

Henderson, J. V. & Y. M. Ioannides 1983. A model of housing tenure choice. *American Economic Review* **731**, 98–113.

Hill, M. & G. Bramley 1986. *Analysing social policy*. Oxford: Basil Blackwell.

Hills, J. 1991. *Unravelling housing finance: subsidies, benefits and taxation*. Oxford: Oxford University Press.

—1993. *The future of welfare: a guide to the debate* York: Joseph Rowntree Foundation.

—& H. Sutherland 1991. *Banding, tilting, gearing, gaining and losing: an anatomy of the proposed council tax*. Discussion Paper WSP/63, Welfare State Programme, London School of Economics.

Hirsch, F. 1977. *The social limits to growth*. London: Routledge.

Hooper, A. 1985. Land availability studies and private housebuilding. In *Land policy: problems and alternatives*, S. Barrett & P. Healey (eds), 106–126. Aldershot: Gower.

Hooper, A., P. Pinch, S. Rogers 1988. Housing land availability. *Journal of Planning and Environmental Law* (April), 225–39.

Huang, S. 1973. Short-run instability in single family housing starts. *Journal of the American Statistical Association* **68**(344), 788–92.

Hughes, D. 1988. Green Belts, green belts buckling, or green eyes of little yellow gods. *Housing and Planning Review* **43**(5), 15–17.

Hughes, G. 1988. Rates reform and the housing market. In *The reform of local government finance in Britain*, S. Bailey & R. Paddison (eds), 109–129. London: Routledge.

Ingram, G. K. & Y. Oron. 1977. The production of housing services from existing dwellings units. In *Residential location and urban housing markets*, G. K. Ingram (ed.), 273–314. Cambridge, Massachusetts: Ballinger.

Jackson, A., S. Monk, C. Royce, J. Dunn 1994. *Land supply and housing: a case study*. Discussion Paper 44, Department of Land Economy, University of Cambridge.

Jackson, P. 1982. *The political economy of bureaucracy*. Oxford: Phillip Allan.

Jenkins, W. I. 1978. *Policy analysis: a political and organisational perspective*. London: Martin Robertson.

Jones, G. 1993. Planning and the reduction of transport emissions. *The Planner* (July), 15–18.

Joseph Rowntree Foundation 1991. *Inquiry into British housing. Second report June 1991* [chaired by HRH The Duke of Edinburgh KG KT]. York: Joseph Rowntree Foundation.

—1994. *Inquiry into planning for housing*. York: Joseph Rowntree Foundation.

JURUE 1977. *Planning and land availability* (final report to the Department of the Environment). Joint Unit for Research in the Urban Environment, University of Aston.

Kearl, J. R. 1979. Inflation, mortgages and housing. *Journal of Political Economy* **875**(1), 1115–38.

Kemp, P. 1993. The case and potential for private renting. In *Housing policy and economic recovery,* R. Best (ed.), 12–15. York: Joseph Rowntree Foundation.

Kennedy, P. 1985. *A guide to econometrics*. Oxford: Basil Blackwell.

Keogh, G. & A. W. Evans 1992. The private and social costs of planning delay. *Urban*

Studies **29**(5), 687–700.

King, D. 1984. *Fiscal tiers: the economics of multi-level government*. London: Allen & Unwin.

Kivell, P. 1993. *Land and the city: patterns and processes of urban change*. London: Routledge.

Koenker, R. 1972. An empirical note on the elasticity of substitution between land and capital in a monocentric housing market. *Journal of Regional Science* **122**, 299–305.

Laidler, D. 1969. Income tax incentives for owner-occupied housing. In *The taxation of income and capital*, A. C. Harberger & M. J. Bailey (eds), 50–76. Washington DC: Brookings.

Lambert, C. 1990. *New housebuilding and the development industry in the Bristol area*. SAUS Working Paper 86, School for Advanced Urban Studies, University of Bristol.

Laver, M. 1979. *The politics of private desires*. Harmondsworth: Penguin.

Le Grand, J. 1991. *The theory of government failure*. Studies in Decentralisation and Quasi-Markets 5, School for Advanced Urban Studies, University of Bristol.

Le Grand, J., C. Propper, R. Robinson 1992. *The economics of social problems*, 3rd edn. London: Macmillan.

Lease, H. *Land availability studies: a review of practice*. BA dissertation, School of Town & Country Planning, University of the West of England.

Leather, P. & S. Mackintosh 1993. *Renovation file: a profile of housing conditions and housing renewal policies in the United Kingdom*. Oxford: Anchor Housing Trust.

Lewis, D. 1992. *Access for life: a case for adaptable, accessible homes in a barrier-free environment*. Derbyshire Coalition of Disabled People, Clay Cross, Derbyshire.

Lichfield, N. & H. Darin-Drabkin 1980. *Land policy in planning*. London: Allen & Unwin.

Lipsky, M. 1980. *Street level bureaucracy*. New York: Russell Sage.

Longley, P., M. Clarke, H. Williams 1991. Housing careers, asset accumulation and subsidies to owner-occupation – a microsimulation. *Housing Studies* **8**(1), 57–69.

Lukes, S. 1974. *Power: a radical view*. London: Macmillan.

Macdonald, G. 1978. A private sector view. In *Releasing land for building development* [RTPI/RICS Seminar proceedings], G. Cherry & W. J. Plunkett (eds), 31–6. London: Royal Town Planning Institute.

Mack, J. & S. Lansley 1984. *Poor Britain*. London: Allen & Unwin.

Maclennan, D., K. Gibb, A. More 1991. *Fairer subsidies, faster growth*. York: Joseph Rowntree Foundation.

Maddala, G. S. 1987. *Introduction to econometrics*. London: Macmillan.

March, J. G. & H. Simon 1958. *Organizations*. New York: John Wiley.

Margolis, S. 1981. Depreciation and maintenance of houses. *Land Economics* **571**, 91–105.

Mayes, D. 1979. *The property boom: the effects of building society behaviour on house prices*. Oxford: Martin Robertson.

McDonald, J. F. 1979. *Economic analysis of an urban housing market*, New York: Academic Press.

Meen, G. P. 1992. *Housing and the macroeconomy: a package for the analysis of housing policy options*. Oxford: Oxford University / Oxford Economic Forecasting.

Mendelsohn, R. 1977. Empirical evidence on home improvements. *Journal of Urban Economics* **4**, 459–68.

Merrett, S. 1989. *The Denarius hypothesis: house price inflation in owner-occupied London*. Discussion paper, Housing Finance Project, University College London.

Middlemas, K. 1979. *Politics in industrial society*. London: André Deutsch.

Mills, E. S. 1972. *Urban economics*. Glenview, California: Scott Foresman.

Monk, S. 1991. *The speculative housebuilder: a review of empirical research* [Discussion Paper 31, Department of Land Economy]. Cambridge: Granta.

Monk, S., B. Pearce, C. Whitehead 1991. *Planning, land supply and house prices: a literature review*. Monograph 21, Department of Land Economy, University of Cambridge.

Moore, B. 1992. *New settlements*. MSc dissertation, School of Town & Country Planning, University of the West of England.

Moorhouse, J. C. 1972. Optimal housing maintenance under rent control. *Southern Economic Journal* **39**, 93–106.

Muellbauer, J. 1990a. The housing market and the UK economy: problems and opportunities in *Housing and the National Economy*, J. Ermisch (ed.), 48–71. Aldershot: Gower.

—1990b. The great British housing disaster. *Roof* (May/June), 16–19.

—1992. Why devaluation is the right way. *The Independent* (17 September).

Mueller, D. C. 1989. *Public choice II: a survey*, revised edn. Cambridge: Cambridge University Press.

Musgrave, R. & P. Musgrave 1980. *Public finance in theory & practice*, 3rd edn. New York: McGraw-Hill.

Muth, R. F. 1964. The derived demand curve for a productive factor and the industry supply curve. *Oxford Economic Papers* **16**(2), 221–34.

—1969. *Cities and housing*. Chicago: University of Chicago Press.

—1971. The derived demand for urban residential land, *Urban Studies* **8**(2), 243–54.

Needham, B. 1992. A theory of land prices when land is supplied publicly: the case of the Netherlands. *Urban Studies* **29**(5), 669–86.

Neels, K. 1981. Production functions for housing services. *Regional Science Association, Papers and Proceedings* **48**, 25–37.

Neutze, M. 1987. The supply of land for a particular use. *Urban Studies* **24**, 379–88.

Nicholson, M. & K. Willis 1990. *Costs and benefits of housing subsidies to tenants: a comparison between tenures and income groups*. Housing Finance Discussion Paper 3, Joseph Rowntree Foundation, York.

Niskanen, W. A. 1971. *Bureaucracy and representative government*. New York: Aldine-Atherton.

O'Connor, J. 1973. *The fiscal crisis of the State*. New York: St Martin's Press.

O'Sullivan, A. 1984. Misconceptions in the current housing subsidy debate. *Policy and Politics* **12**(2), 119–44

Oates, W. 1972. *Fiscal federalism*. Lexington, Mass.: D. C. Heath.

Olsen, E. O. 1987. The demand and supply of housing service: a critical survey of the empirical literature. In *Handbook of regional and urban economics* (vol. II), E. S. Mills (ed.), 989–1022. Amsterdam: North Holland.

OPCS 1988. *The prevalence of disability among adults* [OPCS surveys of disability in Great Britain, report by J. Martin, H. Meltzer, D. Elliot]. London: HMSO.

Ozanne, L. & R. J. Struyk 1978. The price elasticity of supply of housing services. In *Urban housing markets; recent directions in research and policy*, L. S. Bourne & J. R. Hitchcock (eds), 109–138. Toronto: University of Toronto Press.

Page, D. 1993. *Planning for communities: a study of new housing association estates*. York: Joseph Rowntree Foundation.

Pearce, B. 1992. The effectiveness of the British land use planning system. *Town Planning Review* **63**(1), 13–28.

Polinsky, A. M. & D. T. Ellwood 1979. An empirical reconciliation of micro and grouped estimates of the demand for housing. *Review of Economics and Statistics* **612**, 199–205.

Poterba, J. M. 1984. Tax subsidies to owner-occupied housing: an asset market approach. *Quarterly Journal of Economics* **99**, 729–52.

Property Advisory Group 1981. *Planning gain*. London: Department of the Environment.

Richardson, H. W. 1973. *The economics of urban size*. Farnborough: Saxon House.

— 1977. *The new urban economics and alternatives*. London: Pion.

RICS 1991. *Guide to house rebuilding costs 1991* [Building Cost Information Service]. London: Royal Institution of Chartered Surveyors.

Robinson, R. 1981. *Housing economics and public policy*. London: Macmillan.

Rolfe, S., S. Mackintosh, P. Leather 1993. *Age File '93*. Oxford: Anchor Housing Trust.

Rosen, H. S. 1978. Estimating inter-city differences in the price of housing services. *Urban Studies* **15**, 351–5.

Rosenberg, G. 1982. High population densities in relation to social behaviour. *Ekistics* **49**, 400–4.

Rydell, C. P. 1976. Measuring the supply response to housing allowances. *Regional Science Association, Papers and Proceedings* **37**, 31–57.

— 1982. *Price elasticities of housing supply*. Santa Monica: RAND.

Rydin, Y. 1985. *Residential development and the planning system*. Oxford: Pergamon.

— 1986. *Housing land policy*. Aldershot: Gower.

Saunders, P. 1981. *Social theory and the urban question*. London: Hutchinson.

— 1984. Rethinking local politics. In *Local socialism? Labour councils and New Left alternatives*, M. Boddy & C. Fudge (eds), 22–48. London: Macmillan.

SERPLAN 1992. *Planning provision for housing 1991–2006*. London: SERPLAN.

Shankland, G., P. Willmott, D. Jordan 1977. *Inner London: policies for dispersal and balance*. London: HMSO.

Short, J., S. Fleming, S. Witt 1986. *Housebuilding, planning and community action*. London: Routledge.

Simon, H. A. 1945. *Administrative behaviour*. Glencoe, Illinois: Free Press.

Sirmans, C. F. & A. Redman 1979. Capital–land substitution and the price elasticity of demand for urban residential land. *Land Economics* **55**, 167–76.

Sirmans, C. F., J. B. Kau, C. F. Lee 1979. The elasticity of substitution in urban housing production: a VES approach. *Journal of Urban Economics* **6**, 407–15.

Smith, B. 1976. The supply of urban housing. *Quarterly Journal of Economics* **903**, 389–405.

Smith, S. 1991. Distributional issues in local taxation. *Economic Journal* **101**, 585–91.

Smyth, H. 1982. *Land banking, land availability and planning for private housebuilding*. SAUS Working Paper 23, School for Advanced Urban Studies, University of Bristol.

— 1984. *Land supply, housebuilders and government policy*. SAUS Working Paper 43, School for Advanced Urban Studies, University of Bristol.

Spencer, P. 1988. *The likely effects of the Community Charge on the UK economy*. London: Credit Suisse First Boston.

Stewart, J. 1976. *Understanding econometrics*. London: Hutchinson.

Stover, M. E. 1986. The price elasticity of the supply of single-family detached urban housing. *Journal of Urban Economics* **20**, 331–40.

Sweeney, J. L. 1974. Housing unit maintenance and the mode of tenure. *Journal of Economic Theory* **82**, 111–38.

Thornley, A. 1991. *Urban planning under Thatcherism: the challenge of the market*. London: Routledge.
Tiebout, C. M. 1956. A pure theory of local expenditures. *Journal of Political Economy* **64**(5), 416–24.
Titman, S. 1985. Urban land price under uncertainty. *American Economic Review* **75**, 505–14.
Topel, R. & S. Rosen 1988. Housing investment in the United States. *Journal of Political Economy* **964**, 718–40.
Topham, N. & R. Ward 1992. Property prices, tax and expenditure levels, and local fiscal performance. *Applied Economics* **24**, 1225–35.
Tsoukis, C. & P. Westaway 1991. A forward-looking model of housing construction in the UK [Paper presented at London Business School International Conference on the Economics of Housing Markets, September 1991]. London: National Institute of Economic and Social Research.
Tym, Roger and Partners 1987. *Land used for residential development in the South East* [report to the DoE]. London: DoE.
— 1989. *The effects of planning delays on private sector housebuilding* [report to the Housebuilders Federation]. London.
— 1990. *Housing land availability* [Planning Research Programme, Department of the Environment]. London: HMSO.

Verbrugge, L. & R. Taylor 1980. Consequences of population density and size. *Urban Affairs Quarterly* **16**, 135–60.
Vorst, A. C. F. 1987. Optimal maintenance under uncertainty. *Journal of Urban Economics* **21**, 209–27.
Vost, T. 1986. The relation between rent and selling price of a building under optimal maintenance with uncertainty. *Journal of Economic Dynamics and Control* **10**, 315–20.

Walker, B. 1981. *Welfare economics and urban problems*. London: Hutchinson.
Walker, B. & A. Marsh 1993. The distribution of housing subsidies in an urban area. *Urban Studies* **30**(9), 1543–60.
White, M. J. & L. White 1977. The subsidy to owner-occupied housing: who benefits? *Journal of Public Economics* **71**, 111–26.
Whitehand, J. & P. Larkham 1991. Housebuilding in the back garden: reshaping suburban townscapes in the Midlands and South East England. *Area* **23**(1), 57–65.
Whitehead, C. M. 1974. *The UK housing market: an econometric model*. Farnborough: Saxon House.
— 1991. From need to affordability: an analysis of UK housing policy objectives. *Urban Studies* **28**, 871–87.
Whitehead, C. M. & M. Kleinman 1992. *A review of housing needs assessments*. London: The Housing Corporation.
Wilcox, S. 1990. *The need for social rented housing in England in the 1990s*. Coventry: Institute of Housing.
— (ed.) 1993. *Housing finance review 1993*. York: Joseph Rowntree Foundation.
Williams, G., P. Bell, L. Russell 1991. *Evaluating the low-cost rural housing initiative* [DoE Planning Research Programme]. London: HMSO.
Wilson, T. 1991. The Poll Tax – origin, errors and remedies. *Economic Journal* **101**, 577–84.
Wiltshaw, D. G. 1985. The supply of land. *Urban Studies* **22**, 49–56.
Winkler, J. 1977. The corporate economy: theory and administration. In *Industrial society: class, cleavage and control*, R. Scase (ed.), 43–58. London: George Allen & Unwin.

Winter, J., T. Coombes, S. Farthing 1993. Satisfaction with space around the home on large private sector estates: lessons from surveys in Southern England and South Wales, 1985–9. *Town Planning Review* **64**(1), 65–88.

Wolff, C. 1988. *Markets or governments: choosing between imperfect alternatives*. Cambridge, Mass.: MIT Press.

INDEX

UNIVERSITY OF GLAMORGAN
PRIFYSGOL MORGANNWG